WHEN FREDDIE BECAME JESUS

Ashes 2009

WHEN FREDDIE BECAME JESUS

Jarrod Kimber

WHEN FREDDIE BECAME JESUS

© Jarrod Kimber

Jarrod Kimber has asserted his rights in accordance with the Copyright, Designs and Patents Act 1988 to be identified as the author of this work.

Published By:
Pitch Publishing (Brighton) Ltd
A2 Yeoman Gate
Yeoman Way
Durrington
BN13 3QZ

Email: info@pitchpublishing.co.uk
Web: www.pitchpublishing.co.uk

First published 2009

A catalogue record for this book is available from the British Library.

10-digit ISBN: 1-9054117-7-4
13-digit ISBN: 978-1-9054117-7-1

Printed and bound in Great Britain by Cromwell Press Group

Dedication: For Elsie, Ken & Bonga Bonga

"Australia isn't as good as they used to be"

Imran, Taxi Driver, Birmingham

Richie's trousers

He was so close to me that I could have turned around and licked his trouser leg. And don't think it didn't cross my mind.

Grey hair. Light suit. Relaxed, yet authoritative demeanour. It was Richie, the Richie. Richie fucking Benaud.

The grandparent that every cricket-loving Aussie and Pommie kid wished he had. When I was young I think I even told kids that he was my Grandpa. But I also used to tell kids I was born on a plane halfway across the Pacific.

It was my first day in an international cricket press box. It was Lord's, the home of cricket. Here I was trying to concentrate and write shit on the cricket and behind me *was* cricket.

The first voice you heard before the game, and the last after it. The man who was so well-respected that his flawed rain rules were kept in the one-day game for years because no-one wanted to be the one to tell him that they were shit. The man who once said, "It should never be permitted to happen again", and "Gatting has absolutely no idea what has happened... still doesn't know", was behind me.

I could have turned around and grabbed his balls. I wouldn't. But I could have done.

There is no greater test in life than how you will perform with the spectre of a legend over your shoulder. It was like I was sitting in front of Buddha, except this was a way more religious kind of feeling.

Every time I said something, I worried about how he would take it. By accident, and completely out of character for me, I said: "That Michael Clarke can be a cunt like that", and straightaway I thought of Richie. Does he think Clarke can be a cunt like that? Does he think I am a cunt? Does he say the word 'cunt'?

It was a pressure-inducing day. Now I knew how Stuart Broad felt when he fucked up that over against the Dutch.

Richie is so quiet in the box: he just sits and watches the cricket, no commentary-style quips at all. There are no conversations about Wilco; he never asks how the kids are or where is a good place to get sushi. He just focuses on the game with the kind of quietness I can't manage even when I'm asleep.

Eventually I felt the need to say hello to the man. I had to wait till there was no-one around of course. I didn't want to come across as some pervy fan boy on my first trip into the box.

I went up and introduced myself, shook his hand, and generally tripped over the English language. It all took only a few seconds, but I was already out of the conversation and he was dragging my ass along.

Luckily, some Channel 5 lackey needed him, and we were cut off before I said anything stupid. For the rest of the day I managed not to lick his trouser legs. But, later that night after a couple of beers, I did wonder what they would taste like.

The day after the Test I was diagnosed with swine flu. All I could think of was that I could be the man who kills Richie. I was depressed for a little while. I kept checking my RSS feeds waiting for the words, "Richie has a two in 22 chance of survival". Luckily for everyone, he survived.

But the other 10% of me was thinking: "Fucken hell, how famous will I be if I am the guy who kills Richie."

What the Ashes means to me

I must confess a deep and dark secret; I am not one of those people who believe the Ashes *are* cricket. I want to believe it, I honestly do. But when I see a Sehwag slash through point, a Mushtaq wrong'un, or a Stephen Fleming trap at point I know that cricket is more important than the Ashes.

Cricket is my sport, and over the years it is the only sport that has stuck with me. It is the Natalie Portman of sports. The physicality of it, the strategic thought, the brutality it brings, the finality of each ball, and the sledging it encourages are what have always kept me in lust with it.

My first memory of the sport live was watching Mike Whitney storm in first ball for the evil New South Wales against the virginity protectors of Victoria. He fell over. The crowd laughed. I never felt the same about another sport from that moment on.

I do love the Ashes, but I'm just not sure that I love it that much more than other Test series. I am drawn to it, though. It is one of the few times the cricket fundamentalists are outnumbered by the casual cricket watchers. Taxi drivers become experts, handymen understand reverse swing, and accountants talk about wrist work. It brings out the wanker in so many people. And any event that brings out the wanker gets my attention.

My first memory of watching cricket on TV is from the Ashes, the '86/87 Ashes to be specific. I remember David Boon nudging the ball off his hip for hours on end, and John Emburey looking very fucking old. Like any kid looking for excitement, it hooked me. Now, when I think of myself as a six-year-old planted in front of that telly watching Boon readjust his box in his familiar facing-up ritual, I am appalled my parents let me watch this filth.

Being in the opposition's homeland while this ancient incestuous rivalry plays itself out really ups its importance. If Australia lose I'll have to put up with all the casual cricket fans making jokes for 16 months. Most of these people have no real love of cricket; their love is simply beating Australia, and they give it their all. Which is fair enough: we are arrogant bastards.

It would remain to be seen how big this Ashes would be. Two ordinary yet well-matched sides could produce a low-skilled yet close death match, or one team could crumble. For me this would be a huge Ashes, even if England were to win 5-0.

My Ashes

It would be my first Ashes in England. My first time writing on a cricket series for money. My first time watching Australia in a Test match outside of Australia. My first time in a press box watching an international match. And my first time getting married.

Not just getting married: mouth breathing cave dwellers can get married. I was getting married at the Oval four days after the Ashes finished. Pretty cool, huh? I had always thought marriage was about as useful as a nightfuckingwatchman, but when you meet the right girl you can overlook that. But nightwatchmen are still useless.

Somehow I had assed three employers for the summer. *The Wisden Cricketer* and *The Times* you may have heard of. Since *The Wisden Cricketer* had started I'd had an online column with them and I somehow convinced Patrick Kidd, the *Times* sports writer, to allow me to appear on the Line & Length blog. Writing for *The Times* was funny: I was told to take out all the swearing and pornography. My main employer, though, was Crikey.com. You probably haven't heard of them – they're sort of Australia's *Huffington Post*. With some bullshit from me, their cricket-loving editors decided to make me their chief cricket correspondent. Although I may have suggested that title myself.

So those were my professional commitments. On top of them and the constant updates to my blog, cricketwithballs.com, I had a wedding to plan. To be fair it was my Wife Elect who did all the fretting over the buses, cravats, novelty cricket bats, and everything else that goes into making a cricket-themed wedding perfect. I had been useless, and it would only get worse. Almost every role I had in it, I ballsed up. She was Allan Border in 89 and I was Nasser Hussain at the Gabba in 02.

When you also factor in the fact that my family was coming over for the wedding – whom my Wife Elect would meet for the first time two weeks before the event, it was going to be a huge Ashes for me. The cricket would be just one small – yet important part. By the end of the series I was hoping to have a new bride, a career and an Ashes victory for Australia, but I've never been all that good at getting what I want.

Of course if all three went wrong there wouldn't be enough bourbon in the UK to get me through it. Before the Ashes I was also lucky enough to captain an Australian XI (the cricketwithballs.com Aussie code of conduct XI) in the inaugural Bloggers' Ashes against the villagecricketer.com's English All Stars. Like Ricky Ponting in 05 I made my share of mistakes. I opened with a lady who hadn't bowled for years, lost the momentum by not making quicker bowling changes, underbowled my spinners and then got out with the finish line in sight. About 1000 quid was raised for the Everyman cancer charity, but who cares; I lost the Bloggers' Ashes (by 28 runs). I was a disgrace.

I made my way to three of the Tests, watching from the stands or the press box, and spent the rest of the time watching on my couch. I was there on Freddie's day, Broad's day, and the last day, and I saw Andrew McDonald bring out lots of drinks.

As an Aussie living in London, who was marrying a Pom, captained an Aussie team in a charity Ashes, watched every ball*, wrote lots of shit for my website, lots of shit for other websites, and wore a CB Fry T-shirt to the game, I think there is no better person to take you through the Ashes. Unless Neville Cardus and Richie Benaud once had a love child.

*Not every ball.

From my Wife Elect:

> *For the whole of summer 2009, I was anticipating a (hopefully) amazing, life-changing match between England and Australia at the Oval. But not the one you're thinking of.*

This summer was always going to be a big one, being an Ashes summer and the first year that my Husband Elect (a phrase coined by me, by the way) would be writing full-time about cricket. The summer became more complicated after Jarrod took me for a walk on the Clifton suspension bridge and when we got to the middle of the bridge, he asked me to marry him. Presumably the proposal venue was because he wouldn't have been able to carry on with life if I'd said no. Happily, I said yes, and one phone call to his parents in Melbourne later, we established that the wedding would be at the end of August.

In terms of location, where better than the Oval? We met through cricket, we live near the Oval, my first birthday present from him was the Wisden *almanack from the year of my birth, and my first Christmas present from him was a cricket boot signed by Sachin Tendulkar.*

We carefully set the date to avoid the Oval Test itself, not just because I already had tickets, but because I didn't want to have one of those weddings where half the wedding party were crowded round a radio following the scores. Like England and Australia, our journey to the Oval wearing white (yes even the groom, of which more later) had begun.

History: 06/07 just as irrelevant as 05

Before the series, I thought the *Guardian* were running a campaign for Michael Vaughan to be supreme chancellor of the world. Lawrence Booth and David Hopps wanted him in the team and Andy Bull said: "Vaughan's experience… gives him a clear edge." It didn't seem to matter that he hadn't made any runs in a year, was falling over himself at Yorkshire, and that the team now had a level-headed captain.

You can understand the psyche. If you are an average English cricket fan you know two things: you lost the Ashes for years, and Michael Vaughan won them. Of course if life were that easy then Paris Hilton could be California's next governor.

Look at the non-Vaughan reasons England won in 05:

• Duncan Fletcher seemed to come up with the ideas, and Vaughan implemented them. His ideas were very strict, and when he no longer had the team to implement them he had nowhere to go. But for that one series he was pulling the strings.

• Andrew Flintoff was at the top of his game, and that only ever happened for two years in his career.

• The ball reverse-swung like a motherfucker from hell. Have you ever seen the ball reverse-swing like that in England since then? Australia have a kryptonite fear of the swinging ball, but the reverse-swinging ball is like kryptonite on steroids to them.

• Glenn McGrath's ankle. Let us not forget the first Test result. Once McGrath went down, a fairly new and inexperienced captain had to captain a squad with a former top-class fast bowler bowling candy floss, an eager wayward quick, and Michael Kasprowicz.

05 was a special series. Even the massive soul-destroying erection-reducing face-smashing 5-0 loss of 06/07 couldn't kill it. Nothing can. England defeated the mighty Australia in their pomp. It was their first win in 18 years and it almost singlehandedly revived a country's love of a sport. Freddie became a superhero before their eyes. KP a pop star. Vaughan a general. This wasn't a series, it was a cultural watermark; remember-where-you-were type stuff; a dance-naked-in-the- street and pour-yoghurt-on-yourself event. It was so big that for about 12 minutes English people forgot about football. England were so excited they all but skipped their next tour to Pakistan. Australia went home, got angry, and then beat a combined world XI.

The long-running joke coming into this series was the 06/07 series. Sky Sports refused to mention it; English newspapers used it only as a punch line. And the average fan laughed about it. So they should. Over two and a half years had passed since then. The last six in Australia's batting order were all new. Only Ponting, Michael Clarke and Mike Hussey had played in 06/07. It was almost completely irrelevant. And if that was almost completely irrelevant, imagine how irrelevant 05 was? In total, there were only six players who played in 05 who would go on to line up at Cardiff. Relevance? Ghosts? Bullshit?

The story of the 09 Ashes should have been the story of two young teams making their way in this big, bad world. It may not have sold as many newspapers or pay-TV subscriptions, but it would have had the advantage of being true. Instead, the English media talked about 05 until I questioned whether 06/07 had ever actually happened. This was Goebbels-esque media coverage: overlook the part of history that does not fit the story, and drill home the glory of the success until people can't actually remember anything else.

The whole Australian team was angry from the beginning in 06/07. They don't like to lose and 05 had been more than a loss: they were mocked by the English media and fans. But 06/07 would have made even English heretics believe in a vengeful god. All the gloating, MBEs, open-top buses and pissing in the gardens at 10 Downing Street seemed to come flooding back like Sodom and Gomorrah. It was pure Old Testament-style.

As a cricket fan, it was a shame. The 06/07 series was probably the most pre-hyped in history. There was actual electricity in the air before the first ball – not bullshit clichéd electricity, actual electricity. 05 was going to be supersized as two mighty warriors went toe-to-toe to prove who was the better side. Instead, one team was a champion prizefighter and the other was a starving, flea-infested donkey.

The disappointment hit me hard. That series actually made me question my love of cricket. Watching England limp around the country finding new ways to make assclowns of themselves was not good Test cricket.

While Harmy's first ball at the Gabba may have ended the Ashes, the Test at Adelaide Oval walked over to England and took a dump on them. Every insecurity of fans and team ever had seemed to come out in one match: "We can't win, we can't draw, we can only crawl up into a ball and die. Please don't disturb us; we just want to be left alone."

Only an Englishman could ever properly articulate the pain of that Test, so I got one in. Rob Smyth, who was live on the *Guardian's* OBO on that fateful night:

> *"You wonder whether they can talk about it yet; whether an innocent newcomer to the dressing-room has chirpily mentioned the increasingly Macbethian word "Adelaide" only to be met with a sharp silence and then the solemn warning, "We don't talk about what happened that day". Because while sport should never be discussed in terms of tragedy, the million-yard stares of the England team after this game told of the most devastating defeat. It is no exaggeration to say that the class of 2004/05 – the best England team for decades – died that day, and they were killed off by that peerless rogue psychiatrist, Shane Warne, who invited them onto his couch and made them think of demons that didn't even exist.*
>
> *It's easy to forget that Warne actually took only four wickets – two lower-order batsmen and one a terrible decision against Andrew Strauss – but he got inside the minds of the England team and extended party, deadening their senses and their bats to a fatal degree. He will deservedly dine out on this for all his days.*
>
> *England, you suspect, turned up expecting an extremely quiet day at work, only to find a particularly harsh spot-test awaiting them. Under pressure, they forgot everything they had learned, retreating miserably into their shells against Warne in particular, and from there it all began to unravel.*

In many ways it had a horror movie feel: for the first eight overs or so England were entirely comfortable, like in the first 20 minutes of Wolf Creek. And then, from nowhere, they walked round a corner and into a swinging chainsaw: four wickets in no time at all and then, after the grim fight for dear life, the inevitable unhappy ending.

Or was it? Once the partisan trauma and numbness had disappeared – it didn't take long, just a year or two – those who had witnessed it came to fully appreciate one of the truly magical nights of sport. That said, most people had gone to bed safe in the knowledge that a draw was nailed-on, and then woke to have the horrific news relayed by teletext, house-mate, partner, radio, David Gower, Blackberry, black dog, whatever. Where were you while Warne was getting high?

In writing the Guardian's over-by-over report, I felt as alone in the world as the bloke in 28 Days Later: first because nobody was emailing in, and then because, after our then night editor left, it was just me and the coffee machine experiencing what was, for all the partisan disappointment, a great night of cricket – the sort of night that makes you want to engage someone, anyone; to come within a whisker of eulogising Warne to the coffee machine; to greet a bleary-eyed cleaner, with whom you had previously shared nothing more than a few workplace formalities, like a long-lost brother and immediately demand whether he likes cricket because OMGHAVEYOUSEENWHAT'SHAPPENED?!?!?! He shook his head. Whenever those who love cricket think back to the events of 5 December 2006, the reaction – for entirely different reasons – is exactly the same."

Australia refused to lose the dead rubbers in that series as well. Australia love to lose dead rubbers. But this was personal; the 5-0 call that McGrath had made before the series was on the line, and as this was his retirement call, it had to be honoured. 05 would be wiped from the earth. McGrath would restore his pride. Warne would go out on top, and Australia would have to work out how the fuck they would ever win without them.

Neither of the previous two series should have much impact on the coming one. The ball won't reverse swing, Freddie is a photocopy of his former self, Ponting is older, hairier and wiser. The teams are different, the hype is different. And, most importantly, both of these sides are quite shit.

Australia have lost to South Africa and India. England have lost to India and the West Indies. These aren't two wild animals being shoved into a cage to fight to the death; it is an argument on the train between two office workers for the free paper that someone else has left.

Where 05 and 06/07 had greatness. 09 has Ravi Bopara and Nathan Hauritz.

How the teams shaped up

The leaders

Australia: Ricky Ponting

In the few years he's been in charge, he has mocked the South Africans, upset the English, fought with the Indians, and ignored Pakistan. Plus, and I base this on drunken conversations with cricket fans of many nationalities, he has a very disagreeable face. Add that to a surly demeanour, hairy arms, punchy conversation style, and the fact he is leading the number one ranked cricket side in the world as they try to claw onto their mantle, and he is bound to be hated.

Besides, Australian captains are generally grumpy: think of Border, Waugh and Chappell.

Ponting still has that mongrel in him; he is a street-fighting kid from Launceston and, as much as Cricket Australia have tried to clean him up over the years, you feel he is never that far from a scrap with someone. Cricket Australia's ideal captain would be the much more corporate-friendly Michael Clarke, but they also realise that in the short-term Ricky Ponting will win them more games. The corporates like this, too.

Contrary to public opinion, Ponting's leadership has improved over the years. The problem is when he first took over, Australia won almost everything, and no-one noticed how god-awful his captaincy was. When all the stars left, his captaincy got better, but who cares when you are losing?

In South Africa he was mostly top-notch, and completely outmatched Graeme Smith, who according to the mainstream media is the best captain in the world. Ponting seemed to learn much from his two testicle-destroying losses at the MCG and the Waca. In both of those matches he was uninspired and never seemed to know when to attack or defend.
In South Africa he came up with a new gameplan of strangling the opposition. Knowing that South African batsman are mostly defensive, he

choked the game and made them take risks. Andrew McDonald and Ben Hilfenhaus bowled almost as one-day bowlers, and Peter Siddle and Mitchell Johnson had fairly defensive fields and cover when they weren't on top.

Ponting has to be congratulated for this, even if it wasn't his idea, it was still a bold move to go into the game with an anti-Australian defensive mindset, knowing that the press would eat him alive if it didn't work. But it did work. South Africa couldn't find a way to score at more than three an over, and Australia then attacked them when they were weak. Ponting never seemed to get the credit for this; Johnson seemed to be the poster boy for the returning heroes.

That is the thing with Ponting; the public's perception of him is always a bit askew. When he was a real son of a bitch no-one seemed to really hate him, now that he is a maturing humble loser (listen to the press conferences he gives after losses) he is enemy number one.

England: Andrew Strauss

Andrew Strauss probably should have been given the captaincy before the massacre of 06/07. For the second time in England's recent history – KP was the other – they decided to follow the Australian template of giving the captaincy to the best player. In 06/07 it was shown to be a shocking mistake. Not that Andrew Strauss had a great run there either. Random Rudi Koertzen was giving him out for fun, and even when he wasn't, there weren't many runs for the opener.

The word was he had been worked out, and for the next few years he struggled to make any real impact. But then he tweaked his game, made one of cricket's ugliest modern-day hundreds against the Kiwis in early 08 and the world was his oyster again. Still, he was overlooked despite having extensive captaincy experience with Middlesex. But there seemed to be no real push for Strauss at that stage – even Rob Key got more mentions.

When KP imploded Key was hardly mentioned. Strauss was the man, everyone was certain.

The moment he won the captaincy has to be in the aftermath of the Mumbai terrorist attacks, when Strauss stood up and said that the team should go back to India. Strauss seemed the coolest and most logical player in the ECB set up. Harmison and Flintoff seemed nervous, and KP took too long to get on board. Had Strauss not been so strong England may have not gone back.

Then when he arrived in India he stiff upper lipped back-to-back hundreds in the first Test as his personal one-finger salute to terrorists, even if England still lost that match.

In the old days Strauss would have been the automatic choice to captain England. He has the breeding, public school affiliations, cool head, and smooth exterior of many who went before him.

Apart from a short-lived spell when Freddie and Vaughan were sidelined, his first Test as captain was when England were 51 all out in Jamaica. It was ugly, but Strauss said all the right things and England dominated the rest of the series. Problem was that they didn't win any Tests and while Strauss' stern wing-commander demeanour was impressive, his declarations were pathetic. Twice he cost his team victory by setting the West Indies team a chase they would never get to. To be fair to Strauss, though, twice he got his team to within one wicket of victory.

Some captains would have probably taken out a fatwa on Fidel Edwards after he was the man not out in both draws.

When the returning series was in England very little captaining was required. Peter Andre could have captained that side, and he was going through a painful public break-up at the time. So it was too early to tell how he would go in the Ashes. Some Australians asked how a South African-born captain would perform in the Ashes, but they just did that to piss the Poms off; Strauss is more English than mustard on your crumpets.

The coaches

Australia: Tim Nielsen

When you start coaching a side with a captain who has been in charge of the team for five years, and the last coach has turned into a coaching superstar, it is hard to make your mark on the public. Ponting and John Buchanan were seen as a partnership; Nielsen is seen as Ponting's deputy.

Nielsen was the mainstay of the South Australian team in the 90s, back when they won the odd game. He was the wicketkeeper, but I don't need to tell you that, you can tell. He has that nuggetty demeanour of an Aussie wicketkeeper, even if he was born in London.

Like most wicketkeepers before the Gilchrist revolution he was a 'keeper first, batsman second. He only made four hundreds in 101 first-class matches (two against Victoria, bastard). He wasn't a flashy keeper like Darren Berry, or a big mouth like Phil Emery. He just went about his job without much fuss.

Nielsen is only 41 – to emphasise how young he is it should be mentioned his replacement, as South Australia's keeper is Graham Manou who is the back up to Brad Haddin on this tour. Ponting and Nielsen seem to suit each other well. Both like a scrap, both think technology can help without it being the only answer, and they seem to get on pretty well.

I wish I had some cool stories to tell about him, like the time I saw him throw his helmet at Nugget the South Australian changing room mascot, or how we once sniffed cocaine together off a Sphynx cat we stole from Rupert Murdoch. But they would be untruths. Rupert Murdoch doesn't even own a Sphynx cat.

Nielsen is just a solid cricket citizen who moved straight from an uninteresting, yet dependable, state career to an uninteresting and yet dependable role of coach. It is doubtful he has ever used aspirin, let alone cocaine.

England: Andy Flower

Few of us have taken on dictators, Andy Flower has. He averaged over 50 in Tests when it was still hard to do so (even allowing for the fact that he played only twice against Australia) and carried an awful team. He played in a side that was the plaything of Robert Mugabe and lived in Zimbabwe during the start of the tough times. And he once lived in Adelaide. The man knows hardship. Now he is coaching England. Some people live on misery.

Like Nielsen, Flower is a young coach, and he is also new to the job, but the players seem to respect him.

It is way too early to decide how good he is but he and Strauss seem like an appropriate match: two people who work at their game and their fitness until their knuckles bleed, and who have a natural stoic dignity about them.

When he and Henry Olanga wore black armbands throughout the 03 World Cup, these were their words:

"In all the circumstances, we have decided that we will each wear a black armband for the duration of the World Cup. In doing so we are mourning the death of democracy in our beloved Zimbabwe. In doing so we are making a silent plea to those responsible to stop the abuse of human rights in Zimbabwe. In doing so, we pray that our small action may help to restore sanity and dignity to our Nation."

The CEOs

Australia: James Sutherland

As a youngster I was a junior Victoria member, and the Victorians used to send out all sorts of posters with the players pictures' on them. Bottom right corner was a guy called James Sutherland.

His picture was the one that stood out, even though he was pretty much a nobody as a cricketer, and I doubt I ever saw him play more than a couple of Mercantile Mutual cup games. Because of the poster I always wanted him to play more, but he never did.

Little did I know that he would grow to become the CEO of Australian cricket's governing body and use the phrase "cricket consumer" without irony. If I ever decided to have a mortal enemy Sutherland would be on the nomination list with Noel Edmonds and Lalit Modi.

Sutherland believes cricket is a commodity and he seems much more worried in what the sponsors and corporate dining pigs will say than what the Australian cricket lovers will say. The way he treats cricket in Australia makes me want to get a pitchfork.

Someone who knows him told me he isn't a bad guy, I chose to ignore that.

England: Giles Clarke

Poor Giles Clarke, as if it isn't bad enough his suits never seem to fit he goes and gets involved with an alleged fraudster. If you are the man who runs English cricket, and you know how conservative a place it can be when it comes to the sport, surely you would do a bit more due diligence on some Texan who wants to give you 20 million dollars, no questions asked?

Nope.

During the "opening ceremony" (cancelled due to bad weather) of the World Twenty20 thingy, Giles was up on the stage with some royal dude. He just looked so damn miserable. Whether it was the weather, or just his general demeanour, I don't know, but he seemed haunted.

It is hard to find someone who mentions Clarke without talking about Stanford's millions, but from what I can tell he has been a pretty good CEO in many ways. The one thing that shits me about him is not bringing the cricket to the people. With Sky's contract up he had the chance to bring the cricket back to free-to-air TV.

He didn't. Instead Giles chose the instant gratification of selling the cricket to Sky for millions and taking it away from terrestrial TV. Now he can make the argument that he can use that money to spread the love of cricket around England, but you know what does that free? An Ashes series on terrestrial TV.

How the teams got there

To say that neither team was in form coming into the Ashes is like saying Natalie Portman is kind of okay to look at. Australia had lost to South Africa and India, and beaten South Africa and New Zealand. England had lost to India, South Africa, and the West Indies, and had beaten only the West Indies. The problem with the Ashes is you can't pick the teams. It's Poms v Aussies, for better or worse. You have to hope the occasion lifts the cricket.

England's summer of 2008 ended with a new beginning. Michael Vaughan's reign as captain was ended by losing to South Africa and all the fucken straight balls he missed. England won their first Test under Kevin Pietersen, a dead rubber against a hungover South Africa.

KP declared that if his team played like that they could win the Ashes. I was at every day of that Test; I thought he was injecting crystal meth into his buttcheeks when he said that. But his proclamation wasn't that far off; soon after, Australia and England were so shit that the team that beat South Africa in the dead rubber would have had a good chance of winning.

South Africa won 2-1.

Australia had fallen on hard times. Coming up to the 09 Ashes Sky's commentators couldn't stop mentioning how Ricky Ponting would handle an attack without Shane Warne and Glenn McGrath. They seemed completely oblivious to the fact that these two had retired over two years earlier and most cricket watchers already knew how he would handle the attack without Warne and McGrath: badly, and pretty much the same way he did before, except now with fewer wickets being taken.

Australia's trip to England really started with their tour of India in late 08. It was a car crash with seven babies and four puppies inside. There has been no tour that Australia have fucked up more in the modern era. It wasn't all their fault, though. They finally gave the musical spinning chair to Bryce McGain but he could not recover from a shoulder injury he'd sustained with Australia A. Going to India without your chosen spinner would confuse most selection panels, but Australia's ran down the street naked yelling "the cheese is after us". Cameron White was rushed there in Bryce's place. Suddenly a man who refused to bowl himself for Victoria found himself as the main spinner in India. Jason Krejza, the original second spinner on tour, was ignored after a brutal warm-up game, and Beau Casson, who had taken three wickets in his first Test, was forgotten about. That was about the time Australia lost that tour. Their bowlers never really looked like getting India out, and their only chance in the series seemed to be when Anil Kumble was captaining. The score was 0-0 for the two Tests he was in charge, but when Dhoni captained it was 2-0 to India. Failing to win one Test out of the four was the worst part. Australia have never played that well in India, and the Indian side has always manned up well against them. But no wins at all? Pretty useless.

In four Tests Cameron White took five wickets, and in one Test Jason Krejza took 12 (the weirdest 12-wicket haul I have ever seen). Tim Nielsen said that had Krejza played a week earlier he would not have been ready for Test cricket. One week he wasn't ready, and the next week he takes 12 wickets. You decide.

It was on that tour that it became obvious that the Australian team now inhabited a little bubble of their creation. A magical place where the Australian team eat candy floss off Shane Watson's taught abs, to which the media, fans, and anyone not in the current side could never fly.

No matter how stupid or obviously incorrect their decisions were, they argued that no mistake had been made. On the third day of the last Test at Nagpur, Australia found themselves in a position to win the game. They had India 6/166 in the second innings and were only trailing by 252, with four of the tail to get. Unfortunately, the over-rate was pathetic and Ricky Ponting was in danger of being suspended for their next Test (the ultra important one at the Gabba against the world's seventh-best side, New Zealand). Ponting decided to save his bacon. He brought on White, Hussey and Clarke to get through the overs quickly. The site of Michael Hussey running back to his mark between each ball showed that the sick desperation that Australia had once shown in trying to win matches, they now displayed to stop their captain being rightfully suspended. Dhoni and Harbhajan put on over 100, and Australia were never in the game after that.

Ricky Ponting faced heavy criticism from Allan Border, Ian Chappell and, well, me. But Ponting, Nielsen and Cricket Australia's chief man–in-a-suit all backed Ponting. Australia cricket had been changing for a long time, but never was it more evident than in this upchuck event.

India won 2-0.

Up next was England's much-hyped $20 million match in Antigua against the might of the Stanford Superstar XI. A team that comprised of players Viv Richards liked, and named in honour of the man who may or may not have skimmed the money off an unsuspecting public with the help of something called a ponzi scheme.

It was R-rated pornography (no penetration from the beginning). 'Sir' Allan Stanford arriving at Lord's with a chopper full of fake cash. Graeme Swann thinking about pink Ferraris. A pitch that suited no form of entertainment. KP saying the money would mean more to the Stanford boys. The English players trying to forget about the money. Lights too low for the players to see high balls. Emily Prior sitting on Stanford's lap. The English players getting pissed off at Stanford. Rumours about players getting caught with other people's ladies. A real estate agent coming down from New York to play. And finally Chris Gayle stepping all over England.

KP left that series saying the players had been confused, and his already unsteady relationship with Peter Moores, then the coach, seemed to get worse.

Stanford Superstars won by ten wickets.

When Australia got home from India at the end of 2008 they were playing New Zealand, a team who had given up on Test cricket under John Bracewell but now had a new coach. Australia stumbled on the first day, but early season Gabba wickets can be like that and the home team, ended up winning the series with one foot in the air.

It was a quiet little series. Jason Krejza was dropped after his sub par 12-wicket haul, then he got injured and Australia picked Nathan Hauritz out of grade cricket. A club spinner. Hauritz's first selection in the Test team had come in the match against India in 2004 in which Michael Clarke, the part-time slow left-armer, took six for 9, a match in which Hauritz took only five wickets. Soon after, he was discarded, and he hadn't been anywhere near the team since. Upon returning to his state of Queensland he found life tough, so he moved to New South Wales.

Lots of Australian spinners move to New South Wales. No pitch is more conducive to spin than the Sydney Cricket Ground, and in no other state are the selectors watching so carefully. Stuart MacGill made the move before Hauritz, Beau Casson made the move after. After a while, Hauritz struggled to get a game there. Casson was the better batsman, MacGill was the better bowler (a zillion times over) and a new boy by the name of Steve Smith was pretty good as well. MacGill had retired from international cricket. Casson had put in a terribly ordinary debut. And Smith was still unsure of the meaning of his life, a batsman who bowls or bowler who bats.

With Bryce McGain still injured, Jason Krejza newly injured, Dan Cullen underperforming, Cullen Bailey not performing, and Xavier Doherty bowling stutter balls in one-day domestic cricket, the selectors made a bold move by picking Hauritz to play against the Kiwis in Adelaide. It was the official sign of the death of the Australian spinners; the unofficial sign was when Cameron White missed the pitch in India.

Haurtiz's first-class bowling average with Queensland had been 49. Terrible, but on a pitch made for seamers, not that unheard of. His bowling average for New South Wales was 46, on the spinniest pitch in Australia. Get a shovel.

In his last state game he had been overlooked for two other spinners. His best figures for that season were 3/116. In 50 first-class matches he had never taken a five-wicket haul. His strike rate in first class cricket was a wicket every 15 overs. From the 04/05 season (the season he returned a

Test player) till the 2007/08 season, he took ten wickets.
Ten fucking wickets in four seasons of cricket. Not a great way to introduce
Australia's Ashes spinner. But I didn't make up these stats.

Iain O'Brien's blogging loomed as the highlight of this series. Although that
was ruined soon enough when he was called a faggot (which he misspelled
as fagot) by the crowd at the Gabba and it made international news. The
NZC boys then firmly stood on his blogging throat from then on in.

Australia won 2-0.

England went to India in November 2008. After the fifth of seven ODIs ,
the terror attacks hit Mumbai. The remainder of the one-day series was
cancelled (the only good thing to come out of the attacks) and England
went home.

The English team were obviously split on whether to come back or not for
the Tests. Andrew Strauss (not the captain, remember) was not. He came
out publicly and said that cricket must defeat terrorism, or something like
that. He sounded like an intelligent Republican, but he was right. Cricket
did come back to India and Strauss flashed his moral righteousness all over
the ground in the comeback Test at Chennai.

England still lost. Harmison and Flintoff obviously never wanted to go back
to India. When Sehwag, Sachin and Yuvraj Singh hit the English attack
everywhere, terrorism wasn't England's only problem. KP seemed to think
that Moores' lack of tactical nous had cost England the game. KP's non-
existent tactical nous was also laid bare. The next match was drawn. KP
had therefore been in charge for a game where his players lost 20 million
dollars, and for a series loss.

India won 1-0.

Then South Africa turned up in Australia in late 2008. Australia seemed
to have forgotten all about the trip to India and were looking good again.
Mitchell Johnson had become their best bowler, and in the first Test at the

Waca he destroyed South Africa with an old ball spell of five for 2 and set up Australia for a win. But Australia didn't win; instead they let South Africa score 4/414. Johnson was the only bowler who looked like getting a wicket. Brett Lee still looked heartbroken after his marital problems. Peter Siddle was in his second Test, and Jason Krejza's second Test had him leaking runs at will.

Two weeks later, in the Boxing Day Test, Australia found themselves in another great position. South Africa were 7/184 after Australia made 394 in their first innings. Three more quick wickets, and Australia might have locked up the series at 1-1. Instead, JP Duminy squeezed 275 more runs out of the tail, and South Africa went on to win the series.

For the last Test of this series, Australia changed their line up. Brett Lee's heart was now not the only thing injured. Andrew Symond's knee was ruling him out. Australia won the match, but it was too little, too late for this series.

South Africa won 2-1

Around the happy new year-point KP told the ECB that he couldn't work with Moores. And that is when the real fun started. The ECB seemed to agree with him, so they fired Moores. But then in a decision that only the ECB could make, they decided that they didn't want a captain who asked for coaches to be sacked, so they sacked KP too. "We agree with you Kevin, but we don't like your tone".

It was all odd, and yet it made perfect sense.

The Australian way of picking the captain was tossed out, and the English way was reinstated. So the best educated public school boy was Strauss, and he took over a team with two ex-Test captains and one ex-one-day captain. His unofficial vice-captain was Alastair Cook, who hadn't made a Test hundred in over a year at that stage.

England flew to the Windies in February 2009 for what became an accidental five-test series, only to give up the first game with a second innings total of 51. England's No. 3 in that Test was Ian Bell. If you were breeding a technique for the No. 3 position you would struggle to find a more complete package for it than Ian Bell. Based purely on his artistry as a batsman, he is a pleasure to watch. If I were a mad billionaire who hosted parties that people came to just because there was lots of booze and freaky shit going on, I'd hire Ian Bell for the event, strip him naked, oil him up, and make him practise his cover drive for hours on end in a giant birdcage.

Test cricket, though, isn't quite that simple. Having an elegant technique is only one small part of making the big time. You also need to make ugly runs, build on your good starts – and you need to have presence at the crease.

It doesn't really matter what presence you have, just that you have it. You can be a tough little bastard like Ricky, an emotionless patient freak like Rahul, or cool-ass motherfucker like Kumar. But you need something. Bell has none of these attributes. He is the sort of person you reckon you could talk into jumping off a building if you felt the need. Shane Warne sees weakness better than most, and he gave Bell the Sherminator nickname with good reason.

Bell has constantly teased the selectors into thinking he is a No. 3. He passes 50 there quite often. He just doesn't go any further. His average of 31 from the position is below par. The worst thing about Bell is he just doesn't seem to get "it". He was dropped in the Windies after the massacre of 51, but still seemed to think that he was a scapegoat, not someone who deserved to be dropped.

Ian Bell's dropping let Owais Shah take over. Oh Owais, you magnificent nervy bastard. If you have ever seen him in full flight you will know how good this bloke can be. If you have ever seen him in full flight internationally you will know you have seen an eclipse. In domestic cricket, Owais is a force of nature. In international cricket he is a yet-to-be-specified nervous condition. His running between wickets is like Snakes on a Plane, so shit it should be funny, but it isn't. And his arm cramps? Fuck me, stop gripping the bat so damn hard. I think that when a batsman holds the bat so hard it makes him retire hurt, he should see a hypnotist.

Shah had his chance in the West Indies, and you will never get a better chance to make runs than in this series. There were runs there for everyone: Brendan Nash, Tim Ambrose and Denesh Ramdin, but not Shah. With respect to that three, Shah could buy them, sell them, rent them out, and then sell them at a discount with his talent, and yet Shah could only contribute 133 runs at 22 with a top score of 57. The pitches for the last three Tests were made not of grass, but of marshmallows made especially to ensure that the Windies' 1-0 lead could be retained. You and I could have put on a partnership of 30 on these wickets. Now I don't know who you are, but I am pretty sure we could have, and I am no superstar with the bat. That is just how the wicket was. Shah couldn't.

It seemed the universal opinion that if Shah couldn't make runs against the West Indies on these wickets, he wasn't going to make runs against Australia, ever.

It was a weird series, and the West Indies first series win in more than five years against a real Test-playing nation. That is embarrassing. It also included a non-Test at the Sir Vivian Richards stadium, built for the 2007 World Cup, because the bowlers' run ups were too sandy. There were good signs for England: Broad and Anderson seemed to come on a bit, Swann jumped Monty in the pecking order and Bell was finally dumped. Freddie got injured again, but was still going to be fit enough to play in the IPL – to the delight of everyone.

West Indies won 1-0.

By the time Australia got to South Africa in February 2009 their bowling line-up had been completely revamped. Not one of the bowlers had been a Test player 18 months earlier. For the first time in 20 years they were playing a bits-and-pieces player in Andrew McDonald. Marcus North was picked because he could bowl a bit, and Phillip Hughes had the worst technique of any Australian batsman, perhaps ever.

Australia rushed Bryce McGain back from injury to fill the spinner's slot, showing that they were far from whelmed with Hauritz's performances against New Zealand and South Africa at home. Bryce was clearly not ready to make his international debut. At this stage Bryce was the only Australian spinner who could argue that he is a better player than Hauritz. In 22 first-class matches he had a bowling average of 36 with four five-wicket hauls. He also gets his wickets five overs sooner than Hauritz on a home pitch – the Melbourne Cricket Ground – not as suited to spin.

Of course, my love for Bryce McGain often clouds over a couple of facts: Bryce is older than Jesus and Bryce had possibly the worst debut in the history of Test cricket.

Small facts, but I wouldn't want to sound biased or anything. The worst debut is the reason why Nathan Hauritz is still around.

South Africa, showing the subtlety of a horny Doberman, beat Bryce up. They didn't just want to end his career, but end the career of all future McGains in one brutal batting display. Bryce was a hamster, and South Africa were concrete slabs dropped from a great height. By the time they had finished there was just a red bloody stain with a few hairs stuck to it.

That was the day that Nathan Hauritz was picked as Australia's Ashes spinner. There was still no guarantee that he would play. Even if Australia thought that Bryce was their best spinner, they were still going down the path of picking a batsman who could bowl a bit of spin, for South Africa. Marcus North wasn't exactly setting Shield cricket on fire with the bat when he was picked for Australia, but he was the best-performed spinner in the country at that stage. His average in Shield cricket for Western Australia is 48, which falls nicely between Hauritz's averages for Queensland and New South Wales.

Of course, Australia won that series. Johnson and Siddle were brutal, and they outmuscled South Africa's attack. It was a stunning form reversal. North, Johnson and Hughes made hundreds, McDonald was hardly hit off the square, and Siddle bowled so well that Lee and Clark were hardly being mentioned.

Australia won 2-1.

The Windies then travelled to England for the return series in 2009 as stand-ins for the stand-ins. The Windies were both unwilling, and unable. Chris Gayle arrived in England so late that the toss almost had to be put back. The Windies played pretty well on the first day, but they couldn't catch, and then they couldn't be bothered at all. From that day on the Windies had the appearance of kids who had been forced to visit their Grandma. It was possibly the dullest series of all time, the main story being that Chris Gayle doesn't like Test cricket as much as Twenty20. As if we couldn't tell that from how he bats.

England won 2-0.

Australia looked like they had the better form of the two sides at that stage, but they had one more ace up their sleeves: the World Twenty20 world thingy. Before that got going, though, Andrew Symonds was sent home for drinking in the day, effectively ending his international career. Interesting preparation, sending home your star Twenty20 player.

In the warm-ups Australia beat Bangladesh and crushed New Zealand. Then the real tournament started. In the group game against West Indies, Chris Gayle kept hitting them into the Archbishop Tenison's school next to the Oval. Australia then failed to pick former unpickable mystery bowler Ajantha Mendis against Sri Lanka. Two games, out of the tournament.

They tried to put their positive spin on it, saying it was better to be out practising than in and slogging. The truth was Ponting doesn't really care about twenty20 cricket. Nothing showed this more than the way his team played, and the way his team was selected (Dirk Nannes?). This tournament is not yet that important and so it didn't mean much, but Australia would have liked a more reasonable start to their English jaunt.

England's time in the tournament wasn't much better. They did something that no other team could have done: they lost to the Netherlands (the complete outsiders), then they beat Pakistan (the eventual winners), lost to South Africa (the perennial underachievers) and then knocked out India (the favourites). England had more impact on the tournament than any team other than Pakistan, and yet didn't make the semi-finals.

Like I said, this Ashes series is not between the best two teams in the world, but between two teams that play the Ashes. Is it too late to invite South Africa and India?

Hopes of the nation

The Ashes is no place for a fresh-faced debutant. It is for men with scars and facial hair. Who have been around the traps, have a story to tell, and can perform when they are called up.

Australia and England have no such men. Instead the Ashes rests on the shoulders of young men who have no idea what the Ashes will do to them.

Test cricket is a dominatrix; it is tough, painful, embarrassing, but exhilarating if you survive. The Ashes is a conveyor belt of dominatrixes.

Four of the key players in this Ashes were virgins, not ideal, but necessary.

Phil Hughes

I get sensitive about Phil Hughes. I am the one who discovered him you see. True story. I saw him make runs against Victoria and said he would be a superstar. He was ugly, unconventional, and yet he made runs against a top notch Victorian attack, four of whom have since represented Australia, and was so good that England's Darren Pattinson couldn't even get into the line-up.

All day he jumped, swerved, swatted, heaved, and scored slowly. It wasn't an entertaining innings, or even one Hughes would tell to his grandkids, but it just had grunt. Real grunt. It was not an easy day for batting. Even Simon Katich, who broke the runs record in Shield cricket that season, couldn't find his form, but Hughes stood out. Being there felt like some religious experience. I told all my mates about this kid, started mentioning him on my website, and waited for Matt Hayden to retire so I could start the Phil Hughes bandwagon.

It should also be noted that I hate NSWales cricketers. Especially the young ones who seem to jump the queue of all the hard-working and more deserving players (from Victoria). Hughes was this prototype through and through. From the moment he played for NSWales it was obvious the Australian selectors had pencilled him in.

But unlike the rest of them he truly deserved it. Teenage batsmen who come into Shield cricket often have trouble making real runs. They put in good performances, but the oppressive nature of the competition usually means they play a few cameos and disappear. Hughes didn't do that. He made serious first-class runs.

Other than his little baby face there was nothing young about him. His runs didn't come in the way that other young prodigies have made them, with piss and vinegar – his seemed to come from intelligent batting and freakish hand/eye co-ordination. There was a gentle buzz about Hughes, but not the normal Australia-wide scream when a young batsman rips it up in the Shield.

The reason was simple. Not one great former Australian cricketer had come out and said Phil Hughes was a "once-in-a-generation cricketer". That phrase is so overused in Australia that it makes the English equivalent – "the next Botham" – feel underused. In the current Australian set-up there are five: Ricky Ponting, Michael Clarke, Shane Watson, Brett Lee and Mitchell Johnson.

I got so upset by the phrase at one stage I started calling them all once-in-a-generation teddy bears. How can five players in one team all be once in a generation? Exactly. Yet somehow even making a century in a Shield final before he had turned 20 was not enough for someone to bring out the moniker for Hughes. Because being called a once-in-a generation player guarantees you will be selected and persisted with.

The reason, yet again, was simple. No former cricketer was going to come out and back Phil Hughes with his "technique". I have actually set a new world record in writing the most words on the man without bringing up his "technique". I am sure you have seen it, but for the blind people who are listening to this on audio tape (they say I sound like a young Damien Fleming, you know) I'll explain it as best I can.

Hughes is essentially the Don Bradman of tailend batting. He backs away to every ball, giving himself room through point where he likes it, and then he throws everything he has at the ball and generally smacks it for four. When the ball is short he responds as if it is a wasp, and he a teenage girl, flailing his hands in the general direction while contorting his body into positions that don't make sense.

It is probably the ugliest way of playing short-pitched bowling I can remember seeing. The second ugliest would probably be Steve Waugh (ohhhh, he went there, yes I did). Waugh played short bowling in a similar manner but he was nowhere near as frenetic as Hughes.

To say that Hughes looks like he hates the short ball is fair, but then it should be mentioned that he looks like he is afraid of full balls on the stumps as well. When he bats he is often twitchy, all nervous energy and cut shots. About the only time he looks comfortable is when the ball is two feet wide of off stump, the rest of the time he is pure anxiety.

That didn't stop him slapping around South Africa, a far superior bowling unit to England, in his opening Test series. Or dominating the fast bowling love shack that is Shield cricket. He even made runs in county cricket, albeit in the boondocks of division two.

Very little else about Phil Hughes is mentioned other than his "technique". So when he was bowled by Pepler Sandri (a county cricket journeyman from South Africa) I wasn't surprised to hear that the BBC Sussex commentators had worked him out. Bowl straight and full with a fast bowler and he will eventually play around it. Their revolutionary plan of straight and full worked in the second innings as well when Pepler bowled him again.

That buzz lasted until the next game against the England Lions when Steve Harmison started beating him up with the short ball. Twice he took the glove into the cordon. Both dismissals were ugly, but Hughes does have a habit of only getting out in truly ugly ways. It didn't matter though; he couldn't play the short ball. It was fact.

So much so that on the basis of these two wickets, Harmy was even being mentioned as a possible bowler for Cardiff.

Hughes had somehow gone from golden goose to lead albatross without a Test being played. The media from both countries ran with the story that he couldn't play short bowling. It was a feeding frenzy.

On my site, our resident English correspondent, the skiver, had this to say before the Ashes:

> *"Burst onto the scene against a South African side who had hardly seen any footage of him and scored plenty of runs against an attack somewhat lacking in either brains or guile. Even so, he showed some weakness against the rising ball bowled from around the wicket and moving into him. England's attack might not be as pacy as the South Africans', but Broad and Anderson certainly have more wit about their bowling than Steyn, Morkel and Ntini, and Flintoff specialises in the sort of ball Hughes has trouble with."*

Nonsense. Every word of it.

Coming into the Test Hughes would have to survive a barrage of short balls from Freddie and a barrage of short-ball questions from the media.

Mitchell Johnson

When Mitchell first came onto the scene I was pretty damn excited. A proper left-arm fast bowler. Australia hadn't had one since Bruce Reid's wispy moustache was on show. Then he disappeared and I gave up on him. He was involved in the heady world of plumbing for a while, but when that industry busted he was back on the state scene.

His state record was blah. Average of 31 bowling most of his time on the green early-season North Texas (the other name for Queensland) wickets as well. When he was picked it was under the aforementioned once-in-a-generation clause. He *did* do well in one-day cricket. He seemed to find more zip off the wicket, wobble the ball around a bit, and generally troubled most batsmen.

So when Australia had their mass exodus when Warne and McGrath retired he was tipped as a Test bowler. And straight away he looked like one of those "good with white, rubbish with red" bowlers you can see scattered around world cricket. The guys who make the white ball sing, and the red ball cry. Almost every spell he bowled for Australia early on he let off the pressure. It hurt too, as Brett Lee had finally started reaching his potential and Australia's resident proctologist Stuart Clark was still making life uncomfortable for batsmen.

Yet, Mitchell got wickets.

Mitch didn't even have the normal left-arm skill of bring the ball back in. He just sprayed it around, mostly three feet wide of off stump. No one, bar Ricky, was talking him up.

I was savage on him. Actually, I was savage on the selectors for gifting this guy (who had done fuck all in state cricket) an armchair ride when he was obviously not quite ready for the big leagues. The Australian team was clinging on to the title of world's best team by a whisker at this stage. I couldn't see how they could give someone unproven such a run when players like Douggie Bollinger and Peter Siddle were tearing a hole in state cricket and couldn't get a game.

There were few times when he didn't look nervy in this period. You could see he was always working on something mid-match: seam position, arm height, and follow through were often practised on his walk back to his mark. It was excruciating as a fan. Test cricket is not the place for on-the-job training. This, coupled with his almost docile "I'm not sure what I'm doing here" expressions, drove me up the wall.

Then Johnson changed. It was subtle at first. He just reined in his line a bit. Then he seemed to stop working on every aspect of his bowling out in the middle. Not long after he looked confident. Then he looked happy.

On the tour of India he was Australia's best bowler. Three Tests later he was the spearhead of the attack. Suddenly his stats seemed pretty damn good. In 08 he got 63 wickets in his first full calendar year of cricket. More than four wickets a game and most of his Tests were against the Indians. Early in 09 he was just as good against the South Africans and was the difference between the two sides when Australia won.

Then there was his batting. Overhyped by some, undervalued by others. He started off looking like a lucky slogging tailender. Then South Africa brought out the best of him. He made runs against them with ease, and made Paul Harris look more like a one-armed gimp than he already did. Small grounds helped, but Johnson hits the ball so far, small grounds is almost a cop out.

The hyperbole then started about how good his batting was – people were even saying that he could bat top six. He can't bat top six. He won't ever bat top six (in Tests anyway). If he keeps developing he could bat at seven. Right now he is a Neanderthal batsman. The ball comes down; if he likes it, he tries to smash it, if not he leaves it or defends it. He doesn't think like a batsman, and seems to do his best work when he is simply hitting rather than having to guide the tail.

With Freddie's spaghetti lower half, Jacques Kallis' form slump, Daniel Vettori's change into a batsman, and Dwayne Bravo's continued absence, Mitchell became the poster boy for modern all-rounders. It was either him or Shakib Al-Hasan. He was big-hitting. Fast. Good looking. Marketable. And has a lady so pretty she melts you.

He was the only discernible difference between these two pretty ordinary sides. A man who could win a game with bat or ball, and drag the Ashes out of the mediocre swamp it might inhabit.

He was even going to turn up in England with a fabled inswinger, a ball he had mastered on no fewer than four occasions in South Africa. It was going to turn him from high performing Australian all-rounder to Golden God. Look at what he had achieved without an inswinger – with it he could sweep Australia back to their rightful place at the top of the heap.

When he did arrive in England, he seemed to have a great deal of trouble hitting the actual pitch. The only match he looked like the Mitchell of South Africa was the Twenty20 warm-up against New Zealand. The rest of the time he looked like the young Mitchell Johnson who struggled for control, confidence and my love.

There were many factors. First Ashes series; the inswinger being all-consuming; most bizarrely, a public spat with his mother about why he didn't talk to her as much as a son should.

The Ashes one is hard to quantify; the inswing one seems right on the money. Or maybe he was fine with it until his mum implied he was under the thumb and a lousy child.

Australia backed Mitchell to find form by the Ashes; they also brought him a hot water bottle and a blanket. He had the power to win the Ashes for Australia, which also meant the opposite was true.

Ravi Bopara

I was at Ravi Bopara's coming out party. A hundred against the Windies at the home of cricket while the rest of his top order took the day off. That was the only day in that series the Windies really tried to win the Test. So while it is easy to say he milked a poor team, he did milk them on a good day, which makes the milk sweeter (got into a bad analogy there, couldn't get out).

England didn't really care who he made the runs against, just that he made three figures' worth. It was something that Ian Bell was allergic to, while Owais Shah would have run out four team-mates on the way. Ravi was assured, confident, technically efficient and had scores on the board. England had their No. 3; Vaughan and Robert Key never got a look in.

There is a lot to like about Ravi. He has this ripping cockiness, giving KP batting tips after his second Test ton, hits the ball very well and likes to attack. He also this weird nervy streak in him. He reminds me of a likeable

Dean Jones, ego and vulnerability all wrapped up in one. And he has one of the best sad faces of any modern-day batsman when walking off. I could imagine him using that face to get girls to look for his lost puppy.

What he doesn't have is the real No. 3 strut I mentioned earlier. England players just don't seem to have it. Ravi wants everyone to like him. Against the Windies he couldn't stop chatting to their team when he was batting. I don't mean sledging, I mean actual chatting. He wants to be liked; you can see it in every part of his personality.

I am not saying Ravi is too nice to bat in that crucial position. Rahul Dravid is a No. 3, and you won't find many nicer men than he. You don't have to be an anti-social asshole to bat there. But you do need presence.

The position is not just for batting, it is for stamping the game with your initials. Ravi doesn't seem to get that. He seems to follow the lead from the batsman at the other end or the opposition. The innings against the Windies was a perfect example. It was a fine innings, but devoid of batting personality – don't laugh because I just made up a new cricket phrase.

Batting personality exists. Let me set up the game for you. England batsmen never really got started, Ravi batted through the first day without any help from decent partnerships. He made his hundred, but it was just a hundred. It never felt like the kind of rearguard effort like Rahul Dravid would have made; no real counterpunching to it like Ponting would have tried. Kumar would have given the innings a sense of cool: "I've got this." Ravi just batted.

And while there is nothing wrong with just batting in general, at No. 3, you want a little more. England still went on to make a good total. It wasn't like Ravi's hundred was useless – it set up the game – but it just felt a bit average. A week later he made another one, with simple accumulation.

While Ravi might worry about his batting personality it was his war with Shane Warne that really would have bothered him. Not that it was a war as such, more a full frontal assault by an ex player with an agenda to grind. Nothing Warne says is without agenda or grudge, which makes it fun, but Ravi must have felt like a cow in the headlights as Warne opened up on him.

Like a lot of Warne's best work it wasn't a hard ripping leg break that got the job done, but a slider out of the front of the hand:

"Bopara is a good first-class cricketer," he said, "but he is not an international cricketer. I think he's got all the talent in the world, but I just don't think he's got the temperament. He can be put off his game too easily and he's too worried about how he looks.

"Let's hope England aren't relying on Bopara [for the Ashes] because they could be in trouble."

Perfectly pitched. Unlike Mitchell's mother, Warne knew what he was doing. It was a surgical strike.

Stuart Broad

I don't get Stuart Broad. No player gets more unanimous anal lickings from the Sky team than he, but I just don't see it. Maybe you need to be a commentator who is personal friends with his father to see it. Yes, he looks classical with the bat at times, but more often he looks nervy and edgy. Yes, he is exceptionally clever with the ball, but he doesn't get wickets.

Regardless of my opinion, he is here to stay. If you are six-foot heaps, bowl at 90mph, look like an Aryan boy-band member and can play back-foot drives sweeter than honey, people keep you around even when your results aren't that fantastic.

When I think of the tour of the West Indies all I can think of his Stuart Broad coming around the wicket, rolling his fingers on one and being called a genius. He did bowl well in the Windies. Not that it mattered – a Frankenstein bowler built with parts from the West Indies fast-bowling elite would have struggled to take wickets in that series.

In the home series against the Windies he found himself at No. 7. And a more shit-scared No. 7 I cannot remember. His innings at Lord's was pure comedy gold. Dropped three times on the way to 38. I'm not saying 38s need to be chanceless, but getting dropped three times is taking the piss.

Then there was effort of the last over against the Dutch in the Twenty20. He will forever be the face of that game. He had come up with this theory about bowling round the wicket and wide of off stump with a packed offside and it was working. The Dutch had no idea what he was doing, and had no hope of getting him away.

Instead they tried hitting the ball straight back to him and watching him self-combust as they ran. It was ingenious. All England watched this young man with the average record fumble everything and throw wildly.

I wouldn't want to harp on this over, but if I did, it would look like this.

7 runs required from 6 balls. *The first ball is full and Ryan Ten Doeschate can only squeeze it back to Broad who fields, tries to throw down the stumps as they go for a single, but misses from a few metres away.*

6 from 5. *Second ball all Edgar Schiferli can do is hit the ball straight back to Broad, who fumbles it, picks it up at his feet and dives for the stumps catching Edgar a inch or two short. Turns out, though, that Broad has fumbled the ball again a bee's dick from the stumps and his hand breaks the stumps. Not out after 76 replays.*

5 from 4. *Third ball is a shit full toss that could have been hit anywhere but following in the pattern the Dutch had created it is hit back to Broad above his head and he drops it. A tough chance but with all three balls he could have stopped the run or got a wicket.*

4 from 3. *The fourth ball goes straight through Schiferli but the Dutch run a bye anyway. James Foster misses the stumps and the ball comes back up the pitch to Broad. It's not a run-out chance but he still fumbles it.*

3 from 2. *The fifth ball is smacked to mid-on by Ten Doeschate for a single; Broad just looks happy that it has not come back to him.*

2 from 1. The final ball is almost a chapter in itself. Three minutes of Paul Collingwood looking confused; there are team meetings; the helmet is brought out for Foster to come up to the stumps and then the helmet is taken off and Foster is moved back to his original keeping position. Nobody seems to know what to do. Broad comes in, hits the block hole and Schiferli squeezes it straight back to Broad. Where else? Broad dives to save it, takes it clean as a whistle and while still on the ground turns around and with all three stumps to aim at, fires it in, victory in his hands. But he misses the wicket and his throw is so inaccurate it allows the Dutch not only the run, but an overthrow that turns a tie into an England defeat.

Gagger of the greenandgoldrugby.com blog called it a "shat-trick", and for all my trying I couldn't think of anything better.

The aftermath was savage. The average English fan thought Broad was a useless fuck-up. People were walking out of the ground like family members had just died – not me, I walked out like I'd just won the lottery. One friend of mine suggested Broad should go play for South Africa; most people couldn't understand how someone could continually fuck up so many chances. His temperament became the story of the day.

Nasser Hussain was on the front foot straight away, declaring that Broad was a winner and had to throw the ball at the stumps, as all winners would. I thought that was an odd statement. Calling a man a winner after he had four good chances of getting a wicket in one over and failed with them all suggests that Nasser and I have a different take on what being a winner is.

Okay, so Broad wants to win, and he wants to be the main guy, but so do I, so do you. Most people do. Few can. Could you imagine Glenn McGrath making as big a mess of that over as Broad did. McGrath probably isn't half the fielder Broad is either, but he would have got a wicket in that over, he would have stopped at least one more run, and he would have won the game for Australia. That is what winners do. Broad is not quite there yet. And that is okay.

My main problem with Broad is the way he thinks as a bowler. He thinks like a part-time bowler who specialises in batting. Probably because that is what he was until he had a growth spurt. Now he bowls at a good clip, but more like a medium pacer trying to out-think the batsman than a top-class quick who hits the spot and looks for subtle movement.

This is the series for me. Sink or swim. England have plenty of all-rounders in their line up, and on the fringes; his cameos of 30 won't save him if he bowls like Sourav Ganguly against the Aussies.

The tube station adverts have him as the face of Maximuscle, a company specialising in sports nutrition supplements, but it's a confusing choice for sure – I've eaten better built chickens – but he was chosen by them, and by the selectors, because they know he could become the main man.

Swann v Siddle

There are people who think the battle for the Ashes lies between the elegantly groomed hands of James Anderson and the formerly labret-pierced Mitchell Johnson. Wrong. It rests on the shoulders of the leading Test wicket-taker of 2009, and the best performing fast bowler of 2009.

They also happen to be the most entertaining members of either team. Graeme Swann and Peter Siddle. Both men have been significantly involved in the transmogrification of their sides from shit, to better than shit.

England had a horror winter, yet somehow still unearthed the world's best off-spinner (to left-handers), who burst onto the world stage like an 80s rock sensation (with a chin like that he was bound to be a star). Australia were finding Test cricket pretty damn hard in their summer, but they persisted with their working-class hammer, a man with a chest like a Lucha libre star, and somehow Peter Siddle has turned into Merv Hughes without the moustache or beer gut.

Not only are these two probably the most likeable cricketers in either team, they are also the key to the Ashes. If Swann finds it harder to bowl to the

Australian left-handers than he did to Devon Smith, Australia will have a huge advantage. If Siddle's histrionics and work ethic can't wear down England like it did the South Africans, England will be in a very good position.

Yet if they both fire this will be a wonderful series, as both are natural entertainers. I envisage a time in the future when all young English cricket fans want chin implants to look more like their wacky spinner, and all young Australian fans try to stick their chests out to honour their fast-bowling weapon.

May the most entertaining man win.

Selection

Australia

There is an insane confidence in Australia's current batting line-up, if they can honestly bring across only six frontline batsmen to an Ashes series. Two of the six have played five Tests between them and cannot be guaranteed to make runs. Whilst Hughes and North both played matchwinning innings in South Africa, that was just one series. For all Australia know, Hughes will struggle against Paul Collingwood's savage off-cutters.

Then there is Mike Hussey who seems to have been given a legacy position in the Australian top order based on his first 18 Tests (which to me proves nothing other than the existence of the Matrix). Heaven forbid we look at his next 17 Tests where his average comes down from 80 to 30, the level you expected from a wicketkeeper in the late 80s.

This is without even mentioning the fact that Simon Katich and Michael Clarke looked like they were batting on tightropes during the last Ashes, and that Brad Haddin has never played an Ashes Test. That leaves Ricky Ponting as the only player the selectors can rely on, and he is old, if still quite handy.

The selectors are telling us, maybe with a little too much eagerness, that they believe Shane Watson to be the backup batsman. Shane Watson also believes this. Watson is a talented batsman, but he is also Shane Watson: the man who stalks a spot in the Australian team like a carnivorous wolf and gets injured thinking about playing cricket. His Test average with the bat is under 20. And the only time he opened the bat in first-class cricket resulted in much laughing.

Watson being the backup batsman suggests to me that the selectors have no real faith in this new-style bowling attack, even with two old fellas coming back into it. Watson is insurance in case Australia can't manufacture 20 wickets like they did in South Africa.

Nathan Hauritz was picked as the lone spinner. Gavin Robertson, Australia's last spinner picked from club cricket, was retired. Marcus North is only a part-timer really, but one at least as skilful as Nathan Hauritz, and he had made a pretty handy hundred on his Test debut. He was given the spinning job in Australia's victorious tour of South Africa. In a perfect world Marcus North would not be your first spin option, but this is not a perfect world, because Dannii Minogue is famous. If Paul Harris is the ICC's 8th ranked bowler then Marcus North is not a bad choice.

The demeanours of Hauritz and North are worlds apart as well. North is a self-assured man. He looks like a professional, not just of cricket, but from any walk of life: a lawyer who understands and specialises in share schemes and does it with no fuss or fanfare. You feel that he knows he belongs in Test cricket. He has played all over England in county cricket, sometimes as a raging success, other times as a plodder. But he knows his game inside and out. Hauritz is a gentle young man, one who seems unsure of himself or his talent. A blog he wrote for Cricket Australia showed someone with shockingly low self-belief, who felt that he might have been out of his depth (and that was after it was heavily edited by the governing body).

Still, Australia knew that they needed at least one spinner in England, maybe two, so Hauritz was always going to be a chance. The problem was shown up in Hautitz's warm-up games. They weren't good. They were the very opposite of good. Against a weakened Sussex side Hauritz got smashed around Hove. Hauritz doesn't get smashed. His one skill is keeping the batsmen from coming after him. He is a container. Not in this game. In the first innings, the Sussex boys went after him, and although he bowled better in the second, he ended up with 1/158 in 38 overs. Bryce McGain was smashed in his warm-up game in South Africa. The Australian selectors had already begun to see ghosts.

Hauritz's next game started roughly the same way. The England Lions boys went at him hard, and Nathan appeared to have nothing to throw at them: 0/80 off 18 overs. In the second innings he seemed to get into some sort of form with 1/22 off 12.2, but two wickets in two games whilst going at 3.8 an over was hardly what he wanted in order to win over the selectors for the first Test. Cardiff may have been a spin friendly track, but the Australian selectors were already talking about going in with four quicks and North.

Australia stayed true to their normal spare wicket keeper routine for England. The idea was that there are more first class matches on this tour, and a wicket keeper will need a break. Injuries or form can't come into it. The West Indies are the hardest place to send a player from Australia, and there was no spare keeper on that tour; Brad Haddin just kept with broken fingers.

The most likely players to be left out of the first Test are two all-rounders, two bowlers, and a keeper.

England

The home side's squad is never poured over in the same way as a touring squad, but it does tell you who's likely to be in the team. England made the first move when they left Steve Harmison out of the squad.

Of all the current English players, nobody frustrates at such a supreme level as Harmy. He is brilliant at it. In 05 he was a monster, in 06/07 a panda bear that didn't understand its sexuality. His tour of the West Indies had been ordinary, and he couldn't get into the side for the Tests against them at home. Instead his Durham team-mate, Onions, had come into the team and cleaned up the snoozy West Indians.

Harmy had made the late play when he got Phil Hughes out twice in Australia's last practice game. His fans thought that would be enough to get him back into the team but the English management were having none of it. Onions deserved his spot, and Monty was included if they decided to use two spinners.

The back-up batsman was my lubed-up naked caged toy Ian Bell. England cannot let him out of their sight. Others had been playing better in county cricket; Owais Shah had held the position more recently than Bell, while Rob Key is never far from anyone's thoughts. But Bell remains. No. 3 has always been the most important number in the batting line-up even if Jacques Kallis, Sachin Tendulkar and Brian Lara tried to devalue it by moving down their respective orders.

England have always struggled here. Their third top scorer in the position is Mark Butcher. Butcher was a scrapper and someone I respected, but he wasn't a top Test batsman; he averaged less than 40.

So we had the great England No. 3 three audition match, also known as Marylebone Cricket Club v Durham. Rob Key opened the batting, Vaughan (remember him) was at three, and Bell at four. Each newspaper seemed to pick a different horse. They made a combined total of 29 runs, being dismissed by one of other of Durham's Australians Callum Thorp and Mitchell Claydon.

When you add Bopara and Shah, who were unavailable for the game because they were playing in the IPL (Bopara doing well, and Shah occupying the bench) England had five potential number three batsmen, and no clue.

They chose Bopara, the self proclaimed street dog. At least they had others waiting in the wings if he failed.

Reasons Harmy should or shouldn't play in the Ashes

Should: *He is a bit mental.*
Shouldn't: *He is a bit mental*
Should: *He gets freakish bounce.*
Shouldn't: *He bowls to second slip.*
Should: *He is fast, experienced and hungry.*
Shouldn't: *He is a gerbil crossed with an electric tie organiser.*
Should: *Phil Hughes can't play him.*
Shouldn't: *Phil Hughes can't play Pepler Sandri either.*
Should: *Freddie will look after him.*

Shouldn't: *Freddie can't look after his fucken self.*

Should: *Harmy plays good in England.*

Shouldn't: *The first Test is in Wales.*

Should: *Harmy loves playing in the Ashes.*

Shouldn't: *He averages 42 in the Ashes.*

Should: *Will either excite us with great cricket, or make us laugh by playing shit.*

Shouldn't: *Will probably make at least one side cry.*

Going to Wales

The build up

I didn't make my way down to Cardiff. I don't hate the Welsh or anything, it was just that the ECB thought that Crikey.com was not important enough for the Ashes. Having applied for accreditation at the start of April, I only had to wait until the end of June for the final answer. I didn't get bitter of course. If the ECB want to treat one of the few Australian journalists who actually turned up for the Ashes like a mangy dog, that is their prerogative. I am too professional to take a cheap stab at the organisation that went into bed with the Antiguan knight.

The ECB also didn't add the W back into their acronym, even though this was the first Test in Wales. For those who don't know, the full name of the ECB is the English and Wales Cricket Board, but somehow the 'W' becomes silent and invisible when the initials are read out. But Wales refused to be silent forever and put millions into hosting an Ashes Test, and for their money they got the opening game.

Quite a few people were mad, although some of those were misinformed. They thought the series should start at Lord's like it always had. By always they mean in 05 (also known as the only Ashes series ever). Because that was the only time in the modern era the first Test *had* been at Lord's.

Wales wasn't a great choice of venue, not because of the money, the history or Catherine Zeta-Jones, but because the pitch was a shitty slow son-of-a-bitch that tended to produce turgid cricket. That is not how you want the Ashes to start. It's like opening a show with some assclown from *Pop Idol* when you know James Brown is around.

The one good thing was that the pitch was supposed to spin. Probably not good for Australia, but good for cricket. Spinning pitches are cool. Not as cool as bouncy pitches, but cool nonetheless. England had decided on taking two spinners into the side: that meant Monty alongside the man who had ousted him, Swann.

Monty's fall from grace was slow, but predictable. The media should bear as much blame as anyone. They built him up into this amazing creature that would answer every prayer of English supporters hoping for real spinners rather than Ashley Giles-type spinning replicants. Monty does spin a ball. That is not what makes a great spinner though; if it was Anil Kumble would be the CEO of a washing machine company.

Spin is about flight, guile, reading the batsman, finding a weakness, working out the pitch, and then moving the batsman into the position you want him to be in. Monty had very few of these talents. He could land the ball on a low flying gnat at 22 yards, but he was only putting it there because it was a dangerous area, nothing more. He was a spinning caveman. Clubbing the batsman with his spin while everyone else was looking for a touch of subtlety.

It never came. So England turned to the guy who owned county cricket and my personal spinning hero, Grandmaster Mushtaq Ahmed, he of the double-arm twirl and wrong 'un of mass destruction. Shane Warne said of Monty that he hadn't played 38 different Tests, but one Test 38 times.

It wasn't that Monty wasn't intelligent – he'd shit on Shane Warne in an IQ test – it is just that he doesn't appear to have cricket intelligence or creative intelligence. He is very left-brained, which is part of the reason he made it to the top level, and also part of the reason that, once there, he never seemed to learn anything.

Mushie had quite a challenge on his hands. He seemed to relish his role. The media kept showing him in animated one-sided conversations with Monty; generally Monty was nodding. What magic Mushie must have been passing on. The keys to the kingdom being given to Monty every time they met up. Young spinners die for this kind of attention from a Grandmaster.

Unfortunately it was all too much for Monty. He was an automaton, and all this magic mysticism was fucking him up. Almost from the time Mushie came on board, his figures started to slip dramatically. He was varying his pace and line heaps more, but he was also bowling a great deal of crap.

Before he was a spin-bowling machine that could hit the spot for hours on end. Now he was erratic, didn't seem to read the conditions any better, but was experimenting because he knew he had too.

Coming into Cardiff he was a wreck. In county cricket he had been mauled. Adil Rashid deserved the spot far more but there were rumours floating around that he was not the current regime's "sort of guy" and he was never seriously in the hunt. Monty was the man; the English selectors seemed to have no doubts about a man who they had dropped for a Test in the Caribbean that lasted ten balls.

Australia had their selection problems. Brett Lee seemed to be the only bowler in top form coming into Cardiff and his ribs were ruling him out. The only other experienced bowler they had was Stuart Clark and there was a rumour he had lost something called nip. They seemed to have absolutely no faith in Nathan Hauritz and even though this wicket had been fined for excessive spin earlier in the year and England were definitely going to play two spinners, Australia seemed unsure whether Hauritz should even make the side.

They must have believed Clark had lost his nip because he was not selected, while Ben Hilfenhaus and Hauritz were named in the side. England looked a little more settled, Australia looked a little more dangerous. Neither side looked terribly good.

Head to Head

Captaincy

Andrew Strauss is smooth, well schooled, and knows how to handle egos. Ricky Ponting is gruff, quick to anger, but knows how to fire up his boys. Strauss should be the better captain tactically (although there is no proof of that); Ponting is the more inspirational leader.

Opening partnership

Cook and Strauss are not pleasant on the eye, but they do know how to blunt a new ball. Katich and Hughes are way less pleasant on the eye, but they don't just blunt the new ball, they hit it. England should get off to more consistent starts, but if Australia gets off to good starts they could shape a few more matches.

Batsmen

England have an inexperienced No. 3, a matchwinning No. 4, a shovelling No. 5, a plucky No. 6, and an out of form No. 7. Australia have an out-of-form champion at No. 3, a former world No. 1 at No. 4, a prodigy not suited to English conditions at No. 5, a first-class journeyman at No. 6, and an insubstantial hitter at No. 7. Australia have the better batting line-up, even if form is not completely their friend.

Tail batting

England's tail consists of two bunnies, and two players with aspirations of being bowling all-rounders. Australia's tail consists of one all-rounder and three tailenders. Swann and Broad aren't better than Johnson, but combined they make more impact – although three big innings from Johnson could be enough to sway the whole series.

Seam/swing bowling

Anderson (swing), Broad (seam), and Flintoff (heavy balls) are a top collection of bowlers. Yet it is hard not to notice that they all average over 30 with the ball and not one has been a big wicket taker in Tests. Johnson and Siddle are natural wicket takers. They will miss Lee's reverse-swing, but they have decent records even if they don't have the experience of the English attack. The England attack will all need to pull their weight for them to win, Australia will probably have more individual big hauls. The Australians just seem to have more venom, Siddle and Johnson have a combined total of 40 wickets in their last four Tests. Not bad.

Spin bowling

Graeme Swann is almost unplayable for left-handers. Monty Panesar has been lost, but still has a decent Test record. And Adil Rashid is confident enough to make an impact. Australia has three handy part-timers and Nathan Hauritz. North could chip in with a wicket or two a Test, Clarke can bowl okay if his back holds up and Katich bowls tripe, but it gets wickets. Swann is the class, Hauritz shouldn't play, and Monty may get one Test.

Part-time seamers/spinners

Collingwood is hardly a wicket taker, KP can bowl a bit, and I think I speak for everyone when I say I want more of Cook bowling. Hussey, not really, Ponting, Vaughan isn't playing. This isn't a real category.

Wicketkeepers

Matt Prior can bat. Brad Haddin can bat. Neither can keep.

Earnestness can kill you

The Brett Lee story

No one wants to play in the Ashes more than Brett Lee. NO ONE.

All of his hairs (even the pubic ones) stand on end at the very prospect of steaming in with a red nut glimmering in the sunlight at Cardiff. When his mind thinks of Freddie he conjures up visions of past battles won and lost, the friendship, the rivalry and the secret love affair; the thought of Geoffrey Boycott saying his name makes him hum with excitement; he smiles uncontrollably when he anticipates the polite applause he will receive when trotting down to fine leg and he feels giddy when the Lord's slope is mentioned. Thinking of taking guard for the first time gets him all warm and sticky.

But, that damned earnestness, the one that made him fly all round the world hoping Australia would declare him fit, has struck him again. Now on the eve of the eve of the Ashes, Lee is injured. A rib injury, which is biblical in almost every sense, as Lee and the former Mrs Lee have now separated.

Lee is not merely trying too hard; he is trying so hard that every sinew in his body is pushed to the edge. Every orifice is wide open. Every gland is strained. His body is heaved to the limit of its performance by this earnest Ashes-loving man. Something had to give.

A rib, a humble protector of that loveable heart of his. It has happened before, elite athletes pushing themselves so far they break down. It happened to me before the second *Matrix* film. I had geared myself up for it so much, that a few hours before the first showing I pulled an eye muscle. But I soldiered on, used the other eye, and walked out of the theatre proud that I had watched it with one eye down.

Lee is in a similar situation; I cannot imagine a rib injury will stop this man. If somehow he doesn't play, that will mean certain death for Brett Lee. All that furious, earnest energy bubbling around his veins needs to come out, and I fear that if Brett doesn't play, he may well just explode.

That is how he is, and it isn't the first time it has pushed him over the edge. The beamer incident from 2005, when a dangerous ball to Brendon McCullum – the fourth time he'd produced such a delivery in the season – had New Zealand coach John Bracewell warning that he could face prosecution was the perfect example of someone mentally breaking down because he couldn't perform at the level he thought his country needed of him.

When Ponting questioned his commitment, he responded by tearing out the spine of the England Lions team. It was a brutal bowling performance. Few bowlers have a spell like that in them.

Brett has pushed himself so hard to be in the position he is right now. Physically and mentally. With the departure of his wife he seemed even more committed to becoming the Brett Lee of only 18 months ago. He wanted it too much, he tried too hard, and he is broken.

I like Brett Lee, I met him once, and he was so unnecessarily nice. There have been many times I have questioned his place in the Australian team, but never have I questioned how much he wants to be there. When Brett Lee tried, he put in everything he had, and then some more.

Wanting to be in the Ashes as bad as he did is probably the reason he won't be in them.

> And all men kill the thing they love,
> By all let this be heard,
> Some do it with a bitter look,
> Some with a flattering word,
> The coward does it with a kiss,
> The brave man with a sword!
> *Oscar Wilde*

Cardiff

Day 1

Wales has some hot chick opera singer belting out tunes before the game. I never really trust hot classical musicians. I like my musicians weird-looking. Apparently she isn't even an opera singer, as the one qualification to be an opera singer is to sing in operas and she doesn't. She looks like she should be hosting lifestyle-changing bathroom shows. She is that hot that I did a Google image search. I think *Jerusalem* is sung; something about this song bothers me. Perhaps it is the subtle Christian connotations.

Strauss won the toss and decided to bat. There was nothing else he could do. Mitchell Johnson and Peter Siddle hugged and made millions of Australian bogan (chav) cricket fans feel mighty uncomfortable. There was that buzz that you get only when a bowler is coming in to start an Ashes as Johnson skulked in and slungs down a wide ball with no swing that was easily left alone by wing commander Strauss.

A terrible first ball really. It didn't go to slip, it didn't beat the bat, it didn't hit anyone. It was lame.

Hilfenhaus opened up from the other end. His first ball was pretty good, on a spot, swinging in, making Alastair Cook defend it. Then Cook got the first runs, the turn off the pads to deep square for three. The Ashes were well and truly alive.

England opening partnerships are never pretty affairs. There are no better new ball blunters than Strauss and Cook in world cricket at the moment. And blunting the new ball is a great skill; it just isn't that fun to watch. Cook's batting is an interesting case study. He has a tremendous eye, amazing patience, several technical flaws and an ability to never really take the game by the scruff of the neck.

Before the Windies came around it had been over a year since he had made a Test hundred, but he was still made the unofficial vice-captain of this side. It proves that England value two things higher than anything else: public school and patience.

It was Cook's major technical flaw that got him out. His bat was hanging outside off at an angle and doing that to Australian bowlers is like holding steak up to a shark. Hilfenhaus took the edge and Hussey took the catch.

Australia looked pretty fired up at this stage. They knew this was a tough pitch to get wickets on, and that someone like Alastair Cook could lurch over his bat for two sessions without much trouble. They had also got him out with a clear plan. Teams love that. Captains like to come up with a cool field placing or a radical bowling change for a wicket. Bowlers like to bowl an unplayable ball. But nothing brings a team together like a plan working perfectly.

This brought in Ravi Bopara. England's weak No. 3 spot would be tested early. Ravi seemed nervous, and I say nervous because if I say I think I saw him stain his pretty white trousers that would seem mean. Ravi was playing two shots a ball, some were nice, and some were ugly. There was no way he was going to last.

Strauss went before him. Australia have always had the theory that you can get Strauss out with the short one, and Mitchell Johnson, who was interchanging great balls with rotten lettuce and tomatoes got one short, straight and fast that knocked into Strauss' gloves and went to Michael Clarke slowly in his new position at first slip.

Now Bopara's strange innings had to be reined in – he needed some Valium. Instead, he continued with this kamikaze batting display until he was completely done over by the Johnson slower ball. There is nothing worse than seeing a top-order batsman getting out to a slower ball. The dismissal happens in slow motion, the shot always looks terrible, and it makes the batsman look quite stupid. This was a classic case. Ravi tried to drive the ball and instead he looped the ball up to Phil Hughes at point. If you were new to cricket you might have thought that Ravi was trying to get the ball to Hughes in the easiest manner possible.

Not that Hughes' first real taste of Ashes work was well done. He almost fucked it up and ended up catching it inches from the ground when he could have done a handstand and caught it in his asscheeks. Luckily for us Hughes even tweeted about his catch, a rare social networking insight: "Enough jokes about my catch, you either catch it or drop it, I caught it ... just ... hahahha."

Then the game settled down. The Valium that should have been brought out for Ravi was clearly put in KP's drink. He and Collingwood decided they would grind out the middle session. It wasn't pretty, but few Paul Collingwood innings are. Somehow he kept KP in check and the wicket showed its true personality – made for long, dour innings.

Australia brought on Hauritz, and he was fine. Not good, but adequate. Collingwood and KP seemed to handle him with ease, but could not get on top of him. They knew he did not have the weaponry to go through them, so they just pushed him around.

The middle session did not yield a wicket. It brought the game back to a much more even keel. Three wickets in the opening session on what looks like a good pitch for batting had been a bit of a slap in the face to England. This session brought it back.

Not long after tea Collingwood was caught behind. There are few batsmen who get caught behind or in the slip cordon more than him. It was Hilfenhaus again. By far the best of the Australian bowlers, he was taking wickets *and* keeping the runs down. The catch by Haddin was either a terrific catch by a 'keeper who picked it up late, or average footwork covered by a handy dive.

Then KP inspired a million headlines, as only he can. Having eased himself to 69 without too many problems, he had a brilliantly entertaining brain fade. He was facing Nathan Hauritz, and you can only assume he wasn't shaking in his boots in fear of losing his wicket. But as Hauritz hit delivery stride KP got down in the sweep position ready to milk him for a single.

I am not Hauritz's biggest fan, obviously, but there is one skill he does have. In one-day cricket he is quite good at changing his delivery late when a batsmen premeditates a shot. Hauritz is essentially a one-day bowler, so he is used to silly shots being played off him. This one was more than silly, it was arrogant; he might as well have gone down before Hauritz started his run up.

So Hauritz throws the ball wide of off stump, very wide. KP, bless him, refuses to change his shot, leave the ball, or anything that might be construed as backing down. He goes through with this sweep, top edging it into his helmet and it lands in the hands of Simon Katich at short-leg. The pitch map for Hauritz said it all: all the balls just outside off stump, and then one three feet wider.

Sports editors across the country cancelled their shiatsu massages and got back into the office to start the public execution of KP.

While this was happening, Freddie Flintoff and Matt Prior launched an assault on Australia. In 16 overs they scored 80-odd runs. Prior did the majority of the damage. These are not the two most dependable batsmen at No.s 6 and 7, but they are capable of changing the direction of a game, and that is what they do.

Australia picked up the new ball and prayed to Keith Miller that is would do something. It was thrown to Siddle. Since hugging Johnson at the start, he had had a pretty lean day. But Siddle is a motherfucker, and I mean that in the nicest possible way. He loves this sort of situation when the crowd and opposition are against him, and just when it looked like England might be thinking of stumps, Freddie half drives at one and pulls it back onto his stumps.

England decide to protect their No. 8 with a nightwatchman. Fuck off. I hate the very theory of nightwatchman at the best of times. But for a No. 8? They were smashing Australia. Why not continue in this vein, not shut up shop and protect your No. 8's average? Batsmen who want nightwatchmen are pissy little fuckmonkeys who want to protect their average but don't want to do the hard work when required. Opening batsmen don't get nightwatchman (well hardly ever), so why should anyone else in the order? You're a batsman, come in and bat. But Broad is way worse. He isn't even a batsman; at best he is a fast bowling all-rounder. They are supposed to be tough, not afraid of taking their team to stumps. This is more proof that Broad thinks like a batsman. A bowler would have just got on with the job, but Broad needed a bowler with actual balls to get in there and do it.

That bowler was Anderson, who managed to make it to stumps. Prior did not. With Freddie gone and a nightwatchman in, he seemed unsure as to how he should continue. He pushed at a demon of an inswinger from Siddle and was clean bowled. It was a great ball, but if Prior had a little more purpose he might have got something on it. Then Broad came out. I was disappointed. I had my heart set on Monty protecting Broad as well.

That was stumps.

KP was interviewed by Mike Atherton and said that he only got out because the ball came off his helmet, which was unlucky. He seemed oblivious to the fact the ball only hit his helmet be cause he played an ass of a shot. He then went on to say that Hauritz was a top bowler. Justification is a beautiful thing.

The English media predictably jumped into KP.

This is what I posted on my site after a brain fade he made in England's first innings in the Jamaica Test against the Windies, but like Fritz Lang films, it still resonates today.

KP loses another Test

I cannot believe that England are thinking of dropping Bell, Harmison, Monty, or Collingwood.

We all know whom to blame for this loss.

KP. The dumblsog millionaire.

Remember him getting out for 97, of course you do, because the moment he got out you said to yourself, he has lost the game for England, what a massive bellend (apparently this is an English penis joke, as the penis resembles the end of a bell, not Ian Bell, who is an actual penis).

His wicket, while trying to hit Sulieman Benn into the IPL, was so obviously the cause for England's collapse on day four that it is hardly worth mentioning.

From that moment on, no intelligent cricket fan could have thought that England were going to win the game.

97; a massive failure.

While other English players were going out in more traditional ways, through fear and defensiveness, KP yet again snubbed the traditions of English cricket.

Who does he think he is?

When England lose they like to keep the spirit of their cricket alive, but going out on 97 while trying to bring your hundred up with a 12 is not in that spirit.

He should not only be dropped, but England's top fencer, Richard Kruse, should take KP into Trafalgar Square, and carve out that English tattoo in front of a crowd of drunken chavs.

Because that is more English than getting out for 97.

Other things more English than getting out for 97 include:

1. Bowling great line and length, almost never getting hit off the cut strip, and taking no wickets (RJ Sidebottom).

2. Failing in both innings of your debut as full-time captain (AJ Strauss).

3. Earning money for nothing because you once held an important title. (MP Vaughan).

4. Being given the second most important job because you went to a toffy-assed school (AN Cook).

5. Getting the love of the English public for the odd breathtaking performance and being a great drunkard (A Filntoff).

6. Starting off as the saviour before the whole of England slowly turns on you (MS Panesar).

All these things are good and proper English behaviour. Top scoring, and saving your team from a terrible first innings score, is not.

Shame on you KP, 200 years ago you would have been sent to Australia for this behaviour. Now you just get slated in The Times.

Day 2

People were split on what the first day actually meant. Australia took seven wickets in two sessions, England scored 300 in the day. Everyone agreed, though, that too many English batsman gave their wickets away. Funny that Freddie's shot, which was shit, got a lot less publicity than KP's, which was shitter, even though he made more runs. The Australian bowlers were described as honest toilers. And Ricky Ponting spat on his hands 24 times in the middle session (he licked his hands another 12 times).

The commentators spent most of the first day telling everyone how much the ball was spinning. It seemed like wishful thinking. The pitch was spinning a bit, but nowhere near the amount that they wanted it to. It was spin about spin.

Broad started the day okay for England, but after a few quick fours Mitchell Johnson bowled him off his thigh pad. In recent years, that has happened to a lot of batsman. I never questioned why. Blogger The Old Batsman has a theory.

> *"Over the past year, Pietersen and Broad have gone the same way, and so did Lendl Simmons in the World T20 semi-final. It even happened in a club match I played in a while back. The reason's obvious: batsmen move across the stumps far further now than they did even ten years ago, meaning more balls hit that area and then fall correspondingly closer to the stumps.*
>
> *The answer's simple enough. Why doesn't someone just redesign the thigh pad? Instead of the traditional curved bottom edge that the ball seems to catch in and roll around, just extend the pad down and taper the bottom. A decade ago it wouldn't have been worth doing, but it is now.*
>
> *NB: Can the manufacturer that implements it send the royalty to this address. Cheers."*

The thigh pad roll was all that Australia got for a while. From there the nightwatchman Anderson and Graeme Swann went crazy. Mostly Swann, because Anderson has the natural attacking instincts of a brick wall. Swann likes to hit in the air, and he went over the top a few times and then decided to take Hauritz on. Three balls in the row he took Hauritz to the boundary, the last one was a reverse sweep that seemed like a slap in the face from one offie to another.

There is a certain joy watching Swann bat. He is a joyful dude in general. You can see that he doesn't take his batting that seriously, but he does have talent. With the flat decks of Test cricket he could easily knock up the odd 40-60 without too much trouble. He is probably my favourite English cricket personality because he is in a band of questionable musical integrity that looks like fun, plays every Test "like he may not play another" to use the cliché, and he seems to actually have a personality.

Swann just seems to love it all, and when someone like that is on top of you, and his smile is tattooed to his face it must really piss off the opposition.

For a while it looked like Anderson and Swann could frustrate Australia way into the afternoon session. Unfortunately for England Anderson got infected with Swann's devil-may-care approach and suddenly believed he could do anything with the bat. He gave Hauritz his second wicket of the match when he danced down the wicket way past the level of his talent and bunted the ball to mid-on.

Monty didn't last long; Hauritz took his third wicket, the first one where the batsman didn't gift it to him. Although some people could say that Monty's wicket is in fact a gift.

Swann ended up on 47 not out and 435 was the total. Pretty good for a first innings in the Ashes, but England probably could have scored over 600 if someone had got a big hundred, and this was the pitch for big hundreds.

Australia sent out their two openers, Ugly and Uglier, technique-wise – Simon Katich is a good-looking man and I am sure Phil Hughes gets the girls. England opened up with their two boy band members, looks-wise, Anderson and Broad. Anderson's first ball was nice, curved back into Hughes and hit him on the pad. It wasn't out, but it was a good ball.

All the talk about Hughes struggling against the short ball at his body seemed to be forgotten as the pair gave him plenty of width and he smashed them through cover and point. Broad and Anderson were off after six overs and Australia made it through to lunch without much trouble.

After lunch Freddie came on. His first ball was a tasty bouncer. The ball wasn't as vicious as the Freddie spray was. He let rip at Hughes, questioning his sexuality, parentage, species and everything else from what I could see. But why would you care what I have to say when I can give you an insight into this psychological examination by Hughes himself: "Got some good tips from Freddy after his first ball too LOL. ROFL,☺LMAO," he twittered later. ROFL,☺LMAO.

Suddenly England looked like a Test side in the field. Freddie put everything into his first over, and it seemed to lift the team. The only problem seemed to be that England had forgotten about the Krab Katich. He dug his way into the crease. This is his kind of wicket. Slowish, dusty, and friendly to his brand of squirting and slapping. It is an SCG-style wicket, and getting him out at the SCG is not easy.

Freddie and Broad seemed to be bowling quicker to Hughes than they were to Katich. Broad had been ordinary in his first spell, but with Freddie unsettling Hughes verbally, Broad had started hitting that chest cage length. Hughes looked uncomfortable, but he always does. The commentators were giving birth to kittens. Cardiff had come alive. People react to good short fast bowling in a Coliseum kind of way. Everyone wants blood, or a wicket. Sometimes both.

Then Hughes got out. The crowd loved it. Apparently people loved it so much that they didn't realise it was just a standard Freddie-length ball and not a fiery delivery rebounding off his gloves. Hughes had got to 36, hardly an abject failure, but people were already stating that the short ball had done him in, through "referred pressure".

Enter Ricky Ponting. Ponting's batting is not at the superhuman levels it once occupied, but he usually makes a hundred in each series, and that is usually it. His eyes are as good, his skill levels are as good, but he just needs something else to fire him up. First innings of the Ashes is that kind of time.

He and Katich got down to business. They got through the Freddie and Broad spell, milked the spinners easily, and had no real problems for the rest of the day. England's top order should have seen it as a template for how to bat on a slowish pitch.

England's bowlers were poor. Especially their spinners. Swann bowled more full tosses than I could ever remember seeing from a Test offie bowl. It was terrible. Monty just looked easy to play. Very easy. Two days into the match and England's two Test-quality slow men had been outbowled by the club cricketer. Batting had something to do with it as well. Both Katich and Ponting were batting for their country, but there were personal issues at hand as well.

Katich's last tour to England had almost ended his career (I thought it should have). He was thrown back to Shield cricket, and most people assumed he would never fulfil his potential. Instead, he tweaked his already over-tweaked Krab-like technique, made more runs than anyone had ever made in a Shield season and demanded another go. That is how he became an opener. The selectors wanted him in the team, and the spare spot at the time because of an injury to Matthew Hayden was at the top. Then he made hundreds.

Ponting was different. His spot hadn't been in jeopardy in more than nine years. His name is etched in just below those of Lara and Tendulkar. But his captaincy has never received much acclaim. Days before this Test, I was at Lord's for a media breakfast when Jeff Thomson described his captaincy as crap. I laughed, but by the time I got home it was all over the internet. It is something that Thommo and countless other ex-players have said and is a conversation that you will hear in quite a few pubs in the summer.

There must have also been that nagging feeling that Ponting knew that he had ballsed up the last Ashes in England. Even if he thought he did a good job, which is doubtful, mistakes he had made four years ago were getting a lot of air time. Ponting is a prickly guy, he hates losing, and not in the clichéd sports way – losing actually affects his chemical balance. And being the face of failure would never make him happy.

The press had mentioned that Katich and Ponting had not always got along. For some time when Ponting wanted Katich to bowl he had got Michael

Clarke to ask him, the same Michael Clarke that Katich had tried to choke in a drunken misunderstanding over the singing over the team song after the Sydney Test against South Africa earlier in the year. Why Ponting couldn't ask Katich to bowl was never really addressed by the media.

My personal theory – and one not backed up by a pinch of evidence – comes back to the fact that Katich, who leads NSWales, thinks he is a great captain, and Ponting isn't. Katich is a pretty forthright sort of guy, and I don't think he keeps his doubts to himself. Before the title was used on Ponting, Katich was touted as a future Australian captain. Unfortunately due to illness, loss of form, and that fucked-up technique he never really gave himself a chance.

None of this potential animosity helped England, though. Katich and Ponting may have melded themselves into one unit of desperation and class but England were poor, and they knew it.

The fuck you hundred

There are many different kinds of hundred: the attritional, the lucky, the captain's, the rearguard, the gritty, the matchwinning, the match-saving, the effortless, and heaps more.

You can add a new one to the list: the fuck you hundred.

That is what Ricky Ponting makes. They are a middle finger to any doubters he has, to the opposition if they get on his nerves, and to the media if they are questioning his boys.

They come from pure frustration and anger, but usually look good to those who watch.

They are also predictable.

Australia know they need something special in India, and everyone knows Ponting struggles there: fuck you hundred.

Australia put in their worst performance for a long time at Perth against the South Africans, and lose Matthew Hayden early in the next Test at Melbourne: fuck you hundred

Australia lose the Ashes in 05 and come home to face the West Indies: two fuck you hundreds in one match.

There are plenty of other examples.

Ricky may not have hit two hundreds in a series since the 06/07 Ashes, but the one constant in him is making hundreds that are filthily determined and magnificently angry. There is real malice behind them; they are scowling hundreds, aggressive hundreds, and doggedly determined.

And if you think I am reading too much into it, check the series in recent times in which he hasn't made a hundred. None against New Zealand, Australia won; none against South Africa away, Australia won. Both of those series went smoothly, but if Australia is losing, looking like losing, or something pisses Ponting off: fuck you hundred.

From the moment Ricky came to the wicket at Cardiff he looked like he was going to get a century; he had the fuck you feeling in him, and he wanted to give it to the English.

If Australia were to go on and win this Ashes comfortably, it wouldn't have surprised me if Ponting didn't make another ton.

Day 3

The hyperbole of the spinning pitch had reached iPhone proportions. There was little else the English commentators could, or would, talk about. They even had this new tool that was a super close look at the surface of the pitch. It showed it was dusty, but you didn't really need a special camera for that.

You could understand England's excitement: they had two world quality spinners in their side and were due to bowl last on it. Less time was given to the fact that Graeme Swann's bowling had been horrible and Monty Panesar looked unlikely to trouble even tailenders.

England started the second day fairly well. Not because of spin, but because of Australia's one consistent weakness, swing bowling. Katich was hit plumb in front by a huge inswinger by Anderson, and shortly after Australia's walking wicket Mike Hussey pushed tentatively down the wrong line to one that moved a bit. Then Ponting, on 150, gifted Panesar a wicket, dragging a short ball back onto his stumps.

It could have been a comeback: three wickets in the first session was a top effort from England, and Australia were still over a hundred runs behind. England looked more spirited and together, and Anderson was swinging it. But the curse of the middle session was about to strike. On the first two days not one wicket had fallen between lunch and tea.

The same thing happened again and with it went England's chance of winning the match. Clarke and North had no real problems as England's Jekyll and Hyde routine showed it was here to stay. When the ball swings they look like a proper Test team, when it doesn't they're pathetic.

Clarke was smooth. His trip in 2005 started well but went downhill fast. He came on this tour with a reputation that he couldn't really handle batting in England. But that was the old Clarke. That one was fast and loose; only at home when Australia was cruising; the one that couldn't keep still and had to be at you all the time.

This new Clarke was settled, a vice captain, capable of pulling Australia out of trouble, patient and an overall much better player. This was Clarke's sort of pitch as well. He is at his best on pitches that spin, and like Katich, he relished one that was slow and low track.

At the other end for almost the entirety of Clarke's innings was North. I know this because of the 27 times the word "organised" was used by the Sky commentators. He looked technically sound, and with Swann still bowling fairly ordinary, there seemed to be no one who could get him out.

Australia's only real problem seemed to be it kept raining. Eventually Clarke and North had to play for stumps, and this was always going to be England's best chance of getting Clarke out.

Clarke has one of those brains that functions fine when batting normally but turns to porridge when thinking of batting for time. It is the one part of his game he cannot seem to fix. The young Clarke comes out in him and he suddenly looks jittery and nervous and finds ways to go out. This time it was at the hands of a short ball in the dark from Stuart Broad after the second rain interval. Clarke seemed to play six or seven shots as it came down to him. Eventually he just gloved it through to Prior.

The most obvious problem for England was the fact they only took four wickets – a total of five wickets in five sessions. That was obvious. The subtle problem was Ricky Ponting's face. The Welsh crowd rose as one and clapped Ricky off the ground when he was out. Ricky was having none of it; he had a snarl on.

He looked like someone whose friend had just left the bar on their shout, or someone who had come back to his car to find a bird had shit on the door handle. This was not a good sign for England. It takes a special person to be pissed off after making 150, and England would have noticed it, and it might have made them a little worried.

The wife theory

Michael Clarke was destined for great things; it was beyond my control.

When he started he was just a once-in-a-generation batsman, one with a sparkling smile, bottomless enthusiasm, and a nickname that newspaper writers loved using.

He was all energy and runs, loved fast cars, was mates with Warne and Brian Lara, and was the young guy in a team of champions.

Clarke was fond of saying he wanted to go his whole career having never been dropped from the Australian team. Even Warne and The Don had been dropped, but Clarke had grander ambitions.

His grand ambitions never had any basis in reality, especially when his form fell away. Eventually, having no sense of history, the Australian selectors dropped him.

His exile was short-lived as Shane Watson got injured (I am as surprised as you).

Clarke was brought back. This time he was a lot less cavalier, and even though he only seemed to make runs when Australia was already firing, no-one seemed to notice.

This should have been the issue, but instead the story was about his new-found maturity, and before long he was the unofficial next captain of Australia.

I didn't even notice it at the time. One minute he was the inconsistent batsman with the glamour model girlfriend (Lara Bingle of "where the bloody hell are ya" tourism-ad fame), who was lucky to be in the team, the next he was a settled career cricketer with a long-time girlfriend and with aspirations of captaincy.

Since Ms Bingle and Clarke had become settled he had become a better batsmen, more reliable, more patient, with much better shot selection. Perhaps Ms Bingle was a batting guru.

The same thing happened with Ponting, he was a better batsman than Clarke, but he was a bit punchy after a few drinks, but after a makeover and a steady relationship he improved as a cricketer and soon was ready to take over the Australian team.

I wonder if there are people inside cricket Australia who encourage the players to "settle down". And is it just wives that do the job? What about a demanding cat, or a strict gay lover?

On Allan Border medal night (Cricket Australia's awards) they should think about giving an award to the WAG who has transformed her man the most.

Day 4

My English friends had begun to give up on the Ashes. They had seen enough: this was going to be another Ashes where they thought they had a team as good as Australia, but their players couldn't perform when it mattered.

It was too early for a sane person to give away the Ashes, but English fans are not sane.

They are a special breed that needs desolation to believe it is reality. This was a great first Test for them. Had the team started too well, they would have had a spiral of despair waiting for them. This was perfect. The same had happened in 05 – the first Test was pretty much all Australia – and the English fans could wallow in their misery a bit and sound self-deprecating while their team went ahead in the series.

Some of the despair was fair enough. On day three Strauss had looked like he had run out of ideas. On day four he looked like he had run out of common sense. He started the bowling with his quicks using the old ball. Australia looked very comfortable with this decision. Then he brought on the spinners, who for the first time in the innings looked in form. So Strauss took them off and gave the new ball to his tired quicks and let North and Brad Haddin score hundreds.

Few people are harder on Ricky Ponting's body language than I am. Ricky is an emotional guy, and when Australia are struggling you don't have to look at the scoreboard to see it. Strauss is at the other end of the scale; he doesn't show much at all. Maybe it's his Radley upbringing, that look of control that public school boys are taught.

Strauss' demeanour must calm the English boys down in times of need, but it also is a mask he uses when he has run out of ideas. When Strauss is under pressure he plays with things in his hands, his necklace, his hat, a cricket ball, anything he can grab. I've seen him do it up close in a press conference. Starting with a ball in his hands he puts it down for easier questions, and picks it up the harder ones. When he wasn't sure what to say he was whipping the balls between his hands like a mad man.

Sure, this is amateur psychology. But it is what I noticed about day four. Had Australia been in the same situation Ponting would have lost it a few times, sledged, got tough with a bowler, thrown a ball a bit too close to a batsman. Anything to make his mood well known.

Strauss just hid behind this mask of calm. That is fine if in his actions he is actively going for a wicket. Strauss never appeared to be doing that either. He just went through the motions, never trying anything too radical, never really looking like he had a plan.

At no time did England put enough pressure on Australia to take a wicket; never did they stop the scoring for long enough, and in general they looked like they were playing for rain. It was pathetic, and the only thing that makes people forget this sort of captaincy is winning the Ashes.

I should also mention there were batsmen involved. North went on as the foundation of the partnership, and he brought up his hundred without too much trouble. At the other end was Haddin. I had tipped him to score more runs than Gilchrist in 05, and he almost did in one innings. He smashed the dispirited and clueless England all around for 120 off 151 balls. Only giving his wicket away after he and North brought up their 200-run partnership.

Ricky decided that was enough punishment and declared 241 runs ahead.

That left the Australians four and a half sessions to bowl out the English, and maybe have a bat again if that was needed.

Surely England would be able to bat for at least four sessions on this wicket. It wasn't tough, it wasn't falling apart, Nathan Hauritz was the spinner.

There was rain about to give them some breaks. However, once England came out to bat you would have sworn the wicket had been changed.

The pressure of Test cricket is a wonderful thing. The English batsmen should have been looking at the way the Australians had scored with such ease and thought to themselves that this would be piss easy. Instead they did what happens so often: they reacted to scoreboard press and fell apart.

Cook's wicket was terrible. He was beaten for pace on a powderpuff pitch by one that could not have been more straight if it had been John Wayne. He just edged across the crease and failed to play straight, another technical flaw, although this also seemed to have a mental edge. England have only three defensive specialists – two of them are at the top of the order and one is out before tea.

Then Ravi Bopara was gone as well. He was unlucky – the ball hit him very high – but he looked like getting out every ball, so it was probably an act of mercy from the umpire. When tea was taken England needed to bat out four full sessions with eight wickets in hand. Australia were on fire. Their team of inexperienced quick bowlers is still learning the trade, but when they are good they do get on a roll, and had the weather stayed on their side England might well have been five wickets down at the close.

Instead it rained for the rest of the day.

Australia now had three sessions to get eight wickets. England's best two batsmen were at the crease, and would be well rested. But an Australian win was the favoured result. They had demoralised England on day four. In 41 overs they had made 195 runs for the loss of a charity wicket, then in seven overs of their own had taken two England wickets for 20 runs.

Day 5

In my Ashes podcast (I defecate over so many mediums) I said that Paul Collingwood had my Australian neck hairs nervous. He is built for such an occasion. Not many middle-order players are made for draws, but

Collingwood is. I just had a feeling, although Strauss and KP are better batsmen, and more than capable of drawing a match on a pitch like this.

By lunch, I didn't give a shit. KP had got out in a way that was guaranteed to piss off the English media; leaving a straight one. A few overs later Strauss was gone as well. His dismissal was far less likely to cause a commotion, but he did manage to edge a short ball from Nathan Hauritz, which isn't entirely honourable either. Prior was out before the interval as well, trying to cut a ball out of the rough that spat up and took his glove.

Five wickets for Hauritz in the game. Wow. If I wrote that in a sci-fi script no-one would believe it.

England limped to lunch five wickets down with Collingwood and Flintoff keeping the ball out. On day four it had looked like Australia's biggest problem would be the rain, but in fact it was to be the curse of the middle session. In four days now only one wicket had fallen in this period. Australia needed more than one. Three more wickets should win the game, two keep it open.

For a while Australia might have thought one would be hard to get. Collingwood continued to define the word "gritty", and Flintoff was resolute, although Ponting had brought back Mitchell Johnson, who had gone past Freddie with his slow off cutter.

Bowlers with a slingy action can be the hardest to pick when they bowl the slower ball or cutter. Johnson's was pretty good. It wasn't so slow that you could pick it by speed alone, and it usually moved off even the most placid wicket. More than a few other players had been bamboozled by it.

Maybe it was my imagination, but the slips seemed to move up before the ball Freddie got out to. Mitch came in and cut the ball away from Freddie, who just mindlessly prodded it straight to Ponting at slip. Australia were back. Johnson, who had struggled for line, length, consistency and parental approval, had taken a wicket in the session of death. Australia couldn't party yet, though. Broad came in and he pretty much did what Freddie had done, reined himself in and kept up an end.

Collingwood was just nuggetty at the opposite end. He is rarely more, and only occasionally anything but. His whole innings was a struggle, but that is how he likes it. He just about kept out the good balls, handled the average balls and tried to rotate the strike with the bad balls.

It was coal-mining cricket. I am not sure if the phrase has been used before, but that is what he is. Get in, get dirty, risk your health, and then shower off and go for a real ale in the evening.

His face seems to be chiselled out of granite. It has the same expression on it at all times: when he gets out, when he takes a wicket, when he makes love to a woman, or when he finds a 20-quid note in an old pair of jeans. Apparently there are lots of people like him in Sunderland.

A friend of mine once tried to tell me a story about people from Sunderland. It was about some old sailor named Jack Crawford who saved a bunch of people under heavy fire from possible death in a naval battle in the late 1700s. He became a hero – there is a roundabout named after him – but he refused to make easy money by recreating the event for a live audience. The way this guy handled the event is the way these sort of events are supposed to be handled in Sutherland. With no emotion or fuss. I am sure this sailor dude would be proud of Paul Collingwood's defiance. Although Crawford did end up a drunk who rode pigs and died of cholera. Something for Collingwood to look forward to.

Of course I still wanted Collingwood out, the little ginger prick.

But it was Broad who went, beaten by a skiddy one from Hauritz. The baby-faced conman had broken through again. Australia had taken two wickets in the middle session; surely victory was assured now.

Graeme Swann came to the crease. This time, his giddy rollercoaster ride batting was not what England wanted. They still had over a session to survive. This was when Peter Siddle came on. There was a rumour in county cricket that Graeme Swann didn't like the short ball. I assume the Aussies knew of this, and when Swann turned his back on one you could see Siddle salivate.

Victorian fast bowlers are quite often vicious creatures. The modern team had "Dirty" Dirk Nannes (the fastest bowler at the World Twenty20), Shane Harwood (who I had nicknamed "the angry man"), and Mick Lewis (who loved the sound of leather on raw meat), all of whom had been, at various times, under the tutelage of the proper mental North Suburban firebrand Rodney Hogg – the Australia quickie from the 1980s was so mental he subtitled his autobiography *Inside the Mind of a Lunatic Fast Bowler).*

Siddle was not. But he has the spirit of Rodney Hogg in him. He wants to hurt people. He is an animal out on the field, not as funny as Merv Hughes, or as theatrically crazy as Andre Nel, but vicious all the same. He either seems to be smiling or snarling when he's bowling, and when you start your international career by hitting Gautam Gambhir on the skull, you are showing your intentions.

When a batsman shows a huge weakness it is like parading Cynthia Nixon – she of the freakishly long neck from *Sex In The City* – past a vampire. So Siddle seemed to forget about getting Swann out and just decided to inflict pain. Siddle is capable of bowling long spells of short bowling when he gets the blood lust. One spell to JP Duminy in South Africa was fast, short and hostile until he finally got Duminy out. Siddle obviously expected Swann to go the same way. It didn't happen. Swann playing the short ball may have resembled Steve Waugh imitating Phil Hughes, but Siddle could not get him out.

Instead Swann played out 20 overs, and even took on the new ball before he got one that kept a little low off Hilfenhaus and Australia were back in the game, again. This time the tail was going to be exposed to the new ball, and surely that would be enough.

Collingwood was finally removed from the crease by playing a loose cut shot off Siddle that Hussey juggled in the gully. It seemed wrong somehow. Even as an Aussie I had to respect his single-mindedness. Collingwood got a standing ovation, but left the field thinking he had lost the game.

Paul Collingwood – the Bruce Willis of Nudgers

There is 1% of the world's cricket fans that have never bagged Paul Collingwood. These are sick people, a lot of them ginger and/or from the north of England, but there are others who like him so much they want him elected.

I am not one of those 1%, I often bag him, I love it. He is an easy target with the MBE, ginger hair and that face. And his batting, oh my fucking god. He makes the prettiest shots look like a car wreck.

He does it for hours too, sometimes never making more than a handful of runs. But he was the player I thought could stick around and piss off Australia. And that is exactly what he did. It was a tough, proper Test-batsman innings.

He held up his team without ever looking that *in* himself. Watching the flashy and more-highly regarded fall away as he fought like hell to keep his head above water. For most of his innings he looked like going out way more than a top order batsmen should, but he didn't.

You could argue, rather successfully, that on pure natural talent there are eight batsmen in the English line-up better than him. And Jimmy might be pissed I left him off that list. But the little bastard just tries harder than people with four times his natural ability. He is never going to be free-flowing but as a determined, fighting son of a bitch, he has few peers.

He's the Bruce Willis of nudgers; the Clint Eastwood of nurdlers. The Toshirō Mifune of batting ugly.

If he was a character in a film it would be Louis Dega from *Papillion*. Throughout the whole movie you want to punch him in the head, but without him it wouldn't have been much of a film.

One Wicket

Australia now had only one wicket to get, and Montybot Panesar and

Jimmy Anderson were at the crease. There were hundreds of simultaneous heart attacks across England at the very thought of this. Australia had a newish ball, Peter Siddle with some confidence and just over 11 overs. England had two tailenders, one a proper bunny, and one a goodish No. 10.

It wasn't a fair fight.

Panesar looked nervous. First ball he did everything he could to edge the ball behind. His feet resembled some early 90s Russian dance move. He survived the over, and the next few. Siddle went after both tailenders and Hauritz tried his hardest but Australia also had a new enemy: batting again. England had crawled their way to within a handful of runs of making them have to.

Ponting, though, didn't seem that worried about the runs; he just needed the wicket. He knew that two overs would be taken off if England went past them, but that meant shit if they couldn't get the wicket. So he kept the field up.

Eventually Anderson got a boundary through slips, not a real chance, but it meant that should Australia get the wicket, they would have to bat again. Siddle was a bit spent at this stage and Hauritz wasn't looking like making the breakthrough, but Ponting kept them on when a change was called for. Hilfenhaus had been the best bowler in the match, and Mitchell Johnson, while wayward, was still capable of taking wickets. Ponting may not have been thinking straight.

North eventually replaced Siddle. Not Mitch. Not Hilfy. It seemed to be about getting more overs in, and England returned in kind by sending out the 12th man with a message. England were trying to slow the game down – and so they should, this is a fucking Test match, not a village beer match. When North's over finally started it was useless. Monty hit a four and didn't look like getting out. For a minute, I thought maybe Hilfy would be brought on at the other end, but I am not that lucky and Hauritz stays on.

His over took a while to start as well as England sent out Bilal Shafayat, a Nottinghamshire batsman who was there as a specialist fielder, with some gloves as a time-wasting tactic. Funny, I hadn't noticed the England batsmen struggling with their grip.

Then England sent out their physio. The poor bastard. In truth he was a little mooby – he looked like he had borrowed a shirt from someone a little more svelte than him. In my lounge everyone commented on his Bo Derek-style run to the middle.

Ponting might have missed it though. He was too busy abusing Shafayat. In fact, he was in gloriously abusive form I don't know exactly what he said, but the word "fuck" seemed to be used a lot. The umpires were as useless as ever. England were trying to waste time, Ponting was abusing a 13th man and they did nothing. Umpires are worried that technology will relegate their position to something akin to a coat stand, but when shit is actually going down, they do nothing.

Eventually the two interlopers left the field. The next ball was always going to spark a lot of interest, and when it was easily blocked by Anderson, Cardiff screamed in delight. Something about the tension of the situation seemed to get to Hauritz. He had probably dreamed of spinning Australia to victory his whole life, and here he was with the ball in his hand, only a few minutes left and he lost his spin.

At the worst possible time in his career he tensed up. He had played a better Test match than anyone outside his family could have ever hoped for, but when Australia needed him, he just couldn't do it. Just because I don't like him as a bowler doesn't mean I didn't really feel for him. A few overs earlier he'd been turning the ball square.

There was still North at the other end. The man who had been thrown the ball for two overs to perform a miracle. His first over was poor, and his second over was tame. Two okay yet easily played balls were followed by two balls that were left alone. Surely a crime at this stage. But could you blame North? He hadn't bowled in 40 overs, even though the ball had been spinning for Hauritz and had only bowled five overs in the innings before he was brought on to win the match. On the fifth ball he got it right and took the edge, but like a seasoned pro, Panesar played it with soft hands and it landed safely in front of slip.

At this stage Montybot had transformed himself from edgy tailender to a solid lower order batsman. His job was all but complete. Surely England would not lose from here, and there was no reason for Anderson to push for a single. It was Anderson v Hauritz for the last over.

David v David

Hauritz's first ball was the quicker one, slightly down leg. Anderson defended it easy enough. The crowd erupted, the screaming lasting about eight seconds. Then they went silent.

Hauritz threw the next one up, but Anderson easily played it. It is funny how often in this position tailenders suddenly look good. A few overs earlier Anderson was edgy and wafty, now he was resolute and in control. Mind you he wasn't exactly facing Richard Hadlee. Hauritz tossed up another one at middle, Jimmy handled it.

Three to go. So far in the over Hauritz had turned nothing of note. His fourth ball did. But it was too wide and not a real wicket-taking ball. Two balls to go. Hauritz flighted another one on the stumps and Jimmy plays it as safely as you could want if you were an English fan.

Then the last ball: a bye is run. That is how this Test ends, with a bye.

I have no idea why Monty and Jimmy ran this run, but it did remind you of one thing, this innings wasn't kept alive by two sharp-thinking batsmen. These were proper tailenders, who took an unnecessary run. It wasn't a risky run, but had Monty run and Jimmy been celebrating there could have been an unlikely farcical end. Well more farcical than the ending we had.

And the sphincters of millions of English fans relax as one.

The draw

Who wants a result, with an orifice-testing finish like that? "I don't get cricket, five days and then no result," the heretics say. Stick that up your five days and no result. I want that finish, again and again. Bugger the result. Give me the tension motherfucker.

Note to all future Ashes series: start like this, or fuck off.

Australia have flexed their muscles, spun the ball, and shown England that they need to step the fuck up. England have gone within one wicket of an innings defeat, yet at the end Jimmy Anderson pumped his hand like a guy who'd just slept with Natalie Portman. Uncontrolled, illogical emotion.

One wicket. One fucken wicket is all Australia needed. Sixty-nine balls at Anderson and Panesar, and Australia can't win the game. In 69 balls you can get 69 wickets. It's true. I did the maths. Of course there are only ever 40 wickets to get in a match, so the extra 29 balls should be superfluous.

While, as an Australia supporter, it is tempting to take a machine-gun into a crowded building after a game like that, first you have to marvel at two just-better-than-completely-useless batsmen holding up an end to save a game for their country. They had a long time to bat with the knowledge that one wicket is all it takes. Their partnership was worth more runs than the first four, professional batsmen all of them; guys who practise batting for hours each day; guys who eat nice food, drive sexy cars, and bed fine women all because they are in the top six for their country.

It didn't matter that the first four days were coma-inducing – the last one had everything you want. It was a lovely touch by the Ashes, starting slow, then taking us to the edge and withholding the climax.

A result would have been too easy.

Phil Hughes said it best on Twitter: "Well that was close!!!!! Now it's off to Lords nil all, the guys were disappointed but super positive!!!Bring on LORDS I say!!!!"

First Test at Cardiff
Match Drawn

England first innings		Runs	Balls	Mins	4s	6s
*AJ Strauss	c Clarke b Johnson	30	60	90	4	-
AN Cook	c Hussey b Hilfenhaus	10	25	31	-	-
RS Bopara	c Hughes b Johnson	35	52	76	6	-
KP Pietersen	c Katich b Hauritz	69	141	196	4	-
PD Collingwood	c Haddin b Hilfenhaus	64	145	150	6	-
+MJ Prior	b Siddle	56	62	99	6	-
A Flintoff	b Siddle	37	51	66	6	-
JM Anderson	c Hussey b Hauritz	26	40	69	2	-
SCJ Broad	b Johnson	19	20	22	4	-
GP Swann	not out	47	40	54	6	-
MS Panesar	c Ponting b Hauritz	4	17	15	-	-
Extras (13 b, 11 lb, 12 nb, 2 w)		38				
Total (all out, 460 minutes, 106.5 overs)		**435**				

Fall of wickets: 1-21 (Cook, 7.6 ov), 2-67 (Strauss, 19.6 ov), 3-90 (Bopara, 24.4 ov), 4-228 (Collingwood, 65.3 ov), 5-241 (Pietersen, 70.5 ov), 6-327 (Flintoff, 86.4 ov), 7-329 (Prior, 88.3 ov), 8-355 (Broad, 93.5 ov), 9-423 (Anderson, 102.4 ov), 10-435 (Panesar, 106.5 ov)

Australia bowling	Overs	Mdns	Runs	Wkts	Wides	No-Balls
Johnson	22	2	87	3	-	-
Hilfenhaus	27	5	77	2	1	4
Siddle	27	3	121	2	1	5
Hauritz	23.5	1	95	3	-	3
Clarke	5	0	20	0	-	-
Katich	2	0	11	0	-	-

Australia first innings		Runs	Balls	Mins	4s	6s
PJ Hughes	c Prior b Flintoff	36	54	61	5	-
SM Katich	lbw b Anderson	122	261	325	12	-
*RT Ponting	b Panesar	150	224	313	14	1
MEK Hussey	c Prior b Anderson	3	16	24	-	-
MJ Clarke	c Prior b Broad	83	145	176	9	1
MJ North	not out	125	242	357	13	-
+BJ Haddin	c Bopara b Collingwood	121	151	200	11	3

Did not bat: MG Johnson, NM Hauritz, BW Hilfenhaus, PM Siddle

Extras (9 b, 14 lb, 7 nb, 4 w)		34				
Total (6 wickets, declared, 744 minutes, 181 overs)		**674**				

Fall of wickets: 1-60 (Hughes, 14.6 ov), 2-299 (Katich, 84.6 ov), 3-325 (Hussey, 90.1 ov), 4-331 (Ponting, 94.5 ov), 5-474 (Clarke, 136.5 ov), 6-674 (Haddin, 181 ov)

England bowling	Overs	Mdns	Runs	Wkts	Wides	No-Balls
Anderson	32	6	110	2	1	-
Broad	32	6	129	1	2	-
Swann38	8	131	0	-	-	
Flintoff	35	3	128	1	1	7
Panesar	35	4	115	1	-	-
Collingwood	9	0	38	1	-	-

England second innings		Runs	Balls	Mins	4s	6s
*AJ Strauss	c Haddin b Hauritz	17	54	78	1	-
AN Cook	lbw b Johnson6	12	17	1	-	-
RS Bopara	lbw b Hilfenhaus	1	3	4	-	-
KP Pietersen	b Hilfenhaus	8	24	20	-	-
PD Collingwood	c Hussey b Siddle	74	245	341	6	-
+MJ Prior	c Clarke b Hauritz	14	32	37	1	-
A Flintoff	c Ponting b Johnson	26	71	89	3	-
SCJ Broad	lbw b Hauritz	14	47	61	1	-
GP Swann	lbw b Hilfenhaus	31	63	80	4	-
JM Anderson	not out	21	53	69	3	-
MS Panesar	not out	7	35	36	1	-
Extras (9 b, 9 lb, 11 nb, 4 w)		33				
Total (9 wickets, 434 minutes, 105 overs)		**252**				

Fall of wickets: 1-13 (Cook, 4.3 ov), 2-17 (Bopara, 5.3 ov), 3-31 (Pietersen, 10.4 ov), 4-46 (Strauss, 16.6 ov), 5-70 (Prior, 26.3 ov), 6-127 (Flintoff, 49.4 ov), 7-159 (Broad, 66.4 ov), 8-221 (Swann, 86.1 ov), 9-233 (Collingwood, 93.3 ov)

Australia bowling	Overs	Mdns	Runs	Wkts	Wides	No-Balls
Johnson	22	4	44	2	4	1
Hilfenhaus	15	3	47	3	-	4
Siddle	18	2	51	1	-	2
Hauritz	37	12	63	3	-	2
Clarke	3	0	8	0	-	-
North	7	4	14	0	-	-
Katich	3	0	7	0	-	-

After Cardiff (the bullshit)

Cardiff should have sparked a conversation about the brilliant nature of Test cricket. Here were two ordinary teams, one who played shit, one who played good, and on the last day there was an hour of pressure so intense you could have bitten your fingers off.

That wasn't the story.

The story was all about Strauss' time-wasting, and Ricky's concern over the spirit of cricket. It was an artificial construct. But both captains were to blame according to the media.

Australia would have tried to delay the game at that stage. Every side would. It is hard not to snigger when an Australian captain comes out and says: "We came to play by the rules and the spirit of the game, and it's up to them to do what they want to do." I forgot how honest and committed to the true spirit of sport the Australian cricket team has always been.

Strauss was almost as bad. "There was a lot of confusion to be fair," he said. "We sent the 12th man out to let Jimmy and Monty know the fact there was time left, rather than the [number of] overs. Then there were drinks spilt on his gloves and Jimmy called to the dressing-room and we weren't sure whether Jimmy wanted the 12th man or the physio. Just a lot of confusion."

Come on gentlemen, this isn't our first roller disco. We all know how this works. Australia don't care about the spirit of cricket, they care about winning. England also care about winning, and they should be allowed to say: "We wanted only the minimum amount of overs bowled".

Ponting was branded a sore drawer. He wasn't. A reporter asked him what he thought of it, he answered very calmly considering the way he had abused Bilal and then he said it wasn't the reason Australia didn't win. And it wasn't.

There were writers and reporters who weren't happy with England either. Some Australians overlooked the fact that Siddle and Johnson had bowled poorly, that Ponting had captained poorly and that although Nathan Hauritz had played a great Test (for him) he got caught up in the tension when it mattered.

In the English media some questioned Strauss' tactics. They didn't like the game being brought into disrepute with time-wasting shenanigans. It just wasn't cricket. Although it *was* cricket, it was *completely* cricket. When the English fail it is usually because they aren't Australian enough, but when they play like low-down Aussie bastards they get bagged for that as well.

The spirit of cricket is like a big, heavy, imaginary version of the bible. You can use any part of it to prove you are with the spirit of the game, and any part of it to prove your opposition are filthy assholes.

There is nothing more fluid than the spirit of cricket. It is a magical cape that you can wear and tell others that they are dirty cheats. One day it tells people off for sledging, another for time-wasting. Sometimes it talks about walking.

It covers a lot: match fixing, running out batsman who are congratulating team-mates, handling the ball; chucking, underarm bowling, cheating at the toss, taking the fielder's word, bouncing tailenders, moving the fielders backwards instead of forwards, ball-tampering, excessive appealing, batting slowly in a one-day international to send out an opposition team via run rate and appealing for wickets you know aren't out.

This is just the tip of the iceberg, I haven't even mentioned clapping the opposition captain when he comes into bat. There actually is no unified spirit of cricket. How can there be? All these different nationalities play in different ways, so how can anyone expect them all to agree on this concept.

It's great to say cricket has a spirit, but it actually has millions of spirits. If someone created what they believed to be a definitive spirit of cricket guide, if I got 50 cricket fans together from all over the globe, I doubt we would find five who would agree with every point.

And even if all the countries did decide to go with one version, no-one would agree on the way to interpret it – just like the Bible, or the Koran, or the Torah, or the Vedas, or *Red Medicine* by Fugazi.

After Cardiff (the cricket)

There *were* people who talked about the cricket as well. Both bowling units were pretty ordinary. The two most inexperienced bowlers, Hauritz and Hilfenhaus, were the only ones to perform well. Hauritz outbowled Swann and Panesar in every way. Hilfenhaus was okay in South Africa, but he didn't take many wickets. In Cardiff he did.

Anderson and Flintoff both had good spells, but couldn't keep it up. Freddie was not fit, and looked as if he might never be again. Broad was ordinary for most of time and the Australian batsman seemed to enjoy facing him. And Swann and Panesar were tame.

Australia's batting was pretty damn hot. Hussey was still the concern. He didn't look like a batsman who was about to suddenly find form and even if he did, it was likely to be pretty painful.

England's batting was patchy. Strauss struggled in both innings, but he is class. Cook seems to have massive technical flaws; his Essex team-mate Ravi massive mental ones. KP can make runs and still piss people off. Prior seems to hate the ball coming back in to him. Freddie looks better at seven than he ever did at six. And Collingwood was grand.

I think Ponting out captained Strauss, although both were poor. Yes he made some mistakes in the last session that could come back to haunt him, but I think, mistake for mistake, Strauss had him covered.

England were left with the majority of the form worries, Freddie's knee was dragging around behind him and just when I thought he might have to pull out of Lord's, he pulled out of Test cricket altogether. Retiring from the five-day game that had worked his body over. Not straight away. Instant retirements are so 1990s. Now you plan when you are retiring knowing that the selectors, or in this case the doctors, won't rule you out.

Bilal Shafayat gets punched in the beard

While the media was all up in arms about time wasting, the spirit of cricket, and all that other bullshit, they ignored the one interesting story that came out of it, Bilal Shafayat being called a terrorist by a Rupert Murdoch-owned website (I say that not to incriminate Uncle Rupert, but to show it was a major website and not something small like cricketwithballs.com).

David Penberthy, a former political journalist who had left the editor's chair at the *Sydney Daily Telegraph* to take over at The Punch, a website that describes itself as one "for every Australian with a passion for debate", was so pissed off by Australia's failure to force victory, he wrote a post about it. In it, he quoted a friend of his, a mysterious friend named "Steve". He wrote:

> *The question "Did the Poms cheat?" was perhaps put most succinctly by my mate Steve, watching the game online in Chapel Hill, North Carolina, who inquired via text message in the final few overs this morning: "WHY IS THERE A MEMBER OF AL QAEDA HOLDING A F***ING GLOVE, AND A FAT POM IN A TRACKSUIT OUT IN THE MIDDLE?" It's a fair if offensively-crafted question, and one which is now on every Australian mind, none more so than Ricky Ponting.*

I know what you are thinking: how dare Penberthy's friend "Steve" call Steve McCaig, the England physio, a fat Pom. He is Australian. But if you look beyond the fat Pom quote, you may see the reference to Al Qaeda, aimed at Bilal Shafayat. Bilal is a Muslim, which apparently means he is in the perfect candidate to be labelled a terrorist for "comedy's" sake.

I am still yet to find anyone who thinks this is the "fair if offensively-crafted question" Penberthy describes it as. Some people jump to the rather extreme conclusion that calling a Muslim cricketer a member of Al Qaeda is more than offensive – that it is racist – even if he was committing the hate crime of wasting time on the cricket field. However, it was nice of Penberthy to censor the word "fucking", as that would have really offended people.

It was only three years ago that Dean Jones was commentating in Sri Lanka and accidentally let slip the famous "the terrorist has got another wicket" as Hashim Amla of South Africa took a catch. Amla is also a Muslim.

There were rumours that various cricket boards may have been informed of this, and if so, how long would it be before lawyers get involved? Steve's mate Dave could find a nasty letter arriving. And to think all this could have been avoided if Australia had just taken one wicket in the 69 balls they had.

Bloody Al Qaeda.

For some reason I thought that this was a news story. So I offered it to *The Guardian, The Sun, The Wisden Cricketer* and *Crikey*. Only Crikey wanted it. *The Guardian* thought it interesting but not newsworthy, the *Sun* never got back to me, the *Wisden Cricketer* wanted to run it but had never heard of Penberthy and wanted me to get a comment on it from a real news source.

I think I sent it to some other papers as well, a couple with daily in the masthead and I sent an email to Nottinghamshire County Cricket Club. No-one got back to me. I was surprised but I didn't give up. So I went looking for a well known Australian name to comment on the story in hope of getting it out in the mainstream media.

This is what happened when I tried to be a journalist.

Mentally Disintegrated

I now knew how it feels to have be an average medium pacer in the 90s. I went head to head with Steve Waugh, and I wilted like a flower in a hurricane. It was at the MCC's World Cricket Committee press conference. With me was a small number of press, Rahul Dravid, Tony Lewis, John Stephenson, the MCC head of cricket, Geoffrey Boycott and Steve Waugh.

It was about the MCC's idea to bring in a Test championship, and generally sex up Test cricket. During the press conference my questions were well received. The first one even eliciting a "that's a good question" from Steve, which is like saying "well bowled". My confidence was sky high. Then the press conference ended, rather abruptly.

Rahul Dravid and Geoffrey ran off, but Steve Waugh stayed behind, so I ran down to ask him a question. Before I got to him I could see John Stephenson eyeballing me, and as I got down to the floor he cornered me. It seemed my questions about what happens next after the MCC ideas group come up with the ideas got on his nerves. Finally I wriggled out of that.

Then I made my way to Waugh. He was talking to another reporter at the time; I sat behind and steadied myself for the question I had to ask. Just keep it short, sweet, and try to look relaxed. You know he can smell fear, he tastes weakness, and his hairstyle tells you he is not here for nonsense. So keep it light, quick and easy.

It was a hard question; an out of the back slower ball if you will, and I knew Steve wouldn't want to answer it. How many chances do you get to ask Steve Waugh a question though? I might as well ask him one that has some bite to it. When he saw me waiting with a question he was already a little pissed off, trapped on the wrong side of the press conference, and now realised that he was the last "name" in the room.

But fuck it, I had the question ready to go: it was now or never.

"Excuse me Steve, can I ask you a question?" A little nervy.
"Sure" If you have to.

"I'm not sure if you know or not, but Bilal Shafayat was jokingly called an Al Qaeda terrorist by an Australian website after the last test, and I was just..."

Very nervy, I can actually see him turn on me as the question comes out.

"No mate".

And then he gives me the look. You know the look. Anyone who watched cricket in the 90s saw it countless times. That look of complete, pure contempt. He was judging me as a man, and I was failing.

It was the look of insinuated violence – I could break you little man, you know it, and I know it. But instead I will just stare at you until you break yourself. It was the look hundreds of cricketers had had to deal with during their careers, reducing some to tears and making others doubt the very essence of their existence.

At that moment it didn't matter that I am actually bigger than him, he was in charge. I am not a man who scares easily, but I was on my heels. The awkward silence seemed to go on for hours, as he just tore me down with his eyes. I was sort of stuck where I was, I couldn't get around him, and he wasn't in a hurry to get out of my way.

I tried to look him back in the eyes, but they were fucking vicious. Instead I stood next to him like a naughty schoolboy while he dressed me down without saying a fucking word.

Hours later (you weren't there, it was hours) another reporter came in and asked him a question about the Australian bowling line-up and I fucken scrammed. I got out of the building as quick as I could. Another reporter was trying to chat to me, but I didn't want to run into Waugh again, so I bolted out on that conversation as well. Once I was outside I felt whole again, I had survived.

No wonder that bastard was so good at stripping down cricketers; if he had told me *I'd* lost the World Cup at that stage, I'd have fucken believed him.

The end for Freddie

Some people don't try very hard in life. Mostly because they are rubbish at things. But when someone who is very good at something doesn't try very hard, it really pisses you off. "If I had their talent…" That is why a lot of people liked Freddie.

He was freakishly talented, and yet he wouldn't cruise; he would bowl spells that his body couldn't handle, time and time again, and he leaves the game because of how much he put in every time he played for his country. He may not have the record of Jacques Kallis, or even Jacob Oram, but he had more balls than the two of them combined.

That doesn't mean many didn't overrate him, they definitely did. People ignore the fact he only had two really great Test years. Two years when his head and body were in the right space. In those two years he was a monster. He ate up countries in that time. Runs, wickets and scary presence. Four of his five hundreds were in those years, both of his five-wicket hauls up until then also. Batting average of 43, bowling average of 27, and Richter scale of 10. He was a flaming ball of testosterone during that period. No one could touch him. But it took a toll, as did captaincy, drinking, celebrity and his heavy frame.

He was the sort of guy you wanted in your side; the reason he turned from a fat, lazy bastard into Superfred was because Bob Simpson called him a cunt when he was Lancashire coach. That sums him up. He wants to show he is trying to do his best at all times (game day only, not at training), and when Simpson said he wasn't, he stepped up so much that he carried his side to an Ashes victory.

What a heart the big fella must have. An industrial strength organ that can push through freakish pain barriers. That spell in the West Indies when he was clearly injured is one of my all time favourite spells. Watching it was like watching a broken boxer keep throwing the punches: he still had the heart, but the body wasn't there. It reminded me of Ali against Larry Holmes. He knew he had the spirit in him, but his body wouldn't let the magic come out.

Freddie wouldn't stop though, and that is when I thought Freddie was gone. He bowled 15 overs that day, 15 blood-stained overs, and took no wickets. And that is Freddie, all effort, little results. He is more a folk hero than an actual hero. But I don't care, I would pay to watch the big fella hit the wicket any day of the week. If I was picking someone to play for my life, I'd rather have a drunkard with a big heart than a professional cricketer with his eye on the clock.

Test cricket needs guys like him, and Test cricket is a little worse off knowing that he will be leaving it. Thanks for the brutishness Freddie.

Lord's

Where Freddie posed

After Steve Waugh and I bonded, I had a look around Lord's. I saw the Australian tour groups go through the ground. It was not a pretty sight. Fifty-year-old men wearing replica Australia shirts made for more athletic figures, baseball caps with large corporate logos sitting badly on their heads, massive bum bags, and their shorts around their nipples.

They were waddling through the great ground like American tourists at Graceland, carrying all sorts of tacky Lord's merchandise. One guy walked straight past Shaun Pollock because he was looking at his Lord's T-shirt.

I don't think I'd ever seen a bunch of Aussies look so American. But that's a tour group isn't it? They make you get up early, rush you through every possible sight there is to see and at the end you turn into an American.

If someone tries to get me up early on holiday I turn into an American all right – I go all Timothy McVeigh on their ass. They weren't the only Aussies there; also present was the Australian press paddle pool for the Ashes. After the press conference they all huddled up on their own outside. It was like a mini Shepherd's Bush, except without the violence. I stood by them too, perhaps out of an Australian allegiance, or because I knew one of them.

But one thing this is for sure, none of the Australian journalists had bum bags on. This was my first time with Australian journalists, and even with my accent I didn't feel like I really fit in. They had all been in Cardiff together, and probably knew each other from many other Tests; I was just some guy that they didn't know with a similar sound.

This was the first time I had ever been in a Test ground before a Test. I've never had a reason to. I expected the Npower girls to be stretching, the touts scoping the best places out the front and Mark Nicholas hopping from side to side in front of a mirror. I saw none of that.

Not sure why I thought I would see something magical. Why would anything be happening? But walking around an empty Test venue so close to a big event was an exciting feeling. I ended up watching some women cricketers in the nets. Some nice leg spin was bowled. Then I left.

Day 1

Freddie is retiring. Freddie is injured. Hauritz is here. The spirit of cricket is left naked on your bathroom floor. There is rain. Arguments. I'd say we are ready for a Lord's test, wouldn't you?

I have nothing against Wales – I've got really drunk there a few times, but the cricket feels better in England. If the rain stays away this should be a good test. Australia are on top but haven't got the win; England are doing it for Freddie.

Monty was left out. England had brought in the sensibly-faced Graham Onions. A fairly fast line and length bowler, who can seam and swing the ball on a good day. On a bad day, he is a buffet bowler. Andrew Strauss won the toss and decided to bat first. The pitch looked good for batting on, as it had been in the Middlesex games that had been played there earlier in the season.

Australia never lose at Lord's, everyone knew this. If you forgot to mention it in your copy your editor would beat you, justifiably. It was 75 years since England had beaten Australia at Lord's. And that victory, in 1934, was the only time in the 20th century that England had beaten Australia there. To put that year in perspective, the seminal Marx Brothers' film *A Night at the Opera* had still to be released when England last won. Lord's was a cricket Viagra for Australia. At Lord's they occupied a different plane of existence.

Once the day started, it was a massacre. Their plane of existence was now shit. Every facet of Australia's cricket, except rather strangely Ponting's captaincy, fell apart. Mitchell Johnson bowled a spell that Steve Harmison would snigger at. Peter Siddle started well, but then decided Johnson's version of spraying it around could work. Then Nathan Hauritz dislocated his spinning finger. At the time I may have yelled at the TV for him to be put down. I do apologise to his family for that remark.

He was sent off to hospital, not before some weird shots of him sitting out on the Lord's balcony were shown to us. Hauritz had injured his finger by dropping a return catch off Strauss. It was smashed, so almost forgivable, except I don't want to forgive. Australia's fielding was awful and several chances went down. Brad Haddin's keeping was just comical, even dropping one of a no-ball.

While all this shit was going on Hilfenhaus was bowling nine maidens in his first 12 overs. It was like a personal statement to the other two morons who were throwing the match away at record pace. Hilfy had been good in Cardiff, but this was special. Over two controlled spells he kept a lid on one end while Strauss and Cook were dancing topless on tables at the other.

England got to lunch at 0/126 even with Hilfy's great work. After lunch they kept smashing the many many many many loose balls. Strauss was superb. It is easy to point out that he was dropped a few times, and he was, but his innings was class. He had been ordinary at Cardiff, and this was an innings of a man looking to put the pressure back on the Aussies.

It may not have been a Ponting fuck you hundred, but it was just as effective. He saw Australia were choking, and he put his well-polished semi-oxford brogue down on their throat. At the other end was Alastair Cook. Who – even with all the help in the world from terrible bowling and his captain in top nick – was ordinary. It was fitting he didn't get to his hundred, because he truly did not deserve it.

Don't say it, DON'T. Yes, 95 is an impressive score, and yes it takes some skill to get into the 90s in a Test match. But there are runs, and there are runs. Had he got out early on, it would have just gone down as a failure, but instead he managed to not find the slips and gully fielders, not for lack of trying, and then got himself up to a socially acceptable score, but all this did was show how bad a nick he was in. There were some nice shots in there, especially the pull shots, but even when he was well set he was still playing mad shots off the spinners and looking like getting out.

Then he missed a straight one from Johnson. It seemed unfair and fair. When a bowler is bowling as wayward as Johnson and he finally gets one on line and it takes a wicket, people always say: "That was his first straight one all day." Still, whether you bat ugly or pretty the runs are on the board, and a 196 opening partnership is pretty good in my book.

Ravi had scored a hundred against the almost Test standard West Indies side at Lord's in May, but this time he was nervy from the word go. Maybe it was walking past the Shane Warne picture in the Long Room. He was playing shot a ball. Memo to all international captains, if Ravi is playing shot a ball, hold your nerve and keep catchers up. He took 10 off a Johnson over, and if you hadn't seen him bat before you could be excused for thinking you were seeing a top class performer. But Hilfenhaus ended his innings without too much fuss. Ravi was dragged across the stumps and then fed the straight one and was out lbw. Terry Alderman must have been watching and crying at the beauty of such a dismissal.

KP came in, and this should have been good for England, their best two batsmen out in the middle with a huge platform, a shattered bowling attack, and a great pitch. However something was off with KP. There had been a lot of talk about his Achilles, and he seemed to be almost hobbling at times. He got England to tea with Strauss at 2/255.

After tea Siddle got him with a very full ball moving away from him that he nicked behind. It was very similar to his dismissal against Fidel Edwards at Lord's earlier in the summer (if you count May in England as summer). Australia were obviously working to a plan. In came Collingwood, the king of Cardiff.

I have a theory about Collingwood: he bats better when the chips are down, people are calling for him to be dropped, and when he thinks the world is against him. At Lord's he turned up as the hero. If there was ever a man more uncomfortable at being the hero than Collingwood I am yet to find them. A scrappy hero? No, that doesn't work.

Collingwood never really looked like making runs, but his wicket, charging down the pitch and fucking it up straight to mid on off one of Michael Clarke's straight'uns, was ordinary. The sort of dismissal that would have given the English papers days of material if it had been KP. However, Strauss looked far from happy. He was even less happy a couple of overs later when Matt Prior was unlucky enough to be bowled by the Hayley's Comet of cricket deliveries, the Mitchell Johnson inswinger.

Mitchell does have a brilliant knack of bowling bowel loads of nonsense while still getting wickets. Prior might struggle with the ball coming back in to him, but how could he have honestly thought Mitchell would suddenly bowl a huge hooping inswinger that would cannon into his stumps. When Freddie got pushed back on the crease by Mitchell and then hung his bat out at one from Hilfy England had managed the impossible: letting Australia back into the game.

It was a special effort as Strauss was still out there, but at stumps England were 6/364 and while they had a great first-day total, they had been 0/196 on a flat pitch and should never have lost six wickets to an Australian bowling attack as charitable as this.

With Hauritz getting his finger seen to, Australia turned (unintentional pun) to Marcus North and Michael Clarke. A total of 20.3 overs came from part-time spin, 16.3 to Marcus North alone. Clarke was the one to get the wicket, with Collingwood's help, but it was North who looked good. He seemed to have more guile and cunning than Hauritz and nearly all day he made Strauss change his game plan. Life sucks though, so he got no wickets, but Hauritz would have wanted to get back soon just in case.

Australia might have allowed 360 runs in a day, but they were miraculously still in the game. And there were good signs. Almost all the batsmen they had dismissed were out to obvious plans. Cook: full, straight, wait for his balance to go; Ravi: move him across the crease, then fire in the straight one; KP: very full on off stump; Prior: inswing through the vast wasteland known as the gap between bat and pad; Flintoff: push him back with short balls, and then throw it up full.

England's other problem is that the Australian bowlers don't give up. They might lose the plot at times, but they are not the sort to pack up their bags and go home. England's last six Tests were against the Windies. Once England got a good start against the Windies, the Windies packed up and waited for the declaration, Australia don't do that.

A letter

Dear Sirs

This letter is to certify that I do not want to be selected to play for Australia again on this trip. I do understand that this may leave you in a quandary, but I think this is the best result for everyone at this time. I have tried to make this easier for you, but you seem hell bent on picking me. I really do appreciate your loyalty, but I am spent. The team would be in a much better situation if I were not a member. The boys are being very supportive of my decision; I hope you do the same.

Cricket used to be fun, now it isn't. I do love representing my country, but I also like watching Troma films, listening to the Eagles and completing themed word jumbles. I think that at this point it would be better for me to spend my time on these pursuits.

Obviously there are mitigating factors: my mother's press conferences, the pressure of leading the attack in England and the fact that Troy Cooley keeps following me around talking about wrist position. If one more person mentions wrist position to me I might die.

Yesterday was the worst; Steve Harmison called me to tell me he knew how I was feeling. How could another man know I am dying inside, it is all too much for me.

*I didn't sign on for this. Jessica wants me to go to Faliraki
with her, but I am not in the mood. I just wanna crawl
up in the corner.*

*Please just get me out of here.
I've had enough.
No more swing.
No more mummy.
Please. Somebody.
Help me, I want to go home.*

Yours truly,

Mitchell Johnson

Day 2

Mitchell Johnson and Andrew Strauss found themselves as the story of
day one. Obviously for different reasons. Strauss was being heroified,
quiet rightly, and Johnson was being vilified, quite rightly. The job
wasn't done for either side; a few quick wickets, or a healthy lower order
partnership would be enough to swing the game.

Someone, and I can't remember who, said Strauss was not a good
starter on the next day. It isn't something I have ever noticed, but
when you think of it he did go out early on day at Cardiff after surviving
the night session. This time he started way worse. Second ball of the day
he left a ball that knocked over his stumps. You shouldn't laugh, but you
do, everyone does. All that planning, practising, visualizing, video watching
and mental preparation and he gets out second ball without playing a shot.

It got worse, Siddle worried Swann with a short one and he found Ponting
at slip, then Broad dragged on from Hilfenhaus. Australia were well on top
at this stage, and for the next couple of overs Hilfy and Siddle tried to end
it. But Siddle was crook. He looked pale, and he seemed to be on the verge
of a massive chunder. How he got through his last over I don't know.

The Sky cameras were hovering and so was I. I don't think I have ever wanted anything more than one of those 1000-frame slow mos in high definition of Peter Siddle throwing up at Lord's. Chunk by chunk, carrot by carrot, Sky brings you the action. Maybe a nice cut away to a member who is a sympathy chucker also throwing up all over his bacon and egg tie. Then cut away shots of people in the crowd looking ill and sympathy vomiters all losing their stomachs as elderly members shake their head in disgust and pick up their shoes as the stands turn into a sea of vomit. All the speciality cameras could be used. On hotspot, the stream of white hot heat coming out of his mouth showing us how much heat is on upchuck. Snicko for the sound to find out what kind of food makes the biggest noise on impact with the Lord's turf. And then to finish it off a digital version as shown by HawkEye to prove he couldn't hit the right areas and that the spew was hitting the ground at different speeds like when they show all six balls at once.

Had that happened Australia might have been able to re-group and finish off the tailenders. It didn't. So instead Mitchell Johnson came on and Onions and Anderson put on one of those delightful tailend partnerships. Hilfy still fit in a maiden, but Johnson was having none of that. He was determined to bowl how he had the day before, and he did. Eventually Anderson got out and Johnson picked up a wicket with a ball that could have been cut to the fence again. A total of 47 runs off 53 balls with lots of slashes of short and full balls, mostly wide of off stump c/o M Johnson.

So 425 was the damage. Not as much as England should have got, but handy. Australia should also have been pretty happy; the Anderson-Onions partnership might have been annoying, but it proved how good this pitch still was.

Strauss decided to remove Broad from the new-ball attack. His opening spell at Cardiff had been terrible, and Strauss had opted to elevate Flintoff. England obviously thought there was no need to hold Freddie back anymore and they probably wanted Phil Hughes to face him early on.

However, Hughes never got to face Flintoff, instead in the third over he received a junk ball from Anderson down the leg side and tried to help it on its way. Instead he barely gloved it behind. In his two Ashes innings he still hadn't fallen to the Pepsi Sandri full ball or the Steve Harmison short one at his nipple.

It wasn't long before Australia was in troubles with Ricky Ponting given out caught behind. And the decision was incorrect, and yet just. Anderson got one through Ponting with some pace, it went straight off the pad to slip, and Rudi Koertzen checked with the third umpire to see if the ball had carried. Under the rules he could not check whether the ball had actually been hit – it hadn't – so once it was confirmed it had carried to Strauss it was out.

Luckily for Rudi it was out lbw, plumb.

This brought Mike Hussey to the crease. It is never great for the spectators when Katich and Hussey end up together. India were so bored by it that they put eight of their fielders on the leg side so that they could all have a chat while the two of them squeezed out the odd run. This wasn't a day like that, Hussey and Katich went about their partnership fairly briskly by their standards.

Australia made it to 2/22 by lunch. The middle session was mostly rain. I watched a few episodes of *Californication*. When they did get on, Hussey alternated between nice pull shots and trying to get himself out to the short ball. Onions bowled his first spell of Ashes bowling without too much fanfare.

At tea they were 2/87. It was no 0/196, but it was a start.

After tea Katich chased a short one down the legside, not for the first time in England, and pulled it off the top edge to fine leg, not for the first time in England. It was Onions' first Ashes wicket, and like Anderson's it was from a bit of short shit down the legside that deserved nothing.

There are lots of people who believe Michael Hussey's role in cricket is as a statistical anomaly, one determined to keep his average over 50 by any means necessary. When he got to 51 and then left a ball that bowled him, these sorts of conspiracies start to make sense. It was a very fast over from Freddie. He was well above 90mph with almost every ball, although I am not sure that is why Hussey left the ball.

It was funnier than Strauss' leave. Hussey had finally found some form – not the form that got him an average of 80, but form good enough to justify the constant selectorial faith he had been shown. Then he leaves a ball that bowls him. Michael Clarke thought it was so funny he fell into a short mid wicket inswinging trap laid down by Anderson.

Australia were now no longer looking for 425 – at 5/111 they were looking at getting to stumps without losing any more wickets. Marcus North looked like he was going to stay for the long haul. For 13 balls he was almost Buddhalike in his calm, leaving everything he didn't need to hit, and leaning on the odd drive to cover and mid-off. Then he tried to pull a ball that wasn't that short, and he was out.

Now Australia's two most excitable batsmen were out there with the mission to get the team to the close. But England were firing, it was dark, and Australia were panicking. There was also fun, Haddin edged one back in the flap of his pad and then ran around the ground like a dude with his pants around his ankles running away from a sexual predator.

Johnson was getting his first bat in the Ashes at the other end. He looked a little nervy, and England made their plans pretty obvious: they were going to bounce him. They got their field set, and they bounced him. Over half the balls he faced were banged in, and the eleventh he pulled straight into the hands of the man in the deep from Broad. It was not intelligent batting; it was not batting that could be confused with intelligence on any level. It seemed so damn obvious that even calling it smart bowling seemed silly.

With seven wickets down, and fading light it was up to Haddin to make it to the end of play. He didn't. Instead he got out pulling, too. Haddin is a naturally aggressive batsman who doesn't like to defend, but fuck me in the eye; four other batsman had got out pulling or hooking before him, so why the hell would he try it in the dark? How well could that possibly end?

Broad must have been happy. He was unable to get regular wickets, but with Australia compulsively cross-batting anything above their navel, he was back in business. Having lost the new ball, and looking rather docile he needed all the help he could get.

By the end of the day Australia were 8/158 and pretty much stuffed.

Australia had choked.

Five of Australia's top eight had gone to playing the shot they are supposed to play better than anyone else – the pull/hook shot. England had done very little other than put out a deep square fielder and waited for the Australian batsmen to fuck up. It was not a long wait. Australia had given up their Lord's fortress, and probably were now heading towards losing the test.

When the Ashes were done destroying the Australian top, middle, and lower order, they moved onto my site. It was the first time in my site's history that it had crashed because I hadn't done something stupid. It just couldn't handle the hits. My server packed it in, and for 18 hours it was down.

That is what the Ashes does. I knew exactly how Ponting felt.

Pull yourself

Oh come on.

Most of you played this shot when you were in the womb. Back-foot shots are what Australians do. I get not getting swing bowling or having trouble with spinners with mystery balls, but short balls. Fuck off.

Katich and North are from the Waca. The *WACA*. The place of pace and bounce. When they learnt the game this was a wicket that fast bowlers would drool over. If you couldn't play the short ball well there you died, you actually died.

Brad, what was going on with you, you played yours in the dark. In the dark. And you had already seen four others go out the same way. Was there no little voice in your head saying: "Jeez, we are struggling, perhaps I should not try this shot that the whole team has played and fucked up." No, of course not. You are an instinct player. That is why we, and England, love you. Did you see all the happiness you brought them?

Marcus, you were special too. Unlike your brethren you didn't even wait for a short ball, you just attacked one that you wanted to be short. That worked out well for you. You do realise that at some grounds in the world the bounce is rather less than you get at the Waca.

Mitchell, never mind son. Just have a good rest.

Phillip, way to show people you aren't afraid of the short ball, glove a shit one down the legside. Hasn't anyone ever told you it is almost impossible to pull one down the legside, you can't control it. But you are young, I forgive you.

Simon, hasn't anyone ever told you that you can't control a short ball down the leg side you dumb fuck. Come on. You are supposed to be the smart stoic boring one.

What are we supposed to tell the children?

"Daddy, I do not understand, how did we lose to England?"

"Well my dear, you see they all decided to play the hook and pull shots badly on one day."

"Daddy, that is fucked, can we kill them?"

First day in the press box

I am not exactly a proper cricket writer. Unlike the other Aussies covering the Ashes I was not travelling around behind the team. I had no newspaper to report for. No journalistic qualification or ambitions. I am just a writer. I didn't do the hard yards of a cadetship, or report on cheese rolling championships to prove I was a good sport.

I just wrote about cricket on my website, and then people offered me a little work. Not much, but some. The one glaring hole in my CV as a cricket writer was actually being paid to be at the game and report on it. I had reported for free on state games in Victoria, using the MCG's wireless in the grandstand sitting amongst the Vic's WAGs. And when I came to England I had been to a few county grounds, *The Wisden Cricketer* had slipped me into a few press boxes, then I had weaselled my way into the Oval press box for a few Surrey games.

The first time I had ever been paid to write on a game of cricket was day three at Lord's. Not a bad way to get off the mark. While Crikey might not have had the political pull to get me in, yet again the boys at *The Wisden Cricketer* had shimmied me in as their second seat. You see everyone wants to report on the first two days of a test. But by the third day the media don't care.

So I got up at dawn (8am), put my sensible shirt on over my Godzilla T-shirt, and caught the tube in. When I got to the ground the security guard asked me to turn my pass around, as it was facing my chest. When I turned it around she said: "Oh I see why you did that, that is horrible." I tried to lighten the moment by saying that I took the picture in my bathroom and you can see the shower in the background. She looked me with pity.

Then I went up in the lifts to the spaceship thing. That thing is weird. And came out of the lift to see Ian Chappell standing in front of me. It was too early in the morning for his anger, so I went off looking for the seating chart, and went and sat in *The Wisden Cricketer's* seat, knowing that it was supposed to be Gideon Haigh's, but since there was only one mentioned I thought I would sit there. I also figured I could take Gideon if it came to it.

I sat down and then had no idea what I was supposed to do. Play was not due to start for two hours. Hardly anyone was in there. I passed the time by pretending to be entranced by my laptop, and trying to work out how to log into the Lord's Wifi. Eventually people came in, a few people I knew, and then Gideon, who may not have my size, but is probably wirey enough to run me around for a few rounds. We didn't fight though; instead he just stole the next seat, David Frith's. It was weird as it was the first time we had met, even though he had written the foreword to my last book – *The Year of the Balls 2008: A Disrespective* – and risked his reputation.

Behind me, as mentioned in the start of the book, was Richie. Nuff said. Next to me was the cricinfo crew. Andrew Miller arrived late. He had had his laptop stolen the night before, and had to find another one, possibly the first one ever built. I tried to settle in as best I could, and never look over my shoulder. I could also see Peter Roebuck, the Australian (sic) journalist and former Somerset cricketer covering the Ashes for the Fairfax media group, which publishes the *Sydney Morning Herald* and *The Age*, in Melbourne.

I often say jokes at Roebuck's expense, but he is actually a big part of why I am a cricket writer. Back home, the cricket media get swept up in the jingoistic shit storm that is an Australian summer. It can be very hard to hold a dissenting view, but Roebuck, on radio and in print, manages to do it quite well. It couldn't have been easy to be an Englishman in the middle of it all, especially one who couldn't say he was a Test player. Even when I was a kid and he was pointing out that Australia wasn't a country that produced cricket superheroes on a daily basis it didn't bother me. To me he was the intellectual and everyone else was just barracking. That hasn't stopped me calling him "Spanky" (a popular nickname for Roebuck in Australia after his run-in with teenage South African cricketers).

With Richie it took a while for me to get up the guts to speak to him, but eventually I did. Richie isn't real. He is a floating head from another dimension. There is no one who looks or sounds like him. No one who could make a TV career out of saying less. He lives up on that tier where other non-real celebrity demi-gods live. Well beyond the A list. Even seeing him in real life with his laptop and newspaper it is obvious that Richie does not exist in the same way that you and I do.

Roebuck is real, and I couldn't get up the courage to speak to him.

Day 3

The cricket was starting up, I knew that because there was a betting pool being organised. I realised I had chosen the right career. The pool was on how long Australia would last the morning with their final two wickets. I figured that with a flat pitch, Haurtiz who could bat a bit, and Siddle who seemed to make 0 or 20 odd they would last for about 52 minutes. I was also thinking that Hauritz and Siddle aren't likely to hook or leave straight ones, so that limits the ways they can go out.

I won the pool, all 13 quid of it, outlasting Lawrence Booth.

Hauritz and Siddle managed to survive for a while with edges before England got them and Australia were all out for 215. With Hilfy stranded 94 runs short of his hundred. Strauss predictably didn't enforce the follow-on, and England went back in.

It was about this time that I saw Shane Warne in the press box, and what a sight. He was almost orange, I have seen Oompa-Loompas with more natural skin colouring. And his teeth, there has never been a white like this. It was like looking into the centre of the sun every time he smiled. Everyone in the press box was talking about it, and so was everyone who watched Sky. Surely there is no chemical that can induce a white like this. Had he really been at a poker tournament, or was he being worked on by Nazi scientists?

There were those who thought the follow-on should be enforced. There are those that think there are no situations when it shouldn't be. Australians don't always live by that rule, as they know what it is like to be beaten by a team that has been made to follow on. We call it the VVS rule. When the pitch hasn't had much to do with it and the other team has batsmen who can make runs for days, there is no point automatically enforcing it. Thanks to Australia's short innings there was still plenty of the time in the game, so England took the conservative option, but it made sense.

Australia decided to give the new ball to Johnson again. Apparently Australia thought that by continuing to waste the new ball he would learn the errors of his way. After three overs and 17 runs he was taken off. Lesson learned? Say what you want about Strauss' defensive captaincy, Broad stuffed up with the new ball once, and he was relegated. Johnson propelled England along well: at lunch they were 0/57 after 13 overs.

A lot of people want to know what they serve for lunch in the press box. I must admit I'm not really a foodie. My eating habits are slightly more exotic than Shane Warne's. The food looked fancy. I do know I lined up behind Mark Nicholas in the food queue, which was fine, except that he was way more interested in chatting to people than he was in picking up his food.

After the break Alastair Cook got out to Nathan Hauritz. It wasn't great batting from Cook who overbalanced, again as Hauritz drifted one up and straightened it. It was a nice ball, if not brilliantly played. Just as I was getting over the shock of Hauritz getting Cook out, he got Strauss out. It was flighted outside off, spinning away and Strauss nicked it to Clarke at slip. His dislocated finger seemed to be a distant memory. Either that or it had been replaced by one of Shane Warne's. It was a great little spell from Hauritz, and I don't say that easily.

Hauritz's two wickets brought Ravi Bopara and KP together. Being that England were almost 300 runs ahead surely these two were going to keep up the pace and put the game well and truly out of Australia's reach. They were both aggressive batsmen and this was a pressure-off situation.

What followed was one of the most painful partnerships I have witnessed. Not because of the tedious run rate – 73 runs in 28 overs – although that didn't help. It was the pointlessness of it all. It was if the game was on pause. The two of them couldn't score, couldn't get themselves out, and couldn't find any rhythm. Bopara couldn't even score in front of point. Johnson was just as bad, the three of them were all trying to play themselves into form in front of people who had paid 80 quid a ticket to watch them.

When Ravi was dropped by Ricky, Siddle almost combusted. So did I. It was such an easy catch, and it would have ended this torture. Instead the two just kept going. During almost all of the middle session Hilfenhaus bowled 11 overs for 17 runs. It was like he and Mitchell Johnson were two separate species. Throughout the partnership Hilfy was the only one looking like getting either batsman out, in one ball he almost had KP lbw (slight edge) and then KP was so dazed that he wandered out of his crease, but Haddin missed the stumps. KP's innings looked like his lunch drink had been spiked with Ketamine.

Just towards the end of the session, one I am sure everyone wanted to be over, shit happened. Johnson bowled a half tracker that Ravi could have hit anywhere, instead he hit it to Hauritz, on the full, or was it? Hauritz, who has standing only a few metres from Rudi, said he got under it. Ravi never moved.

It was one of those. You know, one that the fielder is sure of, but one that no technology presently available to broadcasters can prove. Most of us have seen the tests where a commentator holds the ball near the ground, and it looks like it is touching the ground, only it isn't. You have your opinion, but since there is no way to tell, they either all need to be referred and given not out, or the umpires need to do a quick character test on the fielder:

Ever told a girl you love her just to get in her knickers?

Do you park in the disabled spot if you are only going to be there for a minute?

Ever pissed in your mum's roses?

Did you catch it?

This one went upstairs, which was unlucky for Australia as it probably was caught, and with a face like Hauritz's, he would never fail a personality test. KP wanted to chat to Ponting about it; it was spirit of cricket day.

England made it to tea on 2/130, 340 runs ahead, and Australia's chances of a miraculous comeback had all but fallen away.

To get my mind off the game at tea I interviewed David Frith the Australian/English hybrid cricket writer. For those who have never heard him speak before, he sounds just like Bud Tingwell, maybe even more than Bud Tingwell used to sound like himself. If you don't know whom Bud Tingwell is rent *Breaker Morant*. Frith had to leave the interview after a while as he wanted to speak to a Victorian leg-spinner, an orange one.

Not long after tea everyone was put out of their collective misery when Ravi got out to another good ball from Hauritz, caught at short leg. What can you do? You see him bowl, you follow his career, you look at his record, and then the bastard takes wickets. And these aren't even the lucky wickets of Cardiff, this has just been good bowling. I decided the best plan of attack was to keep bagging him. If I changed tack he could stop taking wickets. I truly still didn't think he was any good, but wickets is wickets.

Shortly after KP was out dangling his bat in the direction of an average ball from Siddle for the diving Haddin. It was a good thing, because KP still wasn't interested in playing shots, and when coupled with Collingwood, albeit a Collingwood in almost one-day mode, it could have got dire. Instead Matt Prior came out, and he was ready for action.

First ball he edged between Clarke at slip and Haddin, but from then on he made Ravi and KP look like pensioners. He took Hauritz apart, scored off the quicks with ease, moved the field back, and made up for the lethargy of the middle session. Before you knew what had happened he brought up his fifty off 37 balls, and Australia were bowling no-balls, fumbling and looking terrible.

There was little way you could see Australia getting Prior out. They seemed beaten. The partnership was 86 off 12 overs when Prior took on North in the deep and went for two. Somehow, completely against the flow of the game, North hit the stumps and took out the one bright spark of the day. It was poor form from North – even I wanted Prior to make a hundred.

Freddie came in then and at this point Australia were waiting for rain, bad light and stumps. The light got bad, Freddie played some nice shots and Collingwood brought up one of his easiest Test-match fifties.

When Siddle got Collingwood out, it started raining. It was a sign from the aliens that this day's cricket was over. England were 521 in front, and Australia were lying bloodied and beaten on the floor.

During the Prior massacre there was a short time when Ricky Ponting found himself on the long on boundary. Here was an Australian captain at long-on during the last session of the third day at Lord's as two English batsmen scored at will. Not something you would expect to see Mark Taylor or Richie Benaud doing. This isn't what Ricky signed up for. When he took the job he was told he could stand at slip, or gully, point to a bowler and then point to another bowler when he looked tired. The wins would happen on their own.

Soon he will face the questions about what he will do if he becomes the first Australian captain in history to lose two Ashes in England. Few can see him playing under his protégé Clarke. If the worst happens, will he want to stay on as captain? At long on he had plenty of time to think about his response. Australia hasn't lost the Ashes yet, or even this test, but the signs aren't looking good. I had even tried to get a Ricky to retire rumour going, but no-one in the press pool was biting.

The other interesting Ricky moment of the day was that his dropped catch was shown almost every ten minutes. And even through the bulletproof glass of the press box the ironic cheers for it as it hit the screen were almost deafening. Australia were not a team full of well-known faces like they had once been; it was Ricky Ponting and a bunch of guys no-one had heard of a few weeks before. Ricky was the crowd target.

Richie Benaud's raincoat

Just as I was finishing my work Richie came back from his Channel 5 gig with Mark Nicholas to pack up (surely he has people for that?). It was a bit rainy out, and Richie thought he should put on his raincoat, and oh what a raincoat.

It was knee length.

Double breasted.

Giant buttons.

And beige.

I shit you not.

Somehow I managed to keep from cheering at the very sight of it. He is a class act. I so wanted that raincoat.

David Frith and me

It can be easy to start star-watching in the press box , forget about the cricket and go up to your heroes and ask them stuff, so I did. I talked to David Frith. Interviewing him was great, but I couldn't help but compare his rise to my own more unconventional route into the press box.

How we got started

Mr Frith: "It was my dear friend John Arlott who set up my entry into cricket journalism. I had freelanced for years but I was getting nowhere. One evening John rang and asked if I would like to become the editor of *The Cricketer*? I said: "Of course, but it's not going to happen." Then Jim Swanton interviewed me at The Oval, during the Test when Australia leveled the series in '72, and he was satisfied that I had a deep love for the game and a reasonable knowledge of it, so I was taken on as deputy editor. A few months later I became editor."

Me: "After trying to make films about terrible punk bands, post-apocalyptic no-budget action epics, and some infomercials for the Catholic Church I set up my own cricket blog. Amazingly, people liked it. And more amazingly people told me I could become a cricket writer. So I packed all three of my possessions in a bag and headed for England, where I convinced people to give me small sums of money and agreed not to swear or make filthy jokes."

Starting our own Media

Mr Frith: "In 1979 I managed at last to pull off the establishment of a new cricket magazine – *Wisden Cricket Monthly*, with a wonderful editorial board of Arlott, Ted Dexter, Jim Laker, a young David Gower, and Bob Willis, who was soon to become England captain. I had a full hand there. I modelled the magazine in my own image; I produced the magazine I would want to read. It had a good balance of current cricket – colour pictures too, which revolutionised the magazine industry. I included a lot on the game's history, took obituaries seriously, and book reviews and all the rest of it."

Me: "My website was made in my own image: grubby, piss-taking, anti-authoritarian and honest. I had friends involved, but after about a week I realised I was all alone. There was no real plan – it was not meant to make me a cricket writer, or rich, it was just a way for me to talk about cricket in a way that I felt others had not. Now I get paid for it, and my website collapses because of too many hits."

Authors

Mr Frith: "I edited *The Cricketer* for six years nearly, and in that time I wrote a few books. I had a lot of pent-up energy, as at last I was in the game full-time. I wrote *Fast Men* and the Stoddart biography. I had to because my pay was pretty meagre." David Frith has written many cricket books.

Me: "I started a fifth book (all previous unpublished) – a collection of my writings from my website. I assumed it would be easy, a simple cut and paste job. It wasn't. English publishers said it was too Australian and the Australians said it was too international. I gave up and self- published."

For all the changes in the cricket press in the last 50 or so years, one thing remains the same. See the cricket, write your copy, love your job.

One of the comments on this post, originally up on *The Wisden Cricketer's* website, was this: "Love seeing a journo blow another journo." For the record, I never blew David Frith. I have a poor gag reflex.

Day 4

For the fourth day, I thought I would turn up with a hangover. I didn't know much about being a cricketer writer, but I assumed that drinking a lot the night after the game was part of the job. There was rain in the morning. The start was delayed and with that Strauss decided to declare. It isn't Strauss' way to make a hasty decision, but this one did feel like that.

As I explained to my drunken English friends the night before, if Strauss declared at 500 in front, and gave Australia six sessions to bat, they would only have to stay in for two days to make the runs. No it wasn't likely, but this was a good pitch – probably pound for pound a better batting strip than Cardiff and Australia went way past 500 there. This seemed like a risky declaration for Strauss.

Australia wouldn't play for the draw. Even if they did that would be shit at it. They would just bat and see how they go. It would also help England, with the runs at a gettable run-rate. Australia would still go for it until it was not possible. The total was huge, but it won't be long before totals of 600 will be chased down.

And this is why: these days most Test pitches don't get worse as the match goes on. In fact, they seem to get better. South Africa and India both chased huge totals easily at the end of 08. Reaching 400 used to be a battle, but with pitches failing to crumble and the psychological scars slowly disappearing, no total is too much if you have the time. That doesn't mean that Australia are about to pass this total with two wickets down at tea on the last day – they could end up four wickets down.

Not that all Aussies were as positive as me. The night before, my website had quite a few asking about rain. But there is no point hoping for rain at Lord's. Unless it rains for the six hours of scheduled play, the rain has no impact. Lord's has a seven-billion dollar drainage system. It is a variation on the United States' star wars program. The idea is that when the rain comes down a system of automatic lasers comes out and zaps each drop taking out the moisture. They take rain seriously in the UK.

As usual, Phil Hughes had it covered, "Need to dig deep today," he twittered.

England started with Anderson and Freddie again. Anderson went straight for Hughes body, perhaps hoping he would get one wrong down the legside and Hughes would chase it. At the other end Freddie was even more aggressive, and it didn't look like metrosexual posturing when he did it.

Freddie was after Hughes. Being that he is probably three times the size of Hughes, it did look like the school bully abusing the malnourished povvo kid. Freddie's first over to Hughes was just hard. Proper hard. He wasn't just trying to get Hughes out, he was trying to break him.

Hughes isn't a shrinking violet – don't let his poetic Twitter updates confuse you. He grew up playing against adults in country NSWales. The boy is a fighter. He is also used to big bogans (chavs) sledging him. The one difference is that Freddie is pretty damn good. When Hughes gets some lip at home from a tattooed beer-gutted loudmouth who smokes between overs, chances are the guy is shit, slow, and will get tired soon. These are not problems that Freddie has.

Freddie took a wicket with the first ball of his next over, but it wasn't Hughes, Katich slashed a ball very hard, but also straight to KP. Australia were 1/17. Probably not the base you want when chasing over 500. It was about three minutes later that viewers of Fox Sports in Australia noticed something was wrong and Fox Sports passed it on the Sky team, who then showed the rest of us. Freddie had taken the wicket with a no-ball. And not just a slip of the foot that could have gone either way, but a genuine no-ball by some distance.

The umpire, which will surprise you, was "Random" Rudi Koertzen. The man who exudes calm and confidence, perhaps so you don't spot his mistakes. You can never tell what sort of decision Rudi will give. Sometimes I think he gives himself extra time by raising his finger slowly just so he can surprise himself.

After six overs the figures of the bowlers told you the difference in class: Flintoff 4-1-4-1 and Anderson 4-0-25-0. At one end you were facing an extreme psychological and physical examination. At the other you were waiting for the loose balls. The wicket-taking end was surely going to be Freddie's, and he even made sure of that by dropping Hughes off Anderson. Hughes had launched into a drive, and it looked like Freddie could not get down low enough to catch it.

Freddie made up for it the next over getting Hughes to edge to slip. But if only it was that easy. The ball was a nice, typical Freddie length, just doing enough to get the edge to Strauss at slip. Problem was the ball went low, very low. Strauss claimed he caught it, so Hughes took his word and walked. Ponting, the non-striker wouldn't let him. Ricky was thinking of the Hauritz catch, you could see it in his brow, and I was over a hundred metres away.

"Random" Rudi wandered over to Billy Doctorove. Oh Billy. It wasn't a long conversation, but it wasn't as short as it should have been. It looked like it was way closer to the grass than Hauritz's catch off Bopara was. The longer the conversation went on, the more obvious it was that it was going to be sent upstairs, which meant that it had to be given not out based on the fact that everything looks not out on the TV.

The Conversation

Rudi: Billy, Billy, wake up Billy.
Billy: What? Yes.
Rudi: Did you see it Billy?
Billy: See what?
Rudi: The catch.
Billy: Who took a catch, was it good?

Rudi: Andrew took it, weren't you watching?

Billy: Yes, I was.

Rudi: Was it a catch?

Billy: You said it was.

Rudi: Okay, try and follow me, did Strauss take the catch?

Billy: Yes.

Rudi: Are you sure, or should we go upstairs?

(Billy looks around)

Billy: There are no stairs here Rudi.

Rudi: Right. Okay, I think it was a catch, so I am going to say it was a catch, you are going to agree with me.

Billy: Of course, Rudi.

Rudi: This is my hundredth Test, and I say it was a catch.

Billy: Yes Rudi.

Rudi: Ricky, that is out.

Ricky: Aren't you going to refer it?

Rudi: 100 Tests, remember.

Ricky: Listen here you pile of cocksweat, you referred that one yesterday – how about some fucking consistency for fuck's sake?

Rudi: Ricky, please, this is my 100th Test, show some respect.

Ricky: Lick my ass.

So Rudi and Billy decided not to refer it, and gave it out. Of course they did. Why was I even surprised? The whole world thought they were about to refer it, and "Random Rudi" didn't. Made perfect sense.

It meant that Australia were 2/34, but on the plus side they had brought the chase down to under 500. They say you need some luck in big chases.

Ponting was angry at what had happened to Hughes. I wondered if anyone would be gutsy enough to tell him about the Katich no-ball as well.

The online war

After Australia made it to lunch without losing any further wickets, the online war started. Luckily this wasn't a Test match between Australia and India as there would have been calls for Mumbai to change the nuclear landing co-ordinates from Pakistan to Australia. On the Internet, I and the cricinfo boys were deluged with Indian supporters going nuts. Apparently this was karma for what happened in Sydney, when Andrew Symonds was given not out three times when he was clearly out and Michael Clarke and Ponting claimed catches close to the turf. But it wasn't the same thing. It did show though that while the greatest cricket rivalry may be the Ashes, the greatest online cricket rivalry is between Australia and India. Aussies and Indians started abusing each other with vicious relish, while English supporters just sat back feeling uncomfortable.

After lunch Jimmy Anderson improved, bowling a great over to Ponting. He was unlucky not to get him out and then had to watch Ponting play on at the other end to Broad. In the words of one of my mates, Australia were starving. The crowd got loud, the roar of the crowd awaked even some MCC members. The problem with having one superstar batsmen in your order is that once he is out it lifts the opposition. The crowd were already buzzing before Ponting got out, but he took them up several decibels. Australia were still more than 400 runs away from victory, and England knew they could win.

Michael Clarke, though, seemed oblivious to the noise. He was batting like it was a one-day match, pouncing on anything loose, pushing hard with his running and finding scoring very easily. He overtook Hussey in the scorebook, which was not hard, but he did it with no effort while England were flying. The target was suddenly down below 400 and then Hussey was out.

Hussey had not mastered the art of batting in his innings. He was struck on the pads a lot, missed the odd ball, and generally looked uneasy, so when he was taken at slip off Graeme Swann no-one was surprised. What was surprising was the replay that showed Hussey missing the ball, hitting the ground and the ball spinning savagely out of the foot holes. It was pretty clear cut on the replay. Luckily for "Random" Rudi it happened at Doctrove's end.

Australia had now lost four wickets in their chase, three of them to umpiring errors. Ouch. Shit happens though. But ouch. Flat pitch, patchy bowlers, good Test batsman, and 4/120. Eight runs later, North was gone too. This was actually out, one of Swann's straight undercutters that went between the bat and pad.

With the loss of North the atmosphere in the press box changed. The Australian journalists quickly resorted to gallows humour while the English ones were were still laughing at the umpiring. I started looking up movie times. I was now likely to have a free day on the Monday so was thinking of alternative entertainment: either a bit of Michael Mann action in *Public Enemies* or the low budget sci-fi film I had heard about, *Moon*.

While doing this I realised that Clarke and Haddin weren't giving up. They actually looked like they wanted to keep batting, and maybe, just maybe, ruin my plans for a film the next day. I wasn't the only one, though: golf foursomes and lunch plans would be ruined as well.

At tea the two were still around, but a final session that was supposed to last 49 overs was bound to be their undoing. Other than a handful of pessimistic English fans and reporters no one really thought Australia were still in this game. Except Michael Clarke, who kept farming the strike after the interval. In the Lord's press box they have this guy who gives you interesting (well…) factoids about the game. Apparently of the first 78 balls after tea (not sure why it was 78) Clarke faced 61.

What did it mean? It could have been a freak occurrence that meant nothing at all. I saw it as Clarke's continuation into maturity. He knew that Haddin could be prone to a nervous shot early on after the restart, so he did his best to make sure Haddin was settled at the crease. Clarke knew that this was *the* partnership, Johnson might be handy when there was less than 200 to chase, but if he had come in at this stage, Australia might as well have declared.

Clarke must have been onto something as by the time Haddin was allowed to come out and play, he looked very comfortable and the pair were able to put England under pressure.

Strauss seemed to give up about an hour after tea. Even with five bowlers he thought the best option was not Swann and one of his seamers, but Swann and Paul Collingwood. Clarke and Haddin knew they had them.

England's presence in the field suddenly altered. It was like a collective shoulder slump. The predatory team of earlier had been replaced by a confused bunch of individuals. Notably Freddie was not on the field. That was when I realised that England still thought they could lose.

Strauss is not an inventive captain at the best of times; this was far from the best of times. Collingwood did have a plan, some sort of legside trap with two short mid-wickets, but that looked like it was more Collingwood's idea than Strauss'. During this pause in competitive play Clarke and Haddin brought up their milestones, off consecutive balls, Clarke a terrific hundred – by far the best I had seen him make live – and Haddin his fifty.

Swann and Collingwood were kept on until the eightieth over, and then the new ball taken. Strauss called his men in and gave them a blunt talking-to and then a group hug. You could actually see the desperation oozing from them as they embraced one another. Australia had lost half their wickets, had barely half the runs, yet England were resorting to group hugs. Australia had to be over the moon at this situation.

The new ball was in Anderson's hand, but their positioning of only two slips told you much about how England were thinking. But the crowd weren't here for Jimmy. Freddie was brought on at the other end, and he was going to fix this.

Freddie started with a shocking loosener, but then got back on line. He was given three slips, but when he found the edge, it went to the right of fourth. But instead of being happy that Flintoff had got a nick, the team seemed weirdly uncomfortable for one still massively ahead. Haddin flashed another over the slips' heads and England looked disconsolate.

It was clear England weren't going to get another wicket that evening. Australia went to stumps at 5/311 on the back of a chanceless unbroken partnership of 183 off 48 overs, one player on 125, the other on 80. I was there, I saw it all, and I didn't quite believe it. That night I struggled to get out all my pieces – for unknown reasons I felt as ill as a dog – but I thought that in the spirit of Haddin and Clarke I should give it a go.

The ground of the dead

Travelling on the Tube to Lord's is an experience. It is like travelling on a train from 1938, except with dead people. Make no mistake, some of these men are dead. There is no doubt they are just going to the cricket because they have always done it. A beyond-the-grave leisure activity, a chance to catch up with other corpses and talk about how things were better in their day.

I had one seated next to me. I stared at him for three stops, and I was convinced he had passed on. He hadn't moved, or given any signs of life and his skin was a matte grey. I thought someone better do something, so I reached out to take his pulse and just before I got to him he sprung to life with a splutter. When I looked around I realised it wasn't just him, there was a carriage full of them. Each more ghostly than the last, copies of *The Times* or *The Telegraph* in their bony hands, a packed lunch made by their wives sitting at their feet – and three layers of beige on.

You wonder what these guys do the rest of the year. Perhaps there is some special Lord's mortuary, and they are shipped out so that younger members won't get their seats. When you leave the tube you have to dodge them on your way to the ground. They don't walk, they do a shuffle trudge, and they take up the whole footpath, presenting a zombie obstacle course.

Once in the ground, you realise there are thousands of them, still doing this shuffle trudge, getting in your way, taking hours to piss, stopping in walkways, dissing any new (post war) changes, dropping booze and food on their shirts.

When I mentioned this to a friend he said, "You know it is their ground, the members own it, maybe you shouldn't disrespect them". That depressed me. Lord's is the home of cricket. To me it is owned by no one person, no matter how old or rich.

I think that is why Lord's has never really been my ground. It wouldn't even be in my top five. My ground is the MCG, the home of my spiritual awakening. It is known as the people's ground.

Day 5

I was still feeling sick on the morning. so being that I didn't have to be in the press box – I had tickets with friends – I slept in and made sure I got to the game just in time for the start. Unfortunately I was accosted by a Sky camera crew wanting to know what an Aussie fan thought would happen. Served me right for wearing my Victorian shirt.

I said, sorry I'm not a fan, I'm a cricket writer, and tried to pass. But they decided that made me the perfect candidate, and made me answer some stupid-ass questions. My answers were even shitter. I waffled on about the new ball and how great the pitch was. I could tell by his face he wanted to get out of the interview, but I couldn't stop talking shit.

It should be said that if I have five minutes to prepare and relax I am a great interviewee, but on the fly you get waft full of shitness, and this guy got a bucketload. After I stopped talking, he let me go, and I managed to miss the first over. Fucken Sky. I had a lot of hope; on this pitch Australia should only need to beat the new ball, and then maintain some strong partnerships.

The crowd was baying for blood, and as I walked around the ground, I could hear the anticipation of each ball, the scream of an appeal, the groan of disappointment. When I finally got to my seat, Freddie was at the top of his mark. All macho-posturing and three-day growth. I figured Australia only needed to survive 15 overs, win the first hour, and the total was within their grasp. I think I told the kky that, just not in a way anyone could understand.

Four balls. That is all it took Freddie. Four fucking balls. Clarke couldn't shield Haddin early on, and Haddin couldn't keep Freddie out. I had the sense that this whole match was set up just so that Freddie could take it away from Australia, the final big-time performance of the people's cricketer.

Of course the crowd got up and applauded. I just sat there. One-nil down, fuck. How did we get here? You had to give it to Freddie, he was the man for an occasion. His record had been rubbish for a while but when Australia turned up, he dragged England and his knee over the line. England now had that all-important commodity that cricketers never stop talking about: momentum. One on the trot-type momentum.

My friends, all English, disagreed with me. They still saw a chance that Australia could somehow get across the line. They were having flashbacks to Johnson's batting in South Africa. So were quite a few others in the crowd. You could hear the murmurs about Johnson everywhere, and when he slashed Freddie over cover and then later pulled him to the rope, I felt real nervous tension.

Johnson loves batting when there is not the pressure of a result resting on it. He likes to take a full swing through the ball with no consequences. I have seen him make rubbish runs in Australian defeats a couple of times before, and they looked pretty much exactly like this.

Clarke was going okay at the other end, but he wasn't looking like the batsman of supreme quality he was only the day before. Freddie had hit him on the head, he had mistimed a few balls, and missed a few others. Unconsciously, or maybe even consciously, he knew he wasn't seeing the ball as well and that shepherding the tail was not his skill.

Swann was brought on, the third change of bowler at the Nursery End. Freddie remained on at the Pavilion End, and although at the end of almost every over it looked like Strauss was offering to take Freddie off, Freddie would just not come off. But it was Swann who made the big breakthrough.

Clarke tried to come down the wicket, but was completely beaten in flight and the ball went on to bowl him. It was obviously the most important wicket for England, but because Freddie hadn't taken it, it didn't instantly get the ovation it deserved. I figured that with Clarke gone the English fans would sit back and enjoy the win was coming their way.

But they didn't seem able to. One of my friends, I should point out, is an award-winning writer, one known for his analytical brain, and yet faced with overwhelming evidence that England could not lose, he still thought they could – even after the next over from Freddie when Nathan Hauritz refused to play a shot to a ball that knocked his off stump out. He became the fourth batsman in the series to get out not offering a stroke.

At the other end Mitchell continued to swing away. It wasn't brainless tailend swinging, but once an over he would play a big shot and pick up a four. Off drives from Freddie and mid-wickets slogs off Swann. He knew, you could see it in his swing, that Siddle wasn't going to out last Freddie's spell which, considering his knee, was now super human.

Eventually Siddle got out to a classic ball. The crowd went into overdrive and Freddie went into his English saviour pose. Some people don't like it. I'm an atheist and I don't mind it. Him on one knee, arms stretched out, waiting for his people to embrace him. It is not as natural as the Shahid Afridi version. That is more like an eager kid hoping his mother has seen him do well; Freddie's has a pre-planned "I am the English Jesus" feel to it.

Not long after that Johnson fell to Swann for 63, and Australia were caught 114 runs short. The crowd erupted; they had seen exactly what they wanted. Ricky gave a very gracious speech, completely ignoring "Random" Rudi's contribution to the loss and praising the English team. Mike Atherton gave him more than enough openings. But Ricky would not give.

Freddie

Before this Ashes series I thought Freddie was only good for cameo performances, then he announced his retirement, and I thought maybe he could do slightly more. On the final day he did. Way more. Australia would have won this Test had Harmy, Bresnan or Ronnie Irani been playing. Even with Australia's farcical first day, their suicidal second day, and a fourth day when the umpires were unsure of what constituted a correct decision, they had a chance to win this match. But Freddie stood up.

He was the difference between the sides. Watching him run in for over after over with a knee that seems to have no cartilage left in it was herculean enough, but then to take the three most important wickets in the innings, and crush the tail, was astonishing. His spell just seemed obscenely long. After every over I said he must be taken off.

He never was.

Australia went into the last day with hope. Andrew Flintoff picked up their hope, shook it, choked it, and then kicked it out of Lord's. He said in the press conference that he wanted to bowl until the match was won.

You couldn't really take him off, he was presence. His knee must now be ratshit, but who cares, he wasn't allowing Strauss to take him off. At the other end were faceless imitators. They were coming in to bowl, but they had no drama, no pulling power, and no personality. It was all Freddie.

Swann had even taken the wicket of the best batsman. But it wasn't the same. The crowd were shouting Freddie's name, and they were right to do so. Being at the ground made you feel like you were at some ancient altar.

It was Freddie's place; it was Freddie's game, and fuck you if you didn't want to bow down before him. By force of personality and through all pain barriers he was bowling until Australia lost. That takes a special player. Sitting, and standing when he took a wicket, all I could think of was what we had missed from him. Why had he not had this sense of duty throughout his whole career?

Because being there, even when your side lost, was amazing. Sure I am supposed to be disappointed, but I felt like I'd seen something special. His energy and power just won you over. I almost joined in the "Super Freddie" chants. That is what the man does to you. I can only hope Test cricket can find someone else like him.

In bed with Mitchell Johnson

For a little while now you have been hanging out with a young stud. He is well built in every way, very accommodating to your needs, and has a phenomenal success rate when it comes to getting you off.

There aren't many lovers like him. Most of his ilk don't last very long. You know a friend of yours had one like him once and hasn't stopped talking about him since.

Mitchell is great, but he is not perfect. You have had better, but not much better: at this time and place he is far better than any other option you have.

During one particularly savage love-making session he does something that he has never done before, and you melt. He finds your magic spot, and you know if you can train him how to do this regularly, you will never ever want to leave Mitchell.

So you tell him how he did it, and you show him how to continue to do it. He doesn't get it right very much, but when he does you are so damn orgasmic you hardly notice.

Eventually it is all you can think of and every time you and him are in action you ask for it: "Come on Mitchell, give me want I want big boy, I know you can do it."

Sometimes he struggles, but you guide him, teach him, explain it to him, and he eventually gets it right.

Then you go on holiday together, it is your first really special holiday, and all you can think of is Mitchell and your magic spot.

The first few times he can't do it, but he assures you he is just getting used to being on holiday and that he will come good.

You trust him, but you can't help but give him some advice; being the lovely chap he is, he takes it. It doesn't help him though. It just clouds his mind.

Suddenly, even his old love-making skills break down; now, he is like a teenage boy with a hard-on for the first time.

You see him falling apart, and you give him more and more advice, but the more you give him the worse he gets.

Now he is ejaculating before entry, and some of it goes in your eye.

But you remain calm. You know that at times he took you to places few have taken you to before, so you stay by him.

It isn't easy. And you now stop giving him advice altogether, not because you don't want to see him at his best, but because when you do he can no longer get an erection.

When you stop talking to him he does seem to get a little better, now all you need to do is learn to shut up and hope he comes good.

Second Test at Lord's
England won by 115 runs

England first innings		Runs	Balls	Mins	4s	6s
*AJ Strauss	b Hilfenhaus	161	268	370	22	-
AN Cook	lbw b Johnson	95	147	190	18	-
RS Bopara	lbw b Hilfenhaus	18	19	20	4	-
KP Pietersen	c Haddin b Siddle	32	42	38	4	-
PD Collingwood	c Siddle b Clarke	16	36	43	1	-
+MJ Prior	b Johnson	8	10	13	2	-
A Flintoff	c Ponting b Hilfenhaus	4	10	16	1	-
SCJ Broad	b Hilfenhaus	16	26	50	2	-
GP Swann	c Ponting b Siddle	4	6	6	1	-
JM Anderson	c Hussey b Johnson	29	25	47	5	-
G Onions	not out	17	29	40	2	-
Extras (15 b, 2 lb, 8 nb)		25				
Total (all out, 425 minutes, 101.4 overs)		425				

Fall of wickets: 1-196 (Cook, 47.5 ov), 2-222 (Bopara, 53.6 ov), 3-267 (Pietersen, 65.1 ov), 4-302 (Collingwood, 76.3 ov), 5-317 (Prior, 79.3 ov), 6-333 (Flintoff, 82.3 ov), 7-364 (Strauss, 90.2 ov), 8-370 (Swann, 91.5 ov), 9-378 (Broad, 92.6 ov), 10-425 (Anderson, 101.4 ov)

Australia bowling	Overs	Mdns	Runs	Wkts	Wides	No-Balls
Hilfenhaus	31	12	103	4	-	4
Johnson	21.4	2	132	3	-	-
Siddle	20	1	76	2	-	4
Hauritz	8.3	1	26	0	-	-
North	16.3	2	59	0	-	-
Clarke	4	1	12	1	-	-

Australia first innings		Runs	Balls	Mins	4s	6s
PJ Hughes	c Prior b Anderson	4	9	10	1	-
SM Katich	c Broad b Onions	48	93	141	6	-
*RT Ponting	c Strauss b Anderson	2	15	19	-	-
MEK Hussey	b Flintoff	51	91	127	8	-
MJ Clarke	c Cook b Anderson	1	12	21	-	-
MJ North	b Anderson	0	14	33	-	-
+BJ Haddin	c Cook b Broad	28	38	28	3	-
MG Johnson	c Cook b Broad	4	11	13	1	-
NM Hauritz	c Collingwood b Onions	24	36	53	4	-
PM Siddle	c Strauss b Onions	35	47	65	5	-
BW Hilfenhaus	not out	6	14	20	1	-
Extras (4 b, 6 lb, 2 nb)		12				
Total (all out, 267 minutes, 63 overs)		215				

Fall of wickets: 1-4 (Hughes, 2.3 ov), 2-10 (Ponting, 6.6 ov), 3-103 (Katich, 32.4 ov), 4-111 (Hussey, 35.6 ov), 5-111 (Clarke, 36.3 ov), 6-139 (North, 42.3 ov), 7-148 (Johnson, 45.5 ov), 8-152 (Haddin, 47.5 ov), 9-196 (Hauritz, 58.3 ov), 10-215 (Siddle, 63 ov)

England bowling	Overs	Mdns	Runs	Wkts	Wides	No-Balls
Anderson	21	5	55	4	-	-
Flintoff	12	4	27	1	-	2
Broad	18	1	78	2	-	-
Onions	11	1	41	3	-	-
Swann	1	0	4	0	-	-

England second innings Runs

		Balls	Mins	4s	6s
*AJ Strauss	c Clarke b Hauritz	32	48	62	4	-
AN Cook	lbw b Hauritz	32	42	52	6	-
RS Bopara	c Katich b Hauritz	27	93	134	4	-
KP Pietersen	c Haddin b Siddle	44	101	150	5	-
PD Collingwood	c Haddin b Siddle	54	80	118	4	-
+MJ Prior	run out (North)	61	42	50	9	-
A Flintoff	not out	30	27	34	4	-
SCJ Broad	not out	0	0	1	-	-

Did not bat: GP Swann, JM Anderson, G Onions

Extras (16 b, 9 lb, 5 nb, 1 w)   31

Total (6 wickets, declared, 317 minutes, 71.2 overs)   **311**

Fall of wickets: 1-61 (Cook, 14.1 ov), 2-74 (Strauss, 16.2 ov), 3-147 (Bopara, 44.4 ov), 4-174 (Pietersen, 51.1 ov), 5-260 (Prior, 63.2 ov), 6-311 (Collingwood, 71.2 ov)

Australia bowling	Overs	Mdns	Runs	Wkts	Wides	No-Balls
Hilfenhaus	19	5	59	0	-	3
Johnson	17	2	68	0	1	1
Siddle	15.2	4	64	2	-	-
Hauritz	16	1	80	3	-	1
Clarke	4	0	15	0	-	-

Australia second innings		Runs	Balls	Mins	4s	6s
PJ Hughes	c Strauss b Flintoff	17	34	46	2	-
SM Katich	c Pietersen b Flintoff	6	5	15	1	-
*RT Ponting	b Broad	38	69	88	6	-
MEK Hussey	c Collingwood b Swann	27	63	100	3	-
MJ Clarke	b Swann	136	227	313	14	-
MJ North	b Swann	6	25	23	1	-
+BJ Haddin	c Collingwood b Flintoff	80	130	186	10	-
MG Johnson	b Swann	63	75	94	9	-
NM Hauritz	b Flintoff	1	5	5	-	-
PM Siddle	b Flintoff	7	13	18	1	-
BW Hilfenhaus	not out	4	4	11	-	-

Extras (5 b, 8 lb, 8 nb)   21

Total (all out, 473 minutes, 107 overs)   **406**

Fall of wickets: 1-17 (Katich, 3.1 ov), 2-34 (Hughes, 9.2 ov), 3-78 (Ponting, 23.4 ov), 4-120 (Hussey, 32.4 ov), 5-128 (North, 38.4 ov), 6-313 (Haddin, 87.4 ov), 7-356 (Clarke, 98.2 ov), 8-363 (Hauritz, 99.4 ov), 9-388 (Siddle, 103.6 ov), 10-406 (Johnson, 107 ov)

England bowling	Overs	Mdns	Runs	Wkts	Wides	No-Balls
Anderson	21	4	86	0	-	-
Flintoff	27	4	92	5	-	8
Onions	9	0	50	0	-	-
Broad	16	3	49	1	-	-
Swann	28	3	87	4	-	-
Collingwood	6	1	29	0	-	-

After Lord's

Australians were in shock: "How the fuck did we lose at *our* ground?" The English were in shock too: "How the fuck did we win after that fisting at Cardiff?" Cricket writers were confused. But cricket was being mentioned everywhere.

There was hardly a better way to start an Ashes series if you want English people to talk about it than an ass-clenching draw and a surprise English win. .

Australia could take positives out of the game: they were thoroughly outplayed, had problems with injuries and umpires, had a massive self-made collapse with the bat, and they only lost by just over a hundred runs.

Also they must have been thrilled to participate in "Random" Rudi's 100th Test.

England were still inconsistent and hard to work out. They appeared to be amazingly reliant on Strauss and Freddie. But they had one win, confidence and a national treasure in their changing room. KP was soon ruled out of the series with injury. It should have been a huge story, but it felt swamped by the praise of Freddie and the booing of Ricky Ponting.

Lord's had been a weird match, sort of like a partner who is stroppy but great in bed and can get you free movie tickets. This wasn't the same Lord's I had been to before. It had attitude, and was more colisseum than cucumber sandwich.

Npower girls

The Ashes aren't the Ashes. How could they be. If they were the Ashes then a whole swagfull of revenue would be lost. So we have the Npower Ashes. Npower is an electricity company that likes to brand things. It also has the Npower girls. Here they are as described by Npower:

> *"It's a miracle anyone knows what's going on at square leg with girls like these in the crowd. Meet the Npower girls: a bunch of smart, sassy lasses who know their googlies*

from their doosras. During the Tests, they keep thirsty photographers well watered, distribute 4 and 6 cards to the crowds and help us all get behind the boys – and spur them on to victory."

If I was writing a blurb for them it would go like this:

"One look at the pins on these six Aryan glamour models and you won't care if Nathan Hauritz takes an 18-wicket haul. They are so hot that you won't notice your beer is in a non-plastic "plastic" cup when these girls strut by. They know their cricket, but that is hardly relevant. They're hot, blonde, and made to order for drunk, horny cricket fans. After play you won't remember Strauss' cut shot, but you'll remember these fine pieces of sexy product placement. "Go England," squeal the girls when their favourite team pounds away at the opposition."

I do feel sorry for these girls. It isn't their fault. If I was a blond bombshell with long hair, hips that wiggle provocatively and shapely calves I might take up this job. A hundred odd quid a day to go to the cricket? Not a bad gig even if you have to spend that much again on fake tan and yogalates classes. Although, it must get repetitive, the double entendre conversation with drooling idiots talking about polishing their balls, maiden overs, full tosses and stroking the ball through the covers which is followed by other identical conversations with sex-starved drunk. When there aren't any double entendres, it's just shithouse flirting. Guys trying to pick up promotional girls is about the saddest thing you can see, like *Hotel Rwanda* following a news report on burning puppies. Watching the Npower girls operate with these guys reminds me that great *Simpsons* scene in which Homer is at a car show and sees a car with a blonde draped over it.

Homer: "Do you come with the car?"
Model: (giggling) "Oh you."

He walks away and another guy walks up.

Man: "Do you come with the car?
Model: (giggling) "Oh you."

My problem with them is the family-friendly style of ECB sanctioned soft core porn. They aren't there because they know their doosras from their googlies – they'd struggle against Ajantha Mendis – they're there because they are blonde and they are hot and make Npower's red and green outfits look good.

And they're all so one-fucking-dimensional. Can anyone tell them apart? There's not one Asian, African, plus-sized girl, or redhead. They're such great role models for young girls coming to the cricket for the first time: be white, dye your hair blonde, remain under size 12 and apply fake tan and you too can be popular at the cricket.

Maybe there could be an academy where teenage girls are turned into the Npower girls of the future. They could bring in hardened veteran Npower girls who know how to slap away a touchy fan, keep that make-up looking immaculate all day and look so much like the girl next to you that not even their mothers could pick them out.

I think Npower should go down the interracial porn path. Have your six blonde chicks if you want, but also have six strapping black men and six androgynous mixed-race models. Something for everyone. Dress every man in tank top and bike shorts, and give the girls shorter skirts and bikini tops.

They could also have a sunscreen stand where drunk men, gay and straight, drunken women, straight and gay, can pick one of the Npower Hotties™ to rub sunscreen all over them and protect them from the harsh English sun.

During the breaks in play they could put on dance shows. Maybe a shortened version of *High School Musical* – the second one, the first one had plot holes everywhere. Something high energy with lots of lovely male and female parts jiggling around hypnotically. Afterwards they could eat fruit in a provocative way or show people the best way to stretch their groins. The possibilities are endless.

Hot chicks with the same smile tattooed on their faces are always the favourite marketing tool of people who run companies, there is never a shortage of them. Npower are not even the only ones who do it at the cricket. Walking to a ground in England means you get to walk past nearly every glamour model available in the county, a sea of fake tan and cleavage. Inside the ground Marsten have the Marsten Maidens (Npower complained about this as they invented sexy girls in matching costumes) and on the way out of the ground there are usually strippers giving out fliers for their clubs. Cricket tries to be a family sport, but in truth it is as perverted as anything else.

That is okay, because, as you may have noticed, I am a pervert. I am sexually deranged in almost every way. But what place does sex have in a cricket ground, being pimped by an electricity company? Sex is great, sex is wonderful, sex shouldn't be hidden behind closed doors, and people should have it at bus stops. This isn't sex. This is some sick and wrong version of cricketing *Baywatch,* engineered so that drunken dads and loud-mouthed lads can jack off when they are alone later that night. This book might be perverted, but this ain't no family-friendly book.

When I see the Npower girls I generally think of them as cross-dressing Npower executives living out their fantasy of being the prettiest and most popular women at the cricket. For all I know that is what they are. Npower has gone to great lengths to make them not look like real women, just like drag queens do.

I think Dani, one of the 09 Npower girls, explains the whole phenomena perfectly: "I love relaxing in a hot, soapy bath. It's great for unwinding after a hard day."

Who will miss KP the Most?

1 The young fan who wants to grow up and play across the line and have a pop star girlfriend.

2 The breed of women/gay men who feel KP brings a certain level of sexual sophistication to the game.

3 Andy Flower, who believes that KP brings a sense of sexual dynamism to the English batting line-up.

4 The Australian fan who loves to see him hobble.

5 The anti-KP faction who love it when his average drops.

6 His sponsors, especially the VW Phaeton, of whom KP thinks: "Its a fantastic car that lets me travel in style up and down the country, allowing me to arrive refreshed and relaxed."

7 The Australians, who would have been happy that he was looking toothless.

8 The cameramen; now who will be their default shot?

9 Jessica Taylor (his pop star wife), who now has to put up with him 24/7.

10 The *News of the World*, who paid all this money for a gimp who isn't playing.

11 Ian Bell.

This is a trick question, of course; the real answer is the English cricket media.

How to get selected 2.0

Cricket writers are a naturally nostalgic bunch. Many of them laud the achievements of players who died before they were born, and hark back to the simpler times. I am not always inclined to follow the trend, except for a bit of man-love for Keith Miller.

Yet there is one modern development that really gets to me: agents and PR companies trying to infect cricket selection. In the Ashes it came up when the agency representing Stephen Moore put out a press release stating the many, many reasons why Moore should be considered for an England place now that KP was injured.

The idea was to subtly push the media in the direction of speculating that Moore should be in the mix for playing for England. I doubt the idea was to get him into the side – he is an opener and KP bats at four – but his agency just wanted him in the frame, wanting to create some buzz. You know what I am talking about, you've all seen *Entourage*.

They had timed it well – on the back of Moore making a hundred against the Aussies when playing for the English Lions. Moore and Joe Denly had shared an opening partnership of 172 in the first innings, yet afterwards, all the talk was about Denly, not Moore, even though the Kent opener had made only 66 to his partner's 120. There was a good reason for that, though. Denly's innings was one of class, smooth and eye-catching; Moore's was based more on graft and determination.

It wasn't the first time Moore had played in a representative side and all the talk had been about others. During the great No. 3 audition game – the MCC v Durham season curtain-raiser – which featured Robert Key, Michael Vaughan and Bell all battling for that position, Moore top-scored with 45 while the rest of the batsmen fell away. He was barely mentioned. So I understood why his agency were trying to toot his horn. But it wasn't as if he was being completedly ignored: he toured New Zealand with the Lions, played in both Lions games against the 09 tourists and represented the MCC.

Its wording all just seemed a bit desperate:

> *"Only two weeks ago, Moore scored an impressive 120 for the England Lions against a full Australia batting (sic) line up, which included Brett Lee being in irrepressible form. With injuries rife, Ian Bell severely lacking in form and Ravi Bopara proving vulnerable, there is surely no*

one else who has staked there (sic) claim for a spot with
such distinction and, most importantly, form."

It has all the facts there you need, sure, but even a casual cricket writer would see the holes in these two sentences. Yes, Moore did well against Lee, but the bowler had had him plumb in front well before he got to his hundred, and Lee wasn't irrepressible until well into Moore's innings – before then he was pants. Ravi and Belly were both struggling, but using Moore's form was surely a bit much. Form? He was averaging 31 in first-class cricket.

I also wondered how Bell and Ravi would feel. Having fans and the press on your back is tough enough, but now even agents of other players were sending out releases questioning your worth. If I'd been either of them, I'd have been calling Moore pretty damn quick and airing my views on his form and personality.

In India, players and players' families have been known to offer money, toys and sexual favours to journalists get their man into the news.

Somehow, utterly fucked up as that is, it doesn't feel as bad as hiring someone to plug you in this manner. Moore, born in South Africa – if only they could sell their cricketers to help their GNP – is a good bat, but Australia would be over the moon if he were to be brought into the team.

But of all the nonsense in the press release, it was one particular sentence that made me smile like a fool for days:

"For Stephen Moore, a keen musician in his spare time,
the 2009 season is one rich with potential."

He isn't just a cricketer, you know; he is a fully-rounded individual with interests in things that aren't cricket-related, like music.

The swine flu diaries

After my second day in the Lord's press box I was asked out to dinner by some of the other journalists: it was the first time I had been asked to do anything by a journalist in a press box other than to move out the way. I had to decline. I was tired. But that was okay, I was working my ass to the bone and dealing with a militant Bride, I was supposed to be tired.

On the Monday I was feeling good enough to drink all afternoon once Freddie had ruined the Test match, but then I didn't get out of bed for 24 hours. By Tuesday it was obvious that something was more wrong than me just feeling tired from overwork or depressed by the fact Australia couldn't hook or pull.

I was then diagnosed with swine flu.

Diagnosed is maybe pushing it a bit.

If you feel sniffly, you take an online test. At the end of the Test it tells you whether it thinks you have swine flu. If it is positive, you have to call a doctor and repeat your symptoms. Mine was. Then the doctor says you have swine flu, and you have swine flu. That is all.

My conversation with the doctor went like this:

Me: Yes I have a cough, runny nose, am very tired, and have a fever.
Doc: okay then you need a week of bed rest and you need to stay at home.
Me: Oh, so I have swine flu?
Doc: Yes.
Me: But how do you know, you haven't actually seen me.
Doc: You have swine flu.
Me: Are you sure?
Doc: Yes.
Me: Oh, so do I need the viral thingy?
Doc: No, only if you get really sick.

That was it. I wasn't swabbed, touched or measured. I just instantly became a case of swine flu. Shame if I was busy at work and didn't have swine flu.

But I was tired, and I thought fuck it. I bought no medicine, needed no chicken soup, and I survived. For all I know I had a cold and was only being tired because I was subconsciously trying to get a week of sleep.

I think people who are diagnosed over the phone and don't take any drugs should be given a prize for not bothering anyone – a swine flu T-shirt that says: I rode the pig reaper and I survived.

You may even have heard of the Australian cricket journalist who had swine flu. That wasn't me. That was Ben Dorries from the *Courier Mail* in Brisbane. He was told to stay away from the Australian players — as a *Crikey* "reporter" I was already banned from the Ashes, swine flu had nothing to do with it. The closest Ben and I had been from each other was about one metre, and that was outside a MCC press conference. In the press box we were about five metres apart, so there is little chance we even gave it to each other.

There were reports that up to 65,000 people could die from the virus in the UK, but I've had rougher colds. It seemed like a normal flu in every way and I had no craving for bacon – well no more than usual. I was tired, running a fever, prone to afternoon sleeps, and couldn't stop watching bad American action films, so it was pretty much a normal flu. For me.

I was a little worried for David Frith and Richie Benaud, but they both survived. Which is great.

Northampton warm up/down

Australia went off to play the second-division Northamptonshire without their "stars", Andrew Hall and Nicky Boje. Yes, really. It was less glorious than the basking-in-the Ashes-leading glow that the English players were doing. Australia had many questions to be answered. Phil Hughes needed runs, Michael Hussey needed runs, Peter Siddle needed control and Mitchell Johnson needed constant validation and the love of a good mother. Australia had rested Clarke, Haddin and Ricky.

Hughes got his runs, a second-innings 68 while putting on an opening stand of 146 with the redhaired tourist Australia had forgotten, Andrew McDonald.

Hussey retired himself after a hard-working 75 in the first innings. Siddle and Johnson went at 5.57 and 6 runs an over far from respectively.

The two best players in the game for Australia had to be the all-rounders Shane Watson and McDonald. The perennial Baggy Green stalker Watson made an 84 and a 50 (off 35 balls), McDonald making 75 and taking four for 15 off 11 overs before being taken off. Perhaps if he'd got a six-wicket haul it would have confused the selectors too much.

Shane Watson wasn't just in fine form on the field; off the field he was killing it as well. When asked about Hughes's form, he supported him, before saying he could open the batting if required. Shane Watson is a special kind of person, and he doesn't mean to come across as a heartless guy, he just sort of does. Being that he hadn't been asked to open in this match there was no reason to think he would be at Edgbaston, but he smelt a weakness.

Stuart Clark was doing no such press conferences. Even if he had he would have just made some jokes, smirked and then left. He should have been the man most likely to come into the team, while Siddle and Johnson had to be the weakest links. Hughes had failed three times, sure, but one of those shouldn't have been out. Clark's bowling at Northampton was not sensational, but he had taken wickets in both innings and had an economy rate that Siddle or Johnson would have died for. He just didn't seem to be in the running.

The other bowler Australia may have wanted to include was Brett Lee, but his ribs were still ruling him out. So with Clark out of favour, Lee injured, and McDonald seemingly not a serious option Australia seemed to be stuck with the four they had used already, for better or worse. It was telling that Australia had not called for a replacement for Lee. In South Africa, every time a bowler had farted two replacement bowlers were sent over, but Lee had missed two Tests and a first-class game and still there was no cover.

A lot of people may have not known the relevance of this game, but it didn't escape me. It was Australia's first win in the seven weeks of their UK trip. Their last had come against New Zealand in the World Twenty20 warm-up matches. I know, I was there. Mitchell Johnson was on fire, Brett Lee was unhittable and Andrew Symonds hit the winning runs. Oh Andrew, what happened...

Ricky's future

Australia hadn't lost the Ashes yet. They might not. But if they did, what would Ricky do? He would become only the second Australian captain to lose two Ashes series in the UK.

By Christmas he will be 35.

His batting hadn't been top class in the last couple of years, although it hadn't slipped enough for him to be dropped (if Hussey hasn't been dropped how could Ricky be?) or even for it to be a significant worry: he just wasn't as good as he used to be.

His captaincy was probably the only thing that was improving, slowly but surely. But would he want to go on? He wouldn't stay on as a batsman; I couldn't see him playing under Clarke. And that is where Australia would go; Katich would be jumped over like a dead dog, Marcus North would be given as much thought as you give to tantric masturbation, and Michael Hussey would be ignored.

Clarke looks good on a poster, usually says benign things that mean nothing, was a child prodigy batsman, and is already vice-captain, Australia would like every facet of this.

Of course Ponting is a spectacularly vengeful fucker at times. He could stay on till 10/11 or 13 just to try and take a bite out of England. I doubt it, but it could happen.

Look at his team, a rotation of mentally fragile spinners, weird openers, a patchy middle order, a shaved monkey with keeping gloves on, fast bowlers who are too earnest or prone to mental collapse, and Shane Watson.

With Ponting's record, would you play on?

Edgbaston

Where the Ashes got wet

Australia limped into Edgbaston not sure of what team to pick. England came in carrying Freddie on their shoulders (the opposite of what happens out on the field). I did a lot of thinking about the team Australia would pick, and came up with nothing. I doubted the selectors had much more idea.

Then there was the weather, a lot of weather. Edgbaston was under water. Actual puddles. For grounds with the Lord's star-wars system that is okay, but Edgbaston just has the normal drainage. All England was wet – two of the domestic twenty20 quarter-finals were reduced to bowl-outs because of rain, and I got soaked going to my local café.

As if the previous Test hadn't been bad enough for Ponting, he had now arrived at the ground where he cocked up the 05 Ashes, and against his toughest opponent, Edgbaston's curator Steve Rouse.

Steve Rouse is a massive con artist. I suggest you don't ever buy anything from him. Ever. In 05 he told everyone the pitch was going to be a minefield. He said this while stroking a white cat. What he meant was a psychological minefield. Ricky didn't pass that test. He blew himself up before the Test started by electing to bowl as Glenn McGrath clutched his damaged limb.

According to Steve, this time the pitch was like jelly. Is it Steve? Is it in fact made of fruit, pectin, acid, and sugar? Does it wobble and taste delicious? I doubt it. Pitches are rarely delicious, and we know it won't be green: when was the last time you saw a green Test pitch?

What was Steve really trying to tell us? We knew he had a coded secret in there somewhere. Was jelly a subtle dig at Mitchell Johnson's state of mind? Was jelly Steve Harmison's favourite dish? Was jelly the nickname the English have for Shane Watson's body?

Or was it something more sinister? Perhaps Steve was trying to give Strauss the tip that this is a pitch for medium-paced wobblers. Was Strauss calling Mark Eahlam and Dimi Mascarenhas right now? It makes sense. Rig the pitches for the home attack. But surely Steve had noticed that Australia had bought Andrew McDonald along for just such a pitch?

Or is this the double bluff? Make the Australians think this was the pitch for dibbly dobbling wobblers so that Andrew McDonald was picked. Genius.

Yet again Steve was clearly one step ahead; even the fact that this pitch had produced 15 draws in the previous 20 first-class games was merely part of the trap to set up Australia. He had even orchestrated the rain. Steve, I salute your magnificent duplicitousness.

How Steve knew what the pitch was like is anyone's guess, since it had now been covered for a couple of days. Brown and flat when it was first covered, now it could be overrun with weeds for all he knew. The poor ground staff had to work a full 24-hour shift (curries were brought in for them).

There was aura as well. Lots of aura. Here is Strauss on aura:

> *"I don't think this Australian side has got an aura about it to be honest with you and prior to this Test series starting we didn't feel they had an aura about them. That's not disrespectful to the players they've got because they've got a lot of very good players but I think the aura came with the likes of Warne and McGrath and Hayden and Gilchrist, all those sort of guys."*

When Ricky was told about Strauss's comments he asked if Strauss was asked directly, found out he was, and then sidestepped the furore.

Anyone with a passing interest in cricket would have known that Australia lost their aura about the time Cameron White bowled in a Test match. Generally you lose your aura when you lose. No-one says: "That side hasn't lost in three years, but they have no aura. "

It should also be mentioned that auras, like airfares from IATA-affiliated airlines, are non transferrable.

I think people should stop talking about aura and start talking about the momentum of winning one match in a row.

Day 1

Phil Hughes performed a cricketing first today. He was the first Test cricketer to announce he had been dropped on Twitter before the Australian team had announced he was. Let us all stand and applaud this achievement. He got on the back foot, gave himself some room and tweeted:

"Disappointed not to be on the field with the lads today. Will be supporting the guys, it's a BIG Test match 4 us. Thanks 4 all the support."

The Australians were livid that their selection was revealed on a micro-blogging social networking platform before the toss. Cricket Australia finally found out how Generation Y likes to roll — twittering while they are XBoxing, parkouring and LOLing. Well that is what the story sounds like on the face of it. The truth is far from that.

Hughes's manager Neil D'Costa took the blame for the tweet. "How our situation works is we get the Twitter from Phillip and I feed them into our IT guy," he explained. "I spoke to Cricket Australia; they are very supportive of what players do on and off the field. They know this was an innocent situation."

That seems like the most convoluted way of twittering. Neil, buy the dude a BlackBerry or iPhone. If you need three people to put up a tweet, you probably don't need to be doing it. In 24 days, Phil, Neil and the IT guy have tweeted 13 times. I followed it, but not for the cunning insights, but because I was sure that he would say something interesting eventually. Apparently I was right.

Cricket Australia took Phil over their knee. They were probably not happy that they weren't one of the three people to see Phil's tweets before they got posted. Imagine if there was a fourth person looking at the tweets – that would be a terrific use of everyone's time. A Cricket Australia spokesman, Philip Pope, said: "As a young player he will be reminded that he should not be revealing details until the team has been officially announced." To be fair, Phil was probably as shocked as the rest of us that he had been dropped for Shane Watson.

I certainly couldn't believe it. If the idea was that Watson would be opening the batting ahead of Hughes, why didn't he open in either innings of the match at Northamptonshire? In the second innings Andrew McDonald opened. I can't remember him ever doing that for Victoria. He was never ever going to open the batting for Australia, so why didn't Watson open.

The conspiracy theorists, of which I was one, believed it was because Watson was not supposed to be opening in Birmingham. Ponting and Tim Nielsen definitely never gave any indications that Hughes was about to be dropped; he had made a half-century in the second innings.

Allegedly, and I say that because it is just conjecture and because I don't have a phone tap on Andrew Hilditch, it was a decision made by the selectors back in Australia, rather than the panel of Ponting, Nielsen and Jamie Cox in England. The reason Hughes had been dropped was became obvious: Mitchell Johnson was struggling. Watson was brought in for admittedly the weakest link, to strengthen the bowling more than the batting.

However, Merv Hughes, part-selector part-commentator, claimed that Mitchell Johnson's form had nothing to with Phil Hughes (no relation, if you have seen both of them you probably already guessed this) being dropped. "Phil Hughes was under immense pressure, especially from Flintoff. The English bowlers seemed to have his measure," he said. "Watson was picked primarily as a batsman who could do the job and his bowling was a bonus. We just felt the change needed to be made." It seemed like bullshit, mostly because I had seen how Phil Hughes had got out in the last Test. I wouldn't have said a strangle down the leg-side was having his measure.

The Australian selectors were also punting on the fact that opening the batting wasn't as hard as it once was – in modern Test cricket it can often be the best place to bat. The new ball doesn't swing much early on, there is very little seam movement off the pitches, the field is up, and the bowlers ain't what they used to be.

Somehow after all the rain, at 5pm there was some cricket. No-one was quite sure how. At 3:30, there was a test of the outfield where the ball was almost swallowed whole. But the game was going ahead regardless, Ponting won the toss, which must have pleased him immensely, and decided to bat. The pitch looked CEO brown, Watson was confirmed in the side, Hauritz was kept in and England were unchanged.

Or so it seemed. But one ball into the game – Watson shouldering arms to Anderson – there was an announcement that Haddin had a broken finger in the warm-up and had been replaced by Graham Manou. Haddin's fingers do break quite easily for an elite level keeper. In the Caribbean on his first Test tour he got a broken finger, and played on because he didn't want to lose his spot; he very nearly lost his finger.

Strauss had made the gentleman's decision; he was within his rights to say "bad luck" to Australia as the incident had happened after the toss. Had Ricky Ponting been in the same situation he might not have been as nice. It was something for the "spirit of cricket" gentleman's club. Some had questioned Strauss after the catch he took off Hughes in the second Test, but this was showing that he played the game fairly. I would have made Haddin keep.

England had more charity in store. Knowing that Shane Watson was playing his first Test match as an opener they decided to bowl wide enough outside off stump that he didn't have to play many. Then, after England had got his eye in, Watson decided to hit the wide ones for four.

The ball also wasn't moving, so when it was wide Watson could give it everything, which is when Watson is at his best. Katich was having even more fun. England were spraying the ball around and he was cashing in almost every over. There was plenty to cash in on. England seemed to sense they had let go of an opportunity and were playing like guilty eight year olds. Their stroppiness let Australia get to 84 after 18 overs, with Katich, very uncharacteristically, scoring at a run a ball.

Graeme Swann was brought on, and the game changed suddenly; Watson was hit plumb in front, and given not out, then Simon Katich was hit less plumb in front but given out. He had made 46 off 48 balls. Swann was given one more over, and then the quicks were given the ball. Watson continued to punish them, and Ponting stepped in as well. They got Australia to stumps at 1/126.

Why had Strauss taken off Swann? If he was brought on to try to remove the left-handed Kaitch that made sense, but he also should have had Watson out. Surely, with your other bowlers leaking runs, you would have kept him on. At stumps, Shane Watson had a sore face from smiling so much.

England had not bowled well but Watson was very good. He smashed everything on offer, left the wide stuff, and seemed to love every bit of it. His first go at opening the batting was a complete success. He hadn't even got injured. You can't ask for more. The selectors trusted him, and he stood up. Couldn't ask for more than that.

Shane Watson's reasons

Reasons why Shane Watson shouldn't open the batting for Australia:

Shouldn't: *He is Shane Watson.*
Should: *To make me look stupid.*
Shouldn't: *The new ball hurts.*
Should: *He is a better bat than Irfan Pathan.*
Shouldn't: *He might need to bowl Mitch's overs.*
Should: *He doesn't half hit bad balls.*
Shouldn't: *Phil Hughes has got out to two line and length balls and a shit ball down the leg-side.*
Should: *Phil Hughes was the only Australian batsman not to have made a*

50 in this series.
Shouldn't: *Before this match he averaged 19 in Test cricket.*
Should: *His technique is Terry-Test-match tight.*
Shouldn't: *He is simply not an opener*
Should: *Opening the batting is now easier than ever before.*
Shouldn't: *Australia don't do right-hand opening batsmen*
Should: *Australia have had good luck manufacturing opening batsmen in recent times.*

And he is fucking 62 not out.

Day 2

The performance of the first day was that of Steve Rouse. English groundsmen must have some sort of deep love and hate for rain – like firefighters for flames: sure it is bad, but it lets them be badass and try to save the day. People were no doubt backslapping him but the Warwickshire cricket board would have been offering him hookers and cocaine. He had ensured enough overs were played to guarantee no refunds. That's true genius.

There was still four full days of cricket to come, but a result would hedge on one team having a breakdown. The pitch looked good, Australia had proved it was one that you could score quickly on, and there was more rain forecast, a lot more. Logic suggested another draw, and not a cool Monty-saves-the-day draw, just a too-much-rain-and-not-enough-cricket draw.

Strauss made the odd decision of starting with Onions. In a five-man attack someone always gets left out, and at Lord's Onions seemed like that player. Whether Strauss was overcompensating or saw something in the conditions that would help Onions I don't know.

Two Onion balls into the day Australia's top order had fallen over. Most people hadn't even sat down. Well they had sat down, but were yet to find a comfortable angle on their seats. I was eating my breakfast and almost spat it out. Watson got one that cut back on a length and hit him in front.

Then Mike Hussey walked out, left a straight one, and walked back. Two balls, two wickets, and Australia suddenly had their leadership group out in the middle.

Hussey had now left two balls that had bowled him in this series in four innings, a truly special effort. He wasn't so much fighting for his Test career as failing to fight for it. Watson never struck me as someone who likes to restart his innings again the next day – he is a momentum batsman – and he probably wasn't expecting something on the stumps after the friendly opening of the evening before.

The good news for Australia was that Clarke survived the hat-trick and it was only Freddie bowling at the other end. Strangely, Flintoff looked a little off colour. His line and length were scattered and it was Onions who was really worrying Clarke and Ponting. The crowd noise was still louder at Freddie's end.

But then Ricky played a hook shot to a quick one from Onions and feathered it behind.

That moment must have gutted the Australia captain. The ball was just starting to swing, Freddie was off the boil, he had lost two batsmen before the session had really started and now he had got out playing his most dependable shot.

In the dressing-room, he must have wondered if this was his Ashes. He had come here with a young, hungry team but it was all falling apart, Australia were only 4/163, but he could see the collapse coming.

The longer Ponting's career goes on, the more he has to turn himself into Allan Border.

If he doesn't win the big moments, he cannot guarantee that his team will win them for him. This was one of those times. A rearguard innings from Ponting usually lifts the whole team. Unlike the other great No. 3s in world cricket, Ponting doesn't get to bat with the tail much, mostly because if he steps up, so do other members of the team.

He may not look like the talismanic type, but when he bats, his team follow him like they are emo kids and he is some shitty character from *Twilight*. Had he made a century, Australia would have gone on and made a huge total, but without him they were in danger of crumbling. Ricky loved being the man of this side, there is no doubt, it suits his personality. But part of being the man is feeling like you have let down people when you fail.

Around the time of the Edgbaston Test I had seen *Watchmen*, the film based on the comic book. I doubt Ricky would have. The Dr Manhattan character had a bit of Ricky in him: he was a leader based on his other skills, the only character with real superhuman qualities, quick to return to his own world, didn't always handle his role well. Ponting's face had even turned blue in 2005 after a run-out. Ricky had been there before Australia was great, and was there when Australia wasn't great again.

Australian captains feed on losing, and this creates the monsters they become. Ricky was a perfect example of this. Australia was still yet to lose two series in a row. Ricky was the reason. But the other players weren't good enough, or hard enough, to follow Ricky's lead. So he had to drag them with him. You can only do that so much before you lose your will.

While Ricky was in the changing-room not thinking about Dr Manhattan, Australia were struggling with a swinging ball. North and Clarke were doing there best to make it to lunch, but it wasn't easy. Clarke left one that hit the face of his bat and scared Freddie: he was asleep at slip, and it almost hit him.

Freddie had now dropped two catches you would expect a slip fielder of his quality to catch. For some reason the catch wasn't replayed for the crowd every 12 seconds like the Ponting one was, and you could be sure the headline in *The Sun* the next day was not going to be "Freddie's slipping hell".

Clarke had been looking lucky; when he wasn't edging he was missing inswingers. Eventually he missed one too many and "Random" Rudi stepped in. Anderson deserved a wicket, but it was a far from convincing lbw. Clarke, though, had never really looked like making runs; perhaps Rudi senses this and did the kid a favour.

This brought in Graham Manou, the reserve wicketkeeper who only 12 months earlier was about as likely to play Test cricket as I was. Manou's record was pretty ordinary, but anyone who had followed Shield cricket over the last few years knew that was not a true reflection of his talent. His glove work had never been his problem; his problem was his complete lack of runs.

For years he had an average that only a state in complete disarray like South Australia would tolerate. Then he had a breakthrough year. After briefly losing his position and being overlooked for the captaincy, his batting became inspired. The worse South Australia got, the better he became. In 07/08 he was his team's best batsman by a distance, and in 08/09 when others stepped up, he became the icing on the cake.

While this was happening, Luke Ronchi, a prodigiously talented Western Australian, seemed to be having a professional crisis of faith and Australia wanted a back-up for the Ashes. While Tim Paine, of Tasmania, or Matthew Wade, Tasmanian-born but now playing for Victoria, were ideal keepers for the future, Manou was the perfect option for right now. Mentally strong, well schooled in Shield cricket, a terrific gloveman, and pugnacious batsman in great form, he truly deserved his chance.

He came out swinging too, hitting two fours off his first three balls. The swinging ball might have made Clarke uncomfortable and North almost comatose, but Manou wasn't about to let England dictate to him. Manou and North should have formed a great partnership, both older cricketers who were taking their chances and fighting to prove their worth at Test level.

Instead North wafted at an Anderson wide one and Prior took a diving catch. Next ball Johnson mimicked Michael Hussey and was out lbw not offering a shot to a ball that you would have to be mainlining acid not to play at one that straight.

Nathan Hauritz came out to try and survive Australia's second attempt to give an England bowler a hat-trick, and he did. It was just prolonging the inevitable though – Anderson was now firing and he bowled a ball to Manou so good it almost seemed unfair. The paceman went wide of the crease, bowled a rapid one at the stumps which straightened enough to knock out off stump. Manou had just faced one of the best Test deliveries of 09, and the poor dude had only faced 10 others in his international five-day career.

Anderson's fourth wicket took the game to lunch, the damage sustained by Australia seven wickets for the addition of 77. The tourists had collapsed with almost morbid glee. The ball was swinging towards the ends of the session, but few of the batsmen could blame that for their dismissals

Australia had just seemed to mentally disintegrate themselves. England had bowled well, but twice Australia had lost two wickets in two balls, and three of those dismissals were batsmen error alone.

After lunch Siddle played some good shots before playing across Anderson and giving him his five-wicket haul. Hilfenhaus fit a few unconvincing boundaries through gully and then pulled a sitter up to Ravi at cover. Ravi dropped it. If Ravi was your kid, you wouldn't bring him to the next game. He was in danger of being permanently damaged.

Eventually Hilfy's swinging found a fielder who could catch and gave Onions his fourth wicket. It was a well slogged 20, and with Hauritz making 20* as well, Australia had reached the unrespectable total of 263, well under par on this wicket, and unless Australia had some luck, or England panicked unnecessarily, Australia would be behind on the first innings.

Hilfenhaus took the first over, but in a rare act of mercy by an Australian captain, Ricky decided on giving the new ball at the other end to Peter Siddle. I can't imagine Australian captains of the past being so friendly to Johnson; I could see him being told to play good or fuck off. This current team was as pragmatic as any Australian team before them, and would be hoping Mitchell would find his magic, even if at first change.

Siddle's first over made a mockery of Johnson's previous attempts, as he beat Strauss, got Cook off the edge of his dangly bat, then almost cleaned up the England captain with a bouncer. Being that Siddle is not a swing bowler, he won't always get the new ball, but he does like it. It suits his personality. I'd even give him the first over. I like Hifly, but his first overs are a form of delicate probing; there is something a bit more abusive about Siddle.

Australia really needed early wickets, so the Cook one lifted them and with Bopara coming in they would have been very confident. But they just couldn't get through Bopara, and Strauss was impenetrable.

What you notice about Strauss is how good he is at simply getting off strike early in an over. He did this from the first ball for three or four overs at one stage, leaving Australia to work on Ravi for five balls. It isn't his fault Ravi can't do the same, but the good batsmen don't let you work them over very often. I had an old captain who always said: "You can't get bowled at the non-striker's end, so if everyone gets there twice an over we'll score heaps." It isn't an airtight theory, but the best partnerships seem to revolve around this rotation of strike.

The difference at the two ends went way further than that though. At one end was a settled Test player who'd been through some shit but had come back a better cricketer and was now a confident captain, while at the other was a nerdy kid checking movie tickets of much cooler kids during school holidays. Almost everything Ravi did, even his boundaries had an air of, "oh shit I think I did that right".

Eventually Ravi got out, playing yet another poor mental shot. Children shouldn't have to watch this. Surely the only decent thing left was to dig a hole for Ravi to jump into. At around the time Bopara was removed, I got an email saying I could go to Edgbaston for the weekend. Yay, ECB, but surely you could have left it a little later, it isn't even 5pm yet. I watched the rest of the day's play while scanning the internet for accommodation cheap enough that Crikey wouldn't tell me off.

Unfortunately for England more nerves came out to bat. It was if no-one had actually thought the English batting order through. Ian Bell seemed to sweating before he made it to the middle. Bell is the sort of person who looks timid in Test cricket even when he is doing okay, today he just looked timid for him. Australia didn't test him early on, though, and with his fearless leader at the other end, he overcame his anxiety and even hit the timidest man on the field, Hauritz, for six. A couple of overs later he was hit plumb in from a Mitchell Johnson ball with the perfect seam position which swung back in. A truly honest batsman would have walked. On the shin, straight in front, it had the works, but "Random" Rudi said no. Who can argue with him, he has officiated in 101 Tests.

Strauss clipped his way to a very nice half-century. His innings was a top knock that made Australia's total seem even more insignificant than it had before. England made it to stumps with the help of some bad light – all this Test needed, more time taken out of it. The forecast for the next day was not giving anyone hope, but I started to pack for my Brum adventure. Australia were left hoping that rain, or actual Test-standard performances from their bowlers, would save them. Rain seemed the more likely.

England's John Grisham

You can never underestimate the skill required in regularly getting out in the 30s and 40s. There is a poetic nature to it. And while some ill-informed cricket fans think this makes you a shit batsman, the opposite is true. Ian Bell is like the John Grisham of the 30 and 40.

Even if they have different settings, different baddies and different costumes, Bell's innings, like Grisham's novels, have mostly the same ingredients – a few cover drives, some tight footwork, hitting the ball to the fielder at will. And then out.

Sure, both Bell and Grisham are pushing the one-trick as far as they can, but it is their speciality and any wavering from the script would result in mass panic from their fans. To be fair, Bell has experimented more than Grisham. His 199 against South Africa was something of an existential manuscript. But it left his fans in a quandary; they had grown to love or despise him for his trademark and this brazen attempt to cross genres had left them feeling empty.

This time, having tried to get out for 20 odd – sometimes you have to rush one out for the masses – he finds a twist coming. Should he embrace it and write an epic, or go back to what he does best?

This certainly has all the hallmarks of an epic: the comeback, the luck, playing at his home ground, and the Ashes – but the pull of the familiar cannot be underestimated. The man is an artist, but sometimes you have to please your fans.

I know how Bell feels, even as I type this I realise that some of you are saying: "Jrod, this is fine, but where is the gratuitous sex and casual swearing." Sometimes you have to please yourself – not a masturbation joke – and Bell could do that, like Grisham did with *Playing for Pizza*.

If he does, I will miss his 30 and 40 odds.

Day 3

Six fucking am was the time I had to get up in order to catch the train to Edgbaston. I had to travel all morning to get there for the start of play. I hate mornings. Saturday mornings are for beanie baby collectors and people who smile when they are sad. I am a night person.

The ECB had told me I was in the overflow room and had a compromised view; I was looking forward to it.

The train was packed with cricket fans, and I tried to work, but mostly just stared at the rain map. It wasn't a pretty sight. It was one of those trips where it isn't raining on the trip up, but the closer you get, the more overcast it grows and then just as you get to within spitting distance of the station it starts to rain. Luckily, I was entertained by having an attractive girl sit next to me. She wasn't entertaining on her own, but a young guy sat opposite us and spent 30 minutes trying to get her attention, and then the next 60 minutes trying to justify getting her attention.

He failed; she told him she had a boyfriend. If a girl says that after you have been talking to her for an hour, it is never a good sign.

It was pissing down when I got there, and the assclown on the media gate sent me to the photographers' section, which at most other grounds wouldn't have been a problem, but at Edgbaston it is at the polar opposite end of the ground. Then I couldn't find anyone who could give me instructions on where to go, until a photographer told me to go straight across the playing area. I decided not to do that, I'd probably walk in the wrong place, get abused by the groundstaff, or worse, get bogged in the turf.

Eventually I found the overflow room, dropped my stuff on the floor and went to the bar, where my friends beered me up. There I stayed until the day was called off. I should have been pissed off, but I was drinking with friends, and I hadn't paid for a ticket to get in. Plus the bar closed just as it was my shout.

I loved Edgbaston.

I grew up in Melbourne, so I know what a party ground looks like. At a one-day match Mark Ealham tried to pull McGrath and top-edged it for six. The crowd – all 75,000 of them – didn't notice. They were busy watching people get thrown out and trying to start a Mexican wave. Edgbaston is something else though.

By the time I got there, there was little chance of play. At Melbourne everyone would filter out to pubs outside the ground. At Edgbaston, there were about 35 games of wet cricket being played. People found shelter and beer ensuring a good day.

The best game I saw was at the end of the day, a combination of weird French chefs, scary assed clowns and Dame Ednas. The pitch kept a bit low, and the standard of cricket suffered accordingly, but it was the closest thing to a cricket match people got to see. People definitely wanted to watch it. Hundreds. It was almost impossible to walk past and not watch. One of the clowns had a beautiful cover drive.

The drunks, even the non-playing ones, provided even more entertainment. One guy who appeared to have one of Stuart Broad's shirts on stumbled around for 30 minutes while a tent's worth of people watched and cheered on.

At one stage I drank a pint poured by Mike Gatting as part of some sort of promotion. That is something I will tell my grandkids about, and they won't care. There was also vomit, lots of vomit. After hearing from Gideon Haigh about a 10-minute vomit episode he saw (and couldn't walk away from) a guy throwing up, I had my own. In the toilets a middle-aged man stormed in wearing a nice suit and stripey shirt combination and then vomited up and down the cubicle door before getting in to finish off.

Even 90 minutes after the day was called off people were still hanging around, even though the bars were closed. Superheroes, cartoon characters, women with huge fake breasts and Adam's apples, and pirates. I doubt I have ever been anywhere with as many bad costumes as this.

As far as days go with no cricket, this was a great one: beer, comedy, and vomit. It was worth getting up at 6am for.

Eventually I made my way out to find a cab, and I got in one driven rather badly by a guy called Imran. He seemed like a nice enough chap, and even though I had no intention of talking, he drew out of me my career and nationality.

He was one of many conversations I had with people over the Ashes about Australia. And he didn't say anything I hadn't heard before; he just put it so adorably simply I couldn't forget him. "Australia isn't as good as they used to be," he said. Right there, it has it all.

Turned out Imran, a proud Pakistan-born Muslim, loved the Australian team much how I loved his Pakistan team, and it hurt him that they were bad. He spoke for a long time about why he loved the Australian team, but mostly he seemed pissed off that England would win.

"England does not play cricket in the right way", he said. "They think they do, but they do not. They treat it with too much respect. They should enjoy it more."

He had a point. Some of the English – players *and* fans – elevate the game to such a Virgin Mother level that it is almost too much to bear. But in this series England seemed like the team enjoying their cricket, not Australia.

Tomorrow I see Ian Bell (MBE).

Day 4

This worked out much better. It started with an all-you-can-eat cooked breakfast and there are few days that start that way that end bad. There was an actual chance of play. I got a taxi to take me to the ground, and then told a bunch of English fans they could share it. They ended up paying.

I set myself up in the overflow room. My name wasn't on the seating chart, and there were no ECB officials around, so I just sat in the best seat and hoped no-one told me to move. Then I waited for the soap opera on the field to play itself out. It seemed to revolve around Ricky Ponting not wanting to go out and play. The ground was definitely wet, but if England had been 7/82 I think Ponting might have just got on with it.

Instead we had the overacting that must be in the modern Test captain's handbook: "Look how slippery it is when I rub my runners/trainers over damp grass... There is a wet patch at point, if I throw the ball straight into the wettest spot on the ground it might not come back up... This is clearly dangerous, think of all the injuries you can get in the wet." All of this done as the captain walks around imitating a badly balanced person on ice-skates.

All teams do it. But when you are waiting for the cricket to start, it does piss you off, especially when the day before allowed no play at all. Eventually, with the wet spots looking just as bad, it was decided play could start at noon.

Before that though, there was bit more *Jerusalem*. Fuck I hate that song. It makes me think of the star- spangled banner or some guy wearing a flag as a cape and throwing up out the back of a Walkabout.

When they did start Australia bowled three straight maidens, two to Hilfy one to Siddle, and Strauss looked a bit dodgy, getting an edge to slip that fell short. Bell looked worse as Siddle gave him a going over. I think we know what two roles they would inhabit in the playground. Siddle was mixing unplayable balls with rancid rubbish.

One short ball hit Bell on the body and flew down the leg-side. With Prior or Haddin behind the stumps it would have been four, but Manou took it beautifully. It had been so long since I had seen a legitimate wicketkeeper for Australia I had forgotten what footwork, balance and soft hands look like.

Every decent Bell shot was met with almost a standing ovation from his home crowd. When he plays a good shot it makes you stand up anyway, but I doubt they would have stood up for Paul Collingwood, even if he could have matched Bell's style.

Then Hilfy got Strauss, not with a perfect inswinging delivery, but with a short shit ball that Strauss should have smashed, but instead tickled to Manou. Bringing out Paul Collingwood. At 3/141 Australia still had a chance of keeping the deficit at a workable level.

With Collingwood coming in Ponting brought on Johnson. Which pleased the crowd. He had become the comic relief of the Ashes. But this wasn't the lost Johnson of Cardiff, or the wonderfully wasteful Johnson of Lord's, this was the one closest to the demon that played in South Africa. First ball, he swung a ball viciously back into Bell and hit him plumb in front. Not out, a touch of bat involved. Then he tried to take Bell's rib cage out. Bell managed to get a cover drive away to the rope, but he looked far from comfortable.

The next over Bell received only short balls from Johnson, and it seemed like a waste. Bell was on 46 at this stage, but you could tell from the way Australia were going at him they didn't respect him at all. Johnson didn't get him out though, and instead Collingwood got out to Hilfenhaus off the second last ball before lunch playing a lazy drive. Playing a shot like that was his equivalent of KP sweeping a ball into his head from eight feet outside off.

The short session was all Australia's. There was no way to know if the ball would continue to swing after lunch. Ian Bell had reached the sort of score he often departs on, a new batsmen was due in, and Mitchell appeared to have found something, although it was too early to tell what.

Just before lunch was over I went to get some free orange juice from the press catering area. When I got there I realised it was just me and Peter Roebuck in the room. Here was my chance to speak to him, no-one else around, and just thank him for his work. But I just swallowed all my words.

He looked up at me and just gave me the polite professional smile you give someone you don't really know. I figured I had 40 seconds to say something, and I didn't. It was pathetic. Yet again I thought, well it is okay, I will probably get into the press box at Headingley or the Oval, and there I'll grow the required testicles to actually speak to someone who has had a huge impact on my life and doesn't know it. Yeah.

After lunch Johnson still looked good, but would throw in the odd one down the legside just for fun. Eventually he got another one to swing and it was almost identical to the one that "Random" Rudi had decided wasn't out two days ago. This time Rudi loved it. And Bell was out. Everyone in the crowd was shocked; Ian Bell had got a start and not gone on, amazing. It was 5/168 with Johnson flying, Hilfenhaus still spot on, and Australia with just a sniff of redemption about them.

Johnson kept getting massive swing, alternating those balls with short, courage-testing ones. This was the South African killing version for sure. In one over he swung a vicious ball back in at Prior, beat Freddie twice, and then walked down the pitch at Freddie after a very fast bouncer to see if Flintoff wanted a chat. I could be wrong, but I think when you have played two shit Test matches in a row, and for the first time in the series you are bowling well, it isn't the time to mock a national icon.

The crowd started booing Johnson, and they also started with what seemed to me a football chant: "One-nil to the Eng-er-land." I don't even know where Engerland is, but the people from there sound like annoying chavvie cunts.

Johnson's next over was going to be an important one. The crowd was interested now, and with Freddie at the crease, louder even than they would be if Ian Bell was as good as Ricky Ponting. The first ball from Johnson was pretty good, Freddie got it away for a single, and then Johnson abused Freddie and Freddie had some words back. The next ball from Johnson was a mile down leg-side and Manou can't quite glove it.

The crowd went mental. Freddie smirked. He must have known he had Johnson now. Guys like Johnson and Anderson aren't naturally aggressive, so when they do it, if it doesn't work straightaway they crawl into a ball and cry.

Hilfy was still bowling, unchanged all day, but there was just no story there – it was all about Mitchell. First ball of his next over was a cream puff-bouncer and Mitchell gave Freddie the stare. Freddie just laughed in his face. If someone laughs at your macho wanker posturing, you either have to punch them or get them out. Instead, Johnson was taken off.

A double change was made, and it was the double change of death. Siddle replaced Johnson, and bowled a sensational first over to Prior, but Ponting had also thrown the ball to Shane Watson. Only 64 overs into the innings. I am not sure what it says about a bowler when you hold him back that long, but very little of it seems to be: "We really believe you can bowl big fella."

His first over was dreadful. The first three balls were amazingly slow, probably slower than Hauritz, and looked so gentle you'd let them play with your kids. They were all left alone as Watson was bowling in a channel way beyond the corridor of uncertainty. After driving one hard back to Watson, Freddie just smashed the next one. He looked like he was facing one of the commentator's kids, and the only danger was he would hit one so hard that Matt Prior wouldn't be able to get out of the way.

Watson began his next over bowling straight, but Freddie just creamed it back through him for four. But his third – and last – over was the one: half volleys, full tosses, and some of the most amazingly docile bowling I have ever seen in a Test match. I could hardly believe he was bowling this bad.

Australia had Freddie where they wanted him. He hadn't been flowing, couldn't get the ball away, and was due a brain fade but by bringing on Watson, Ponting gave him a bowler to feast on and England – and the crowd – were now right back into the game. Add in some lucky runs off Siddle and Prior and Freddie were eroding the deficit quickly.

Siddle eventually got Prior out for 41, playing a pull shot to mid-on, but Freddie wasn't done. Hauritz replaced Watson but Flintoff cleared the rope from his second ball and a sweep later in the over took England past Australia's score. Siddle tried his best at the other end to kill Broad, hitting him twice in an over, but England knew they had Australia now.

The crowd was flying, Freddie was commanding, and Australia were trying to squeeze their way to the new ball for protection. Johnson was brought back to replace Siddle as England skipped past 300, having scored 100 in their last 15 overs, which had been exactly the moment when – you know who I'm going to say, don't you? – Tasmania's, Queensland's and now NSWales' own Shane Watson had come on for his short-lived spell.

Ponting then decided that he didn't want the new ball to fly off Flintoff's bat, so delayed taking it and kept faith with Hauritz. And bugger me if the little fella doesn't get one to rip out of Mitchell's footmarks into Freddie's gloves and then on to slip. Freddie definitely made a mess of leaving it, but it was Hauritz who had to hit the footmarks and get the spin. Freddie had made 74, and yet, only minutes earlier, before the ball was thrown to Watson, it had looked like he was struggling for form.

England found themselves at 7/316 at tea. They had scored 157 in that middle session and lost three wickets. It was quite some session. How anyone in the crowd had any voice left after that I am not sure.

The new ball was taken after tea, and Ponting, in hope perhaps, threw the ball to Johnson. Twenty-five runs came off his first three overs with it, but also the wicket of Graeme Swann. Johnson was getting more and more aggressive, he was sledging Swann at will, and even Broad was getting involved. In fairness, it wasn't that manly, more like three kids fighting

whether *Transformers 1* or *2* was better. Swann got very worked up, and
Johnson capitalised with his hard to pick slower ball than Swann dry
humped to cover. Twenty-four off 20 balls for Swann though, a lovely cameo.

Anderson came in and kept up his record of 52 innings without a duck.
Then Broad smashed Johnson down the ground, and Johnson gave him
some more verbals, then he flicked one off his pads and Johnson gave him
even more verbals. The pitch had turned into a discussion group, and part
of the exercise was for Broad and Johnson to get as close as they could and
look into each other's eyes. There must have been some teenage girls that
had fantasies about this scene. Thanks to Broad's helmet grill, they resisted
the urge to kiss.

Australia had found their mongrel, but with the scoreboard ticking over
so regularly it was a fairly useless tactic, failing to scare England in any
way. Broad was smashing the ball everywhere; he didn't even stop when
Anderson cut one behind from Hilfenhaus. While Broad was slogging,
England moved to more than 100 in front. It all happened so fast.
Eventually Broad's angry slogs got him out, Siddle picking up a cheap
wicket after Australia had been embarrassed.

Getting embarrassed was bad, but Australia's complete fucken ineptitude
had made this a game that they could lose. England had scored at such a
rate that they now had enough time to bowl Australia out and make the
runs. Australia had become more aggressive, but had failed to slow down
the scoring at any time: England knew they were just four good sessions
away from being two-nil up.

Anderson and Freddie started very well as Australia batted again, tight,
probing, and hard to get away. Katich and Watson were more than aware
that their job was to bat for as long as they could. The early part of the
session was slow, but nice-thick-dripping Test cricket. Then Australia had a
couple of very big overs, with Anderson and Onions getting punished.

But just when it looked like Australia might start slapping England
around, Katich nicked one behind off Onions and Edgbaston erupted. The

opening partnership had given Australia a quick 47 runs, but they needed a lot more.

Then in walked the most despised man in England. From the booing you would have thought he had killed Baby P, slapped Stephen Fry, and slept with Cheryl Cole and not called her back. It was loud, but largely in good fun, more WWE villain than Michael Moore at the Oscars. The place was rocking. Perhaps it was the sudden realisation that they could win, or maybe it was just their arch enemy walking out to bat.

It was beautifully good natured Mobile Vulgus mentality. I think I saw an old woman flip Ponting off. The crowd was loving every moment. So was I. Test cricket in England can get a little polite, but this was anything but – it was lusty and abusive, just how I like it. This crowd could have come to Melbourne and felt at home.

Ponting's innings lasted all of six balls. In that time he was very nearly out lbw but Rudi shook the magic eight ball that said not out and a couple more from Graeme Swann that spun savagely. Then he faced *the* ball.

It was the one that off-spinners wet dream about. A flighted ball that dips late, brings the batsman further forward than he wants to come, then rips back through bat and pad and slaps itself into middle stump. All that was missing was the drift away, but I doubted that Swann would be dwelling on that too much. The ball pitched in the same Mitchell Johnson footmarks that Hauritz had used to get Freddie out with.

Swann looked so happy he could have died after that.

It couldn't have happened to a better cricketer either. Swann was a late bloomer who had worked on his game very hard. At that moment it felt like England had won the Ashes. The boos of a few minutes earlier were now primal screams. The ground was actually howling. I was in shock. Not so much at Ponting getting out, but at the ball that got him. Swann had been a non-event up to now, other than a decent second innings haul at Lord's, and even then he didn't bowl great the whole innings.

Now he had stepped up with probably the best spin delivery that had been bowled by an Englishman in 20 years. Ripping through an in-form Ponting with massive rotation and a puff of dust. The wicket said everything you needed to know about this Ashes, Champion batsman beaten by a journeyman offspinner who was averaging over 50 with the ball in the series.

The wicket was the moment I thought Australia couldn't win the Ashes. It wasn't based on facts or logic – it just felt too tough. On pure talent Australia were at least as good as England, probably slightly better, but it wasn't their series. The fourth day at Lord's told you that. Katich, Hughes or Hussey could have been the difference in the chase. If all three had been given not out, in this hypothetical existential innings that doesn't exist, they might have been able to produce the 120 runs Australia needed to chase down the total.

In Cardiff Australia had had 69 balls to get one wicket. All they needed was one ball from Siddle to keep low, one off break from Hauritz to get a nick, even one piece of proper tailend batting could have done the job. But nothing. Sometimes shit just happens. Australia had created a lot of it themselves, but Swann had proved that bowling pretty ordinarily for two Tests doesn't stop you from spinning the ball through the gate of one of the world's best batsman.

If Strauss had been batting in a similar situation, I had the feeling the ball would have bounced over the stumps.

The cricket didn't magically finish with that ball, though. Mike Hussey had come in, and first ball he pushed hard at one from Graham Onions, the ball took the inside and edge and flew up in the air. If there had been a short leg he could have turned around and moonwalked over and still caught it. There wasn't. Instead Onions threw himself at the ball but just couldn't get there in time. Next ball Hussey timed a straight drive down the ground and at least 392 people in the ground said: "Cricket's a cruel game, isn't it."

Australia was now reliant on its whipping boy and the man with the rapidly descending average. I was far from confident. Watson still looked good, much the same as he had in the first innings, and Hussey was all nerves. But sometimes he looks nervous when he is compiling a hundred.

Then the game changed. Graeme Swann went from hero to fuck up. In one over to Hussey he bowled a long hop that went for four, the ball landed in a puddle, and then he bowled some howlers with the wet ball and Australia suddenly looked to be going okay. It was enough to get them to stumps but not before, in the last over, England decided that a whole six balls of sledging Watson might work.

However, being that it seemed to be Anderson and Prior doing the sledging it seemed to do nothing at all. Sky loved the aggression and showed a super slow mo of Watson's witty retort, "FUUUUUUUUUUUUUUUUUUUUUUU UUUUUUUCK OOOOOOOOOOOOOOOOOOOOOOOOOOOFFFFFFFF".

Watson and Anderson kept up their talk all the way off the field. When men had moustaches, flabby stomachs and violence in their eyes this kind of talk had an edge to it. When it is two pretty metrosexual lads it doesn't quite fool anyone. As a Cricket Australia official said out loud, the only time Watson gets really scary is when there is someone between him and a mirror.

The game had just enough left in it to get people to the ground the next day. Watson was no certainty to last very long nor Hussey. North had played three pretty ordinary innings in a row. Manou was on debut. It seemed that Michael Clarke was going to have to prove himself, again, as a leader of this side, because there seemed to be so little else left.

Originally I was only supposed to stay for the weekend, but the ECB said that I could remain for the Monday as well, kind-hearted organisation they are. So I booked a new hotel, one cheaper and closer to the ground, and then, after writing countless brilliantly prosed pieces about Australia barking but not biting, I went to take a look around Brum. I call it Brum not just because that is what people call it, but because when I try and say Birmingham I say it the way one would say Birmingham, Alabama, not Birmingham, Warwickshire.

My new hotel was the sort of place cockroaches would be embarrassed to be seen in. All the doors near my room had appeared to be kicked in. Mine hadn't but maybe tonight would be the night. The bed was on wheels. I tried to wash and clean my T-shirt and underwear, but there was nowhere to dry it, so the final day would be a wet undie and second-wear T-shirt kind of day.

Before I'd gone to Brum I had heard nothing but bad things. Everyone had told me how crap it was. Some people had talked about all the chain stores. Others referred to it as lifeless and ugly.

I was expecting some grey lifeless city with a McDonalds on top of their McDonalds. What I saw was a fairly nice place. Yes, it was more industrial-looking than Bath but not so ugly on the eyes. Sometimes I think English people think anything that isn't a quaint village or old-looking is ugly.

Brum has plenty of parks. Who talks about the parks? Trees, too. Sure it is grey and dingy in parts, but in others it is quite nice. I felt very comfortable there, and I could understand the accents. Sorry that it doesn't have cobbled roads or fucked-up streets that make little sense, but it is a more modern city and doesn't need to be pretty to feel good about itself.

Generally most of the jokes about Brum are made by locals trying to beat the interlopers to the joke, but you can feel their pain when they say them. People do have a point about the chains. Upon leaving my hotel I walked for 15 minutes without seeing anything but chain eateries. It got so desperate that I almost ate at TGI Fridays; I only left when I saw they had product-placement steak names, like the Jack Daniel's New York Strip. I prefer my steak independent. I ended up at the Beefeater, which probably isn't that much better, but at least it didn't have a fucken Herbie the Love Bug car out the front. They also served me whiskey when I ordered bourbon, so I moved to beers from then on.

A monster

Gerhard Hanz was a German scientist who was smuggled into America after the Second World War under operation paperclip. He worked in Area 51, and all those other dodgy places that the X files talked about, and one day he was holidaying in the Caribbean, and was turned on by the game of cricket.

Its brutality crossed with tactical thinking excited him, so he decided to use his spare time to design the perfect cricketer. He would be blonde, broad shouldered, never a hair out of place, and nice on the eye.

He would bowl fast.

He would hit the ball hard.

His confidence would be that of a Gestapo officer.

He would expect to be the best.

Unfortunately for Hanz, he could not be German, but luckily for Hanz he knew the perfect cricket country: Australia. He briefly considered South Africa, but they already seemed to have players like this and Hanz's creation would not stand out.

This perfect cricket specimen was made from advanced revolutionary frankensteinian techniques: he was a cricketing Gollum. Unfortunately Hanz did not get time to test his creation – the American government were pressuring him to create a new kind of super soldier – so he had to send his cricketer to Australia.

The Australians were happy to receive this experiment, and promised Hanz they would fit him in every chance they got. This was a lovely gesture, but their specimen of cricket perfection had a few flaws.

During the heat of competition he could break down.

Bowling would hurt his back, batting would do his hamstrings, fielding would tear his groin and carrying the drinks would affect his general wellness.

With Hanz dead (eaten by one of his super soldiers), Australia sent their continually unstable creation to North Korea. Fascist dictators always have the best mad scientists.

In North Korea the final touches were put into the creation – leopard hamstrings, porn star's groin and a titanium spine.

Now Australia have this new version of Shane Watson, and we will have to see if the North Koreans know more than Germans about creating super cricketers.

Touts

When I first came to the UK I was shocked to see touts operating in the open outside cricket grounds. At the Oval they have guys outside the Oval tube station and then all the way up both sides of the ground until you get to within about 10 metres of the ticket office. Since the Oval is just a normal footpath area, it is hard enough to get by during game days, but add a few toothless, hairless scarred touts and getting to the ground takes forever.

I couldn't believe how many there were. I counted 20 on my first trip there. Some standing only a couple of metres from the cops, and all saying different versions of the word "ticket" out the side of their mouths. It is a skill, to say it at such a pitch that you are sort of aware they said it, but not 100%. I assume there is some sort of tout school where they are taught this.

They are all also clones of each other. They all seem to be missing a tooth, have a scar on their forehead, be bald or balding and they all have a busy manly walk about them. They are mostly white, although way more culturally diverse than the Npower girls (although no women). What amazed me is that it didn't seem to matter what race the person was, before they even said "ticket" you knew who they were. It is also safe to say that they all looked like Freddie Flintoff fans rather than Andrew Strauss fans. Few wing commander types look like touts.

What shocked me the most, though, was that you could see them at all. I couldn't tell you what a tout looks like in Melbourne. I spend about 45 days a year at the MCG, but since the ground almost never completely sells out, and scalping is illegal in Australia, actually seeing touts is almost impossible.

The AFL grand final is probably the hardest sports event in Australia to get tickets for, and I saw one person selling them. He was hanging around near a tree in the car park, still doing the muttering, but he looked normal. He had hair, teeth, and no scar. He wouldn't fit in with the UK touts. If he did come over it would be much better for him, as touting sports tickets, contrary to popular opinion, is legal here as long as you aren't selling football or Olympic tickets. Although most local authorities require you to have a street trading license in order to buy and sell on the street.

Even the football tickets law isn't to stop touting, but to keep filthy scummy banned football hooligans out of the grounds. In a country where the average sporting stadium is small compared to the demand for tickets, it seems a weird rule. But the police still play a part. They might not arrest the touts, but when you want to talk money with a tout they take you off to a pre-specified area, and just for a second you expect someone to come from behind you and smack you on the head. Luckily I was at Edgbaston, and there weren't that many dodgy areas near the ground, or as many cops around to scare the touts, so I was taken behind a bus shelter.

He offered me a ticket at £110. I asked what the actual ticket price was, and he paused, looked me up and down, and then there was a quick silence. Fearing I had said the wrong thing I said: "No I'm a writer, just wanted to know how it all works." He then looked around, not sure what for; we were just two law-abiding people on our way to the cricket having a chat behind a bus shelter.

He was having none of it though. He didn't want to chat to me. There were tickets to be sold at almost double their face value. I was a distraction. So I watched him for the next 20 minutes. He covered about 400 yards, from the gates at Edgbaston to a major road. He went up and back, loitered near cabs, walked close to every person walking towards the ground, turned his back on cops walking past and nodded or exchanged words with other touts. They seemed to have a system of rotation going on, not that I could work it out.

After 20 minutes he finally got a bite. I was glad, I thought if I stared at him any longer he would think I was perving on him – and his general demeanour didn't give me the feeling he was a progressive thinker on gay rights. He took three guys behind a tree, and while I couldn't see exactly what was happening, it seemed like they were happy with the prices and purchased them all. Even if that was his only sale for the morning, it wasn't a bad 20 minutes. Then it got me thinking about what he makes in a day.

If he sells nine tickets a day at twice the ticketed price, assuming he had to pay £30 over face value for the ticket in the first place, he sells at a £30 profit. That is £270 for three hours' work. That is more than I make working at the cricket all day. And what risk does he have? He can't go to jail. It is an Ashes match, so he knows he is going to sell all the tickets, and if it gets tight towards the end of the day, he can sell them at cost.

They say that touting in the UK is part of organised crime, so you probably have to pass some initiation ceremony to get in. I assume that is when they give you the scar.

Day 5

Starting the day with another great serving of all-you-can-eat cooked breakfast left me full of boundless positivity. Of course Australia could bat the day out, of course they could win the Ashes, of course I could eat more bacon. The world was wonderful.

On the way into the ground I watched England in the nets. They were having a group hug talk. It was all very New Age. England looked nervous. Unlike the last day at Lord's where a result was inevitable, on this day they had to make the pace, had to take the wickets; otherwise a golden opportunity would pass them. Also unlike Lord's they weren't going to be able to rely on Freddie, who had looked proper gimpy the day before. I could be wrong, but at one stage I thought his leg came off and had to be re-attached.

Before play started I had a chat to Gideon Haigh who suggested that England could lose the Ashes based on the fact that they hadn't had a short leg to Michael Hussey. Gideon was quick to point out that almost no sides use short legs straight up anymore. It is just not the current trend, had Strauss bucked the trend, the Ashes might be all but his by now.

Onions and Flintoff opened the bowling. Seems weird that twice in this match Anderson was not used first thing in the morning. Perhaps, like other artistic types, he doesn't like mornings. I now saw why Onions would be used. Because he bowls dead straight, he will make the batsmen play or in the case of Michael Hussey, not play. With the second morning collapse Australia put in the English must have been confident, especially as it was the same two who started it – Hussey and Watson – facing.

Instead the first over had no real bite to it, and neither did Freddie's. It was a gentle stretch of a morning. Watson and Hussey played and missed occasionally, Freddie put in some half glares, and the crowd seemed a little underwhelmed. Strauss seemed to be searching for something as well, and after a four-over spell Onions was replaced by Swann.

This could be the deciding moment of the day. Swann's ball to Ponting would have kept him bouncing off the walls all night, but if he couldn't break through this morning, Australia would be pretty confident of seeing the day out. He started with a maiden, but a tame one. Swann is known for starting a spell with a wicket or two, but this one was barely a yawn. His second over was garbage and Hussey helped himself and gave Australia the lead.

At the other end was Freddie, who had hardly looked more out of shape than he did now. This was one of his I-will-bowl-until-I-can't-walk spells. Every over had an unplayable ball, but it seemed to hurt him to turn around and walk to his mark. At one stage he hit Watson hard on the arm, but even as Watson dealt with the impact of a 90mph delivery, Freddie looked in more pain.

This spell had all the makings of his one at Lord's, but he didn't look like taking a wicket. Through his pain, though, he still had time to abuse Watson, and when he was storming (limping or crawling) in Watson backed away causing Freddie to grimace like they were moving a cabinet together and Watson dropped it on his foot. It might be the single coolest thing I have ever seen Watson do. It also showed the Freddie wasn't on top form, as surely no one would be stupid enough to make the big bearded bear annoyed when he is in top form? That was the last over of his spell, so maybe it was Watson's way of making him feel every inch of the over. Watson was now on 50 and looking sure.

After drinks, Anderson was brought on and the first ball Watson faced after the break he nicked behind. It wasn't the worst shot, but it just felt like the timing of it was poor. Statistically and technically Watson had proved the faith the selectors had had in him, and the massive faith he had in himself, was justified, but twice he had fallen the ball after a break, and that is not good.

At the other end Swann was an interesting case study. He would bowl one or two overs that were hardly scored off, and then would spice it up with an over of full tosses or short shit. I have never seen an off-spinner struggle with length the way Swann does. While he should have been the major threat on a pitch with a bit of rough and buoyed with confidence over the Ponting ball, he was a liability and Strauss had to take him off.

The bowler brought on for him was Stuart Broad, for his first over of the innings. The 51st of the innings. Wow. How do you go from opening the bowling at Cardiff to not coming on before the 50th over in the third Test of the series? That is some demotion. His first ball was a half volley that was hit to the rope, which didn't exactly inspire confidence. But in his next over he got Hussey out; Strauss was probably hoping no-one had noticed it was only Broad's second over.

Australia got to lunch without a further wicket, but England had to be buzzing, they were teetering on the edge of 2-0, one more wicket and Manou was in on his debut. If I'd been Andy Flower that's what I would have been saying to every player as they ate their lunch.

Both teams had bigger problems though as a hoaxer was threatening to blow up the Members' Pavilion during the break. Strangely, the players were not evacuated, but the members were. In the press box it was pure panic. Andrew Miller was running around naked. Lawrence Booth started speaking in tongues. Simon Hughes was writing out his will. And George Dobell, the guy who broke the story, was looking for weapons.

Okay, that didn't happen. I don't think most people even knew about it – it certainly wasn't mentioned as I helped myself to a second portion of prawns. The scare was at the opposite end of the ground, so I was safe even if Ricky Ponting wasn't. I should have noticed something as there were suddenly cops and security everywhere outside the press box. But there also were prawns.

Surely if it had been a really dangerous situation trained commandos would have come in and whisked away Derek Pringle and Scyld Berry.

In the third over after lunch Clarke hit two drives for four. England reached over and pressed the snooze button. Even the crowd couldn't be bothered. Then the Barmy Army started mumbling in unison and Swann and Freddie were brought back on.

England's team doctor must be Victor Frankenstein because I am sure Freddie died out on the field at one stage. The last ball of his second over it seemed that even the work Frankenstein had done failed him. The big fella went down. It appeared his ankle, the original sin, and not his gimpy knee, was the problem. Freddie bowled two more overs, and occasionally, even from 100 metres away, you could see his leg buckling.

It was classic Fred. "I don't care, me. I'm bowling and that's it."

Eventually Strauss replaced him with Ravi Bopara. Clarke and North had brought up their 50 partnership, and Strauss had run out of ideas as the new ball approached. The field was bog standard for a medium pacer and when Strauss had finished with it he put himself at short midwicket and watched Ravi start with a long hop. Next ball he bowled another one and Strauss must have been just about to look to the skies in some archaic religious way when Clarke hit the ball straight to him. Strauss dropped it.

It took four seconds for someone to say: "Has Strauss just dropped the Ashes?" Based on research, one in 12 people who saw the event said the same thing at least once.

Swann and Prior then appealed a catch that missed the bat but hit the toe. "Random" Rudi walked forward and Australians everywhere began to sweat uncontrollably. He called upstairs, got the word and it was not out. Rudi knows not of the tension he brings to a cricket match.

Anderson came back on the over before the new ball was due and had a strop of his own making. He bowled an attempted yorker to North that was dug out back to him. Seeing North was momentarily out of his crease he kicked the ball back at the stumps and it hit North and went into no-man's land. Clarke saw where the ball was, although may not have seen how it got there, and ran. Anderson started to have a go, but there is a lesson for young bowlers out there: don't just boot the fucken ball down the pitch like an idiot.

Onions took the new ball and North and Clarke brought up their fifties within a couple of overs of each other. At this stage Australia looked like they were coasting to a draw. England didn't even look that fired up with the new ball. Having twice taken a bunch of wickets in a single session in this series, you'd think there would be enough to keep them interested, but they aren't.

Strauss all but conceded when he brought on Swann for only the ninth over with the new ball. Stuart Broad is brought on for the one over before tea, but that is the over you give to the shit bowler you don't really like. I have bowled that many a time. Australia certainly like to bat for a draw in style – they scored 121 in the session. Had they tried to bat for a draw like a normal team they would probably be seven down by now.

This is the time in the press box that you stop watching the game and start inventing conspiracy theories. In Lord's I came up with the rumour that Ponting was going to retire, now I had a new one.

During Freddie's most recent spell, not long after he fell over and got up like a 93-year-old, he called Jimmy Anderson over from cover. They chatted for about 20 seconds and then Anderson pointed to Strauss for Collingwood to come out of second slip.

I didn't think much of it at the time, other than thinking Anderson was now well and truly a senior member of the side. Then later on when Freddie was taken off, Collingwood stood at second slip to the other seamers instead of Freddie.

If you had a gimpy physical basket case of an all-rounder who always fields at second slip and had just fallen over almost tearing his ankle from his leg, why would you not have him at second slip?

Had Strauss not been at first slip, this would have meant nothing, but he was. These were two pretty flimsy pieces of evidence, but I have a third far flimsier one. In the press box there have been a few mumbled whispers that Flintoff had become a little larger than life in the changing room – even larger than usual.

The guys who huddle behind closed doors had always said that Freddie was hard to handle in the changing room, but now he was the English Jesus and that his time was almost up he was even worse. Not sure how true this was, but all three pieces of flimsy evidence almost add up to one solid piece – if you squint your eyes and stand on one leg.

At that moment Freddie was walking towards me like a man looking for a zimmer frame, yet he was fielding at long-on. If your Grandpa was out on the field, where would you put him: slip or long-on?

The only thing to counter this was that Freddie had dropped two catches at slip in the last two Tests. But surely his overall record as a slipper was more than enough to balance that out?

While writing about my air-tight conspiracy, North decided to get to his hundred in a hurry. It was starting to get dark, half the crowd had fallen asleep, if they had ever even been awake. North started slogging. Strauss brought on Ravi, probably to hasten the centuries. Sure enough, Ravi's first over went for 17 and both North and Clarke skipped together into their 90s.

North's hundred wasn't to be, instead he slashed at a Broad ball outside off and sent it rocketing to Anderson, at gully, who dived and took it one-handed. It was a top catch, but all I could think was that Freddie could field at gully. It was unfortunate for North because he had taken the game away from England and deserved a hundred, but perhaps his lack of experience had cost him his wicket.

For some reason the cricket continued. There was a voice in my head that was saying: "Get a gun, kill it." I assumed the voice meant the game, and not the Cricket Australia official in full uniform behind me.

Broad had deserved his wicket. While the rest of the English bowlers had given up long ago, he was still coming in and bowling well. Although if you'd asked me about it in the bar later I'd have said it was dark. He should have had Clarke bowled, but the bails didn't come off and he hit Manou on the hand which seemed to worry him a fair bit.

Broad was taken off – I assumed because he was making it too hard for Clarke to make his hundred – and Collingwood was brought on to a standing ovation. It was the biggest ironic cheer ever. Then Ravi Bopara got Clarke to edge to slip; I think that is what happened, it was pretty dark by this stage. But it was a no-ball, or Rudi decided he didn't hit it.

Then they took drinks, which seemed like a completely unnecessary punishment. Then finally Clarke starts scoring, and he brings up his hundred. It was well deserved but a little too late for anyone to care. Test over. Thank fuck.

I went around for my first ever post-match press conference, at the last minute realising I hadn't put my recording device out. When I did put it on the table Ricky looked up at me and wondered who the fuck I was. Malcolm Conn asked the first question because the Cricket Australia official pretty much asked him to.

I didn't ask any questions, only because I couldn't work out what I should ask. Ponting seemed amazingly relaxed and confident. He praised the batting, put out a thinly veiled jab in the direction of Nathan Hauritz and Shane Watson's bowling and then passed over to the hero. Clarke was amazingly tired, and said very little, but talked a lot. Even when Clarke isn't tired he says amazingly little and talks a lot. I can only imagine that all those years of media training from Cricket Australia have turned his brain to porridge.

I went home to the love of a good woman and to change my underwear. It wasn't still damp, although it had been quite damp until lunch. But mentally I felt it was damp. Strauss would know what I meant.

The press box dynamics

I'd been in about ten press boxes across England by now, and they are very odd places. Every English one seems to contain about 15 to 20 old men. Proper old guys between 60 and 90. Most of which come in with apples (not the computer, actual apples) and newspapers. Real life newspapers, like from the 30s or something.

I don't know who these guys write for, or even if they do, but they seem to have legacy positions in the press box. They are delightfully dressed like something out of a Noel Coward play, and a few of them have such red faces you want to pinch their cheeks.

They are people who have often made their whole career out of cricket writing. Something it is very possible to do in England. Yesterday I had been told about Freddie Trueman's hatred for batsmen coming out dressed as knights (with padding on). And there was not a press box in which I did not have a similar history lesson.

The very first time I was allowed into a press box was for a Pro40 game between Surrey and Kent, and next to me was one of these chaps. He was very nice, seemed interested in what I was writing, and then fell asleep after the dinner break. *He fell asleep.* Now the Oval press box has a ridiculous dark cover on it that makes it almost impossible to watch the game at night (and not much easier during the day), but it isn't so dark you need to nap.

A couple of weeks later I was in the press box at the Oval again for a county match, and while everyone was busy typing their reports, one guy got out a phone (an actual phone, not a mobile, but an actual phone), plugged it into a socket and rang his desk to dictate his report: "Surrey's decision to use Shoaib Akhtar. *Comma*. The petulant overrated Pakistani quick. *Comma*. Has come unstuck due to his abysmal physical fitness. *Period*." This was the lunch report, so he was dictating it so that someone could put it up on the web. And he had a laptop, I know, because earlier in the day he had basically said: "Hey there boy, you're young, come here and fix my computer."

At the county games many of the older reporters will only turn up at lunch, eat, chat, and leave. Although to be fair I have noticed young reporters do that as well. At another county game I sat behind a veteran county reporter in his late 50s who spent one whole day on dating websites and chatting with random women. The next day he spent most of it in a local pub, and when he came back he said, "I turned my head and missed that catch, who took it, was it good?" Turned my head, my ass.

For the bigger games the press box turns into a schoolyard. The cool kids – the ex-players and some well know celebrity writers – sit in a cluster and generally make the most noise; the nerds – the intellectual analysis type writers – don't always sit together but often rush over to each other; the teachers – the older writers – often seemed startled when you ask them something and then often ask you long and entirely unanswerable questions, before moving on to ask someone else the same question.

The rest of us try to watch the cricket and form our own little cliques. You can sit next to someone for a few days without knowing their name or who they write for, but you will have bonded over a mutual, if unnatural, hatred of Jimmy Anderson.

When the cool kids come over, you are expected to answer their questions on something they have missed or are unsure about. Once they have worked it out, you are to agree with their opinions. It is not cool to doubt what they are saying (trust me). The nerds usually won't say much, but when they ask you something you know you have to get it right, as if you don't they will never ask you again. You can tell the teachers pretty much anything.

Oh and it's always best to leave one over before lunch – to ensure you don't have to queue for the food. I learnt that from watching Derek Pringle.

One of the things I did notice in the press box was the difference between the ages of the press pool. The Australian journalists are really young.

Not everyone of them, of course: Malcolm Conn is no spring chicken, Gideon Haigh is young at heart but probably not in years, and Peter Roebuck is a little older. But the majority of the others are quite young: Peter English, Alex Brown, and Chloe Saltau spring to mind. England does have some younger cricket writers, but if we did a median age test the Australian one would be young enough to be the English one's child.

I suppose it has a lot to do with the different structures of the countries' journalism. In the UK there is a thriving cricket media. Few get rich from it, but few starve as well. Almost every UK writer seems to have written a bunch of cricket books, and it is not unheard of for them to have worked on almost every major newspaper in the country.

In Australia we don't have as much of a cricket media. Roebuck, Conn, Robert Craddock and Ken Piesse stick out, but none of these are very old chaps who have been writing on cricket for 50 years. Gideon Haigh does not even consider himself a cricket journalist (he probably thinks he is a superhero; he probably is a superhero).

In Australia I had never even got close to being a cricket writer. Newspapers seemed the most logical places to start, and they generally didn't just let you walk in and be a feature cricket writer. The Melbourne papers would never even email me back when I sent in a story. I realised quickly that if I wanted a career as a specialist cricket writer I would have to come to the UK.

Over here it is something a lot of people do. Some writers cover a bit of football or rugby in the off-season, but generally you are a cricket writer, and if you want, and you get some luck – generally via selling books or becoming a newspaper or magazine guy – you can have a long career in it.

One thing I have noticed in England is the lack of women covering the game. Maybe it's because I come from a city that employs a female cricket writer, Chloe Saltau, in its second biggest paper, but where are the ladies? Alison Mitchell works for BBC mostly as an interviewer and tweeter, but Sky and the newspapers don't seem to have any women covering the cricket. The first time I was in a press box with a woman who was actually writing about the cricket was at Lord's with Chloe. Before that, the only women I had seen in the press box were officials and a work experience girl.

Perhaps this is why after a Andrew Strauss press conference the ECB official looked Chloe Saltau in the eyes and said: "That's all guys."

The general mood towards bloggers is mixed. Some hate my kind; some just despise us. If something happened that was trivial more than once someone said: "Why don't you blog about it?" And they said "blog" with an inflection that made it sound a hundred times shitter than the word "write". I did notice a few people taking a sly look at my site though, trying to cover the screen so no one could see the filth. Others seem to be interested in someone with a different style of writing. Even respecting it.

The Shane Warne letter

Dear Sirs / Madams / Troglodytes / Administracrats

I am writing here not for myself, but for a man who has given so much to international cricket, Shane Warne. For years the big-hearted Shane gave so much to this sport and asked for so little in return. Now I think it is time to give him something.

Wickets. Five wickets.

You might ask why Shane deserves these wickets. Perhaps you don't read the news, or don't understand cricket at all. Ravi Bopara came into these Ashes as a beaten man. Shane Warne had made sure of this. His tormenting of

Ravi through the media was the reason that the previously confident Ravi, three hundreds in three Tests against the might of the West Indies, completely lost the mental ability to succeed as a batsman.

I understand that such a statistical feat has never happened before, and that some of the current Australian bowlers may feel aggrieved that they lose wickets they feel they have rightfully earned. The truth is that these are Warne's wickets as much as any he got before he retired. I am sure Bopara would say so under oath.

Bopara's fate was sewn up well before he ever got on the pitch for these Ashes. With that in mind how can any right-thinking ICC official truly give these wickets to the underperforming Australian bowling attack.

The ICC is obviously a mighty organisation, respected by one and all, and being that you are so powerful and omniscient in the cricket world, surely you can see that a grave injustice has occurred here.

Give Warne the wickets, but just the first five, because if England continue to play Bopara after this Test surely the wickets should go down in Geoff Miller's career column.

Faithfully yours,

Jrod

The white Australia team

One of the questions I was asked the most about the Australian team during the series was their whiteness. Not just Mitchell Johnson's teeth, but the whole team, and why there weren't any Asian or Aboriginal players who had ever played for Australia. Jason Gillespie was here during the

Ashes. I can only hope that someone asked him why an Aboriginal player had never played for Australia. Being that he is Aboriginal.

Ryan Campbell has also played for Australia, but I think I am the only person to remember that, so Jason Gillespie is the easier answer to the question of whether an Aboriginal had ever played for the national team. There has even been an Asian: the great Dav Whatmore was born in Sri Lanka; and Stuart Clark's mother is Indian. Although, in Australia, a Sri Lankan would not be deemed Asian. Don't ask why, just accept it.

That usually shuts them up for a minute, but then they say: "But you never have players who aren't really white-looking play for Australia, Andrew Symonds aside." That is pretty true, but we also don't have players who are born in other countries play for Australia very often, Dav, Symonds and Kepler Wessels aside. We aren't the only country like that. South Africa and India, the other two Test teams that are hardest to get into, also don't have many players born outside their borders.

The fact there generally aren't Aboriginals is easy enough to explain. Cricket has never been that huge a game amongst them, whereas Aussie rules football is. Less than 2% of the Australian population is Aboriginal, and yet in the AFL – the Aussie rules league – they make up more than 10% of the players. I'd also say that cricket has never made a big enough push into their communities, unlike Aussie rules. But it is easier for football, with so many Aboriginal stars, to return and market the game.

The Asian situation is a little different. When I played cricket most of the better players I played with didn't have parents who were born in Australia, or themselves weren't born there either. The best ones were generally Asian kids. They were also the least likely to train because of homework, most likely not to be able to play every game due to family commitments, quite often were overseas during key parts of the seasons, and generally the players whose parents put most pressure on them to perform academically.

In Australia missing training or a game is like grabbing your team-mates' testicles and twisting. To get anywhere in Australian cricket you need to train twice a week, play for a district/grade side, never miss a game, commit to cricket above almost all else, and then perform consistently on match days. Then you might get a run around with a state side. In England you can make a few runs for school, end up at a league club, not train, put in some good performances and get offered a chance to train with a county side. Being a professional cricketer in England is a viable career option, in Australia it isn't.

Lisa Sthalekar, former Australia women's captain, who was born in India, recently told the *Sydney Morning Herald:* "Lots of Indians, Sri Lankans and Pakistanis play in the early stages of cricket but many of them drop out when it gets serious to focus more on their work." She added: "It's also the case, certainly in women's cricket, that a lot of Indians don't want to get any darker, and so they don't want to spend any more time in the sun than they have to." As yet no-one has blamed Dean Jones' commentary when Muslims are on the field.

Most of the kids I knew just quit when it got tough with their studies. The really dedicated ones did both, but it was very rare. There is only one Asian Shield cricketer at the moment, a Pakistan-born New South Wales player by the name of Usman Khawaja. A very talented, yet very dour, player who hasn't quite managed to make a name for himself, but has made runs against the Victorians. In the 90s there was an Asian player who was a legend for New South Wales. Richard Chee Quee, who was of Chinese heritage, lit up the domestic one-day competitions with ADHD-style batting before it was popular. He only played 20-odd games for New South Wales and never had a real chance of earning national honours.

It is not the most comprehensive racial record, but Australia isn't some Anglo-Saxon wonderland. In this team is Simon Katich with his Croatian roots, while Ben Hilfenhaus and Nathan Hauritz also aren't Anglo Saxon. Jason Krejza's father was Czechoslovakian and his mother Polish. Michael Kasprowicz, Michael Di Venuto and Len Pascoe were all not Anglo-Saxon. Future Australian player Moises Henriques – trust me – was born in Portugal, and the player who should have opened the bowling for Australia in the World Twenty20 was Dirk Nannes, who instead he did it for the Netherlands, care of his Dutch parents.

England do have a great ethnic mix: Pakistanis, Indians, West Indians, Australians, New Zealanders, South Africans and Zimbabweans. But these are all former colonies of England, and all are active cricket nations. Players like Nannes, Krejza, Henriques and the insanely handsome Theo Doropoulos – he is also a model – are playing cricket in Australia at a high level even though their families often have no background in or knowledge about cricket.

Third Test at Edgbaston
Match Drawn

Australia first innings	Runs	Balls	Mins	4s	6s	
SR Watson	lbw b Onions	62	106	129	10	-
SM Katich	lbw b Swann	46	48	85	9	-
*RT Ponting	c Prior b Onions	38	47	85	5	-
MEK Hussey	b Onions	0	1	1	-	-
MJ Clarke	lbw b Anderson	29	55	94	4	-
MJ North	c Prior b Anderson	12	49	62	1	-
+GA Manou	b Anderson	8	11	19	2	-
MG Johnson	lbw b Anderson	0	1	1	-	-
NM Hauritz	not out	20	50	76	1	-
PM Siddle	c Prior b Anderson	13	26	30	2	-
BW Hilfenhaus	c Swann b Onions	20	31	36	4	-
Extras (5 b, 7 lb, 1 nb, 2 w)		15				
Total (all out, 319 minutes, 70.4 overs)		**263**				

Fall of wickets: 1-85 (Katich, 18.6 ov), 2-126 (Watson, 30.1 ov), 3-126 (Hussey, 30.2 ov), 4-163 (Ponting, 38.3 ov), 5-193 (Clarke, 49.4 ov), 6-202 (North, 51.4 ov), 7-202 (Johnson, 51.5 ov), 8-203 (Manou, 53.5 ov), 9-229 (Siddle, 61.5 ov), 10-263 (Hilfenhaus, 70.4 ov)

England bowling	Overs	Mdns	Runs	Wkts	Wides	No-Balls
Anderson	24	7	80	5	-	-
Flintoff	15	2	58	0	1	1
Onions	16.4	2	58	4	1	-
Broad	13	2	51	0	-	-
Swann	2	0	4	1	-	-

England first innings	Runs	Balls	Mins	4s	6s	
*AJ Strauss	c Manou b Hilfenhaus	69	134	175	11	-
AN Cook	c Manou b Siddle	0	4	6	-	-
RS Bopara	b Hilfenhaus	23	54	66	4	-
IR Bell	lbw b Johnson	53	114	150	7	1
PD Collingwood	c Ponting b Hilfenhaus	13	22	28	3	-
+MJ Prior	c sub (PJ Hughes) b Siddle	41	59	99	6	-
A Flintoff	c Clarke b Hauritz	74	79	117	10	1
SCJ Broad	c and b Siddle	55	64	95	9	-
GP Swann	c North b Johnson	24	20	25	5	-
JM Anderson	c Manou b Hilfenhaus	1	6	5	-	-
G Onions	not out	2	14	20	-	-
Extras (2 b, 4 lb, 9 nb, 6 w)		21				
Total (all out, 399 minutes, 93.3 overs)		**376**				

Fall of wickets: 1-2 (Cook, 1.4 ov), 2-60 (Bopara, 19.2 ov), 3-141 (Strauss, 44.1 ov), 4-159 (Collingwood, 50.5 ov), 5-168 (Bell, 55.6 ov), 6-257 (Prior, 71.3 ov), 7-309 (Flintoff, 80.4 ov), 8-348 (Swann, 87.3 ov), 9-355 (Anderson, 88.6 ov), 10-376 (Broad, 93.3 ov)

Australia bowling	Overs	Mdns	Runs	Wkts	Wides	No-Balls
Hilfenhaus	30	7	109	4	-	4
Siddle	21.3	3	89	3	1	-
Hauritz	18	2	57	1	-	-
Johnson	21	1	92	2	1	5
Watson	3	0	23	0	-	-

Australia second innings		Runs	Balls	Mins	4s	6s
SR Watson	c Prior b Anderson	53	114	182	9	-
SM Katich	c Prior b Onions	26	47	54	2	-
*RT Ponting	b Swann	5	7	6	-	-
MEK Hussey	c Prior b Broad	64	130	153	13	-
MJ Clarke	not out	103	192	281	14	-
MJ North	c Anderson b Broad	96	159	207	15	-
+GA Manou	not out	13	28	36	1	-

Did not bat: MG Johnson, BW Hilfenhaus, PM Siddle, NM Hauritz

Extras (4 b, 6 lb, 3 nb, 2 w)   15

Total (5 wickets, 112.2 overs)   **375**

Fall of wickets: 1-47 (Katich, 13.2 ov), 2-52 (Ponting, 14.6 ov), 3-137 (Watson, 43.6 ov), 4-161 (Hussey, 52.6 ov), 5-346 (North, 103.1 ov)

England bowling	Overs	Mdns	Runs	Wkts	Wides	No-Balls
Anderson	21	8	47	1	-	1
Flintoff	15	0	35	0	-	-
Onions	19	3	74	1	1	-
Swann	31	4	119	1	-	-
Broad	16	2	38	2	1	-
Bopara	8.2	1	44	0	-	2
Collingwood	2	0	8	0	-	-

After Edgbaston

Ah, momentum, so we meet again. Now Australia have it. What an amazing unquantifiable commodity it is. Australia had been lying on the canvas bleeding when Graeme Swann bowled Ricky Ponting; the next afternoon they were up and punching so hard that England were stumbling around. England had still dominated all but the final two sessions of the match, but Australia had *momentum*.

Not only did Australia have that, but it also appeared that Ricky Ponting had rediscovered his anger. There was a report about him smashing the Edgbaston door after getting out to Swann's magical ball. *The Mirror* led with "Ricky Ponting vents Ashes frustration by smashing a door". In the article Keith Cook, Warwickshire's cricket operations manager, wasn't quite as screamy. "We have to make all sorts of running repairs all over the ground," he said. "I've not had any complaints, but if a batsman has lost his temper when he's out it wouldn't be the first time." I just hope they cleaned up all the vomit.

More people were talking about the fact that Freddie might not play at Headingley. Some harsh types may suggest he didn't play on the last day at Edgbaston. Harmy was the like-for-like option in the bowling attack. The places of Ravi Bopara and Stuart Broad seemed under pressure. Broad was saved by the fact that England couldn't lose two all-rounders at once, Bopara was saved by ... I have no idea. In my mind Chuck Norris and Charlie Bronson together couldn't have saved him, but he still looked likely to play.

Australia were making all the noises that said Nathan Hauritz was likely to miss out. Peter Siddle as well. It seemed likely that one of them would be left out, once Ricky Ponting said Hauritz wasn't a strike bowler. Headingley also wasn't known for being a spin-friendly pitch. Brett Lee came out and said he was 100% fit. Which is pretty fit. Shane Watson came out and said he wasn't.

It almost made a splash in the media, but no one could work out the angle. I get the feeling that when Watson comes out and says something stupid like that the Australian players just ignore it. It must be easier that way; otherwise they wouldn't ever talk to him again.

Mitchell Johnson had survived the Edgbaston Test, bowled well at times, sledged Freddie, got laughed at by Freddie and then talked to the media. The fact he could front the media meant he thought he was back, and the Australian camp obviously agreed.

It tells you something about a series when that many players were still fighting for their places after three matches. My four great hopes had been savaged by Ashes expectations: Mitchell had still not turned up, Hughes had been discarded, Ravi was lucky to still be picked and Stuart Broad had been almost ignored by his captain.

The one thing that really fell apart was the Australian game plan. Their theory to beat South Africa was to choke them (not a World Cup joke). It worked. South Africa lost two Tests at home without ever scoring at better than three an over. They were completely suffocated. Then Australia came to England and threw that plan out the window. It appears their new one is to bowl so many hittable balls that the batsmen get tired and eventually play a stupid shot.

It is a variant on the rope-a-dope boxing tactic. It could work if a) the Australian batsmen make 600 b) the English batsmen don't work it out c) if the planet starts rotating around the moon and not the sun.

England had scored at better than four an over in each innings except the one in Cardiff when they were playing for a draw. In the third Test they managed to do it without KP – and with Ian Bell. Andrew McDonald has not played a Test in this series and yet he was the major cog in the defensive strategy that beat South Africa. Stuart Clark has also not played a Test yet and he is Australia's best defensive bowler.

Instead Australia have persisted with their two South Africa destroyers, one of whom has taken two-and-a-half Tests to find his radar and the other who has lost his ability to slow down the scoring.

This tour has proved much more representative of their tour of India: bringing in players to plug gaps and ignoring players who could make a difference. Even though it appeared successful at Edgbaston, Shane Watson's selection as an opening batsman was as sensible as picking Cameron White as a frontline spinner. Neither player had had first-class experience in the jobs. The decisions seemed to come from a mid-tour freak out.

Watson could easily bat at No. 4, replacing a man who remembers what runs are but not exactly what they look like. Hussey had hit fewer Test centuries in the previous 18 months than Hughes had in his five Tests. Whether the panic brought on the high run-rates or vice versa is still unknown, but one thing was for sure: Australia need England to lose a Test, as they look unable to win one on their own.

Even though England was on the verge of winning the Ashes, the major story was more about a cultural identity crisis: whether or not it was okay to boo Ricky Ponting. Giles Clarke wrote in the match programme for Headingley that he wanted Ponting treated with respect and courtesy. The media seemed divided on the issue – some pissed off that Giles had stuck his beak in, others casting their long manicured fingers in accusation at the Barmy Army.

Boo Hoo

It *is* okay to boo Ricky Ponting. It really fucken is. Ricky doesn't care. I don't care. I doubt the average Australian fan cares. A boo is a sign of respect. No one boos shit players.

No one is booing Mitchell Johnson. They are laughing at him.

England are booing Ricky Ponting because he is the face of this team, he has scored over 11,000 runs, he is quick to anger, and he has a face that is easy to dislike. That is okay. If a bunch of uptight suits and hyphens have problems with this, fuck 'em.

Cricket is an emotional game. People love this game, they get fired up and they yell. They feel it. People sitting around tut-tutting and gently applauding is in the past. Now people yell, scream and boo. And so they should.

At the end of the series if Australia have lost, Ponting being booed will be pretty fucken far from our minds.

Boo your hearts out.

Headingley

Where Australia arrived in England

It isn't often you are 1-0 up in a series, are coming off a draw in which you were in front for 80% of the match and you still bring three new men into your squad. England had turned up at Headingley with a new man, Jonathan Trott, an old man, Ryan Sidebottom, and an odd man, Steve Harmison. Trott was an in-form South Africa-born Warwickshire batsman who was brought in to a) replace the struggling Ravi, and b) as a No. 7 batsman for Freddie. The second one was unlikely, even if Trott does bowl little Nathan Astle-style seamers.

There have been a lot of rotten tomatoes thrown at the Australian bowlers this tour, especially Siddle and Johnson. They averaged 40 and 42 respectively. Not very good. England had two bowlers, Broad and Swann, with averages of over 50 – the benchmark of proper shit – and their national hero Freddie had a bowling average of 48. He had taken seven wickets in the series with five coming in one innings at Lord's. It seemed only Freddie's injury could save Broad, while Swann is saved by Monty's terrible county form and the fact that England aren't about to take a punt on a young leg-spinner on debut.

Sidebottom seemed likely to be brought in as a swinging Headingley specialist. Being that Australia play swing bowling like I play the violin, it was a good move, but the ball had hardly swung in the series. Harmy was brought in as the hit-the-deck bowler who intimidates if England wanted a Freddie-like replacement. Harmison was also under an injury cloud as he had a blister on his big toe.

A bad blister. A real bad blister. A very fucking bad blister on his toe. This blister was like Terry Savalas's-in-*The-Dirty-Dozen* bad. It was sabotaging the whole foot. But Harmy braved the blister and played, Ravi played too, and only Freddie was rested from the side.

England's other problem was Graham Onions' mind. During the Edgbaston Test Lily Allen, the singer of pop songs, tweeted that she had heard that Onions can go for days and days, and quite liked the sound of that. Onions was asked about it by *The Guardian's* tweeting expert Lawrence Booth and spit out a couple of meaningless sentences about having a girlfriend and thinking Lily Allen was a great singer. I say this as someone who doesn't mind Lily Allen, but she isn't a great singer. She isn't Jill Scott or Antony from Antony and the Johnsons. She has written some good songs, but I've seen her live and great singing was not a phrase that came to my mind.

More importantly look at the way Onions put this: "It would be great to meet her. I've got a girlfriend." Quite obviously Onions is thinking of himself, Allen and girlfriend in a raunchy threesome. Who wouldn't? He is just some dude who bowls well, and now he has a pop star talking about his potential endurance in the boudoir. Why wouldn't he dare to dream? Sorry to shock you, but men to tend to go to fantasy rather quickly, and look in the top ten list of male fantasies, threesomes are always a big vote winner. Hopefully Onions would have stopped thinking about his healthy sexual fantasies by the time the Test started.

If Lily Allen were a cricketer, she would be a wicketkeeper, yapping in your ear and generally annoying the fuck out of you, but she would make some handy runs when the team needed them.

Over in the Australia camp everything seemed very calm. A little too calm? No, just calm enough. Brett Lee was not match fit, and even though he was 100% fit he was not going to play. The talk was all about Stuart Clark, and his lack of nip, coming in for Hauritz. Australia had lost faith in Hauritz as a wicket-taker. They needed to attack to get the 20 wickets, and they believed in their quicks, not in Hauritz.

Brad Haddin was brought back in, and Manou was now resting with a broken finger. I suppose with keepers they all regularly have broken fingers, it just depends on whether they can keep with them. Michael Clarke was reported to have a stomach strain, but it seemed okay. If it had been really bad Australia would have had a reserve batsmen flown in, as I doubted they would make Phil Hughes bat in the middle order.

It looked as if it would be cloudy for the first day and then sunny after that, so whoever bowled on the first morning could be in a very good position by the end of day one. The scientists and learned types say that cloud cover has no effect on a cricket ball, but it does seem to swing and seam more when there is cloud around, and on the flat decks of modern cricket, a sunny day can mean death for a bowling side.

I was not greatly inspired today. Maybe it was my hangover, but I didn't have my normal zest-for-Test-cricket feeling going on. My whole life was about these Ashes at this time, and neither team was filling me with orgasmic glee. The truth remained that both teams were quite shit. England might have ridden to victory on the back of two special, for different reasons, performances by all-rounders at Lord's. But they are shit. Australia might have all but won at Cardiff, and got so out of the hole at Edgbaston, that they were now favourites. But they are shit.

Trying to make a prediction about this Test would mean I was full of shit. I was, but I didn't know how you could make a guess on this game. I had no idea.

Day 1

The cricket hadn't started and all sorts of whacky shenanigans were going on. Mostly to the poor Poms. At 5am they had to leave their hotel as the fire alarm went off. And then 40 minutes before the game, Prior had a back spasm. I know all about back spasms – they is the Devil. Strauss still won the toss. He is a majestical tosser. England to bat, Prior got over his back spasm, but still gave the reporters something to talk about, especially the ones who hate the players playing football in the warm-up (although it turns out he wasn't playing football in the warm-up).

It was a melodramatic morning. There were rumours of choppers flying Tim Ambrose in, retired keeper Bruce French donning the gloves, and the fire alarm. You couldn't believe any of it, I didn't even believe Nathan Hauritz was out of the Australia team until they got out there.

Luckily, we had the boring cricket to ease our pumping valves back down. Hilfy took the new ball to Strauss and bustled in and bowled one wide of off stump that was left alone and went through to the keeper. No, that isn't what happened. He bowled an inswinger from Hades that smacked Strauss straight in front. It couldn't have been more out if it had bowled him. It took all of Strauss' mental strength not to turn and walk. "Random" Rudi had been replaced with baffling Billy Bowden. Not out.

That was Australia's Ashes; even when they got it right they didn't get any luck.

In the fourth over Siddle did get Strauss, the captain hanging his bat out and handing Marcus North the chance to take a classic one-hand reflex catch in the slips. Australia were jubilant: maybe their luck had changed. Strauss had left his awkward apprentice Cook, who was joined by Ravi, who now was not so much a street dog as a confused rabbit.

By this stage, he was a waste of time. Of course he got out, I felt sorry for him.

Bell came in, and that must have lifted the mood of every English fan. Ponting must have been tempted to keep his two openers on, but instead backed Johnson. Ponting's faith in Johnson had never really faltered, but neither had it ever really been justified. Bell edgily slashed him to the rope, but the rest of his over was pretty testing. Clark was brought on at the other end and uncharacteristically bowled a ball miles down the leg-side. It was too early to tell if he had indeed lost his nip, but he started with two maidens.

While Clark was building the pressure Johnson steamed in, bowling a bouncer at Bell's face that Bell could only guide into the damaged hands of Brad Haddin. This was now officially a mini-collapse. Clark finally went for a run but in his fourth over he did what he does best, finding a weakness and taking a wicket. In his fourth over he does what he does best, he finds the weakness and takes the wicket, the weakness being Collingwood pushing at balls outside off stump, and Ponting does the rest.

Not only were England unravelling before a morbidly quiet Headingley crowd, all four Australian bowlers had taken a wicket and it was 4/42. Then Matt Prior came out, not exactly what he was planning to do after a back spasm only two hours earlier. England were now relying on their young unofficial vice captain to step up and see them through to lunch.

It didn't happen. Instead Cook got an edge to Clarke at slip. In walks the man who looked like the worst Test No. 7 I had ever seen when he played the Windies, Stuart Broad. England were now looking to a keeper who'd had a back spasm and one of their bowlers. I've seen a lot of hesitant batsmen in my time, but Broad looked particularly petrified.

But Broad did what any smart cricketer would do: he started wasting time, doing his level best to get to the interval by playing as few balls as possible. It was a sound theory, but just made him look like a bit of a pussy. Time-wasting before lunch on the first day, as far as an Australian team are concerned, is like chucking a steak into shark-filled water. In response, Johnson aimed one at Broad's throat, and the England player just managed to get it past gully.

If he is going to bat at No. 7 for England, he has to get used to the odd collapse, because few countries do it better. Stuart Clark is the worst bowler to show weakness to. I call him the proctologist because he gets right up there probing away and makes it very uncomfortable. A play and miss was followed by a slightly quicker one that Broad was late on, then swung one onto his pads and the Aussies all went up. Next ball Broad tried to get off strike by pushing one to square leg, but instead pushed it to a diving Katich at short leg and England were 6/72 at the break.

Australia had bowled well – Clark and his lost nip had picked up three wickets, while the others had taken one each and looked good. But it was not entirely their doing: England had panicked. Maybe it was the fact that Freddie wasn't there, or the 5am wake-up call, or the scare with Prior, but this was a pitifully pitiful effort from them. Cook has at least got set, but couldn't handle the pressure, while Broad has just looked proper afraid.

Australia had moved the ball, but not enough to get six wickets, not anywhere near that many. England are supposed to understand swing bowling anyway. No, this was an Ashes pressure collapse. Australia had done it twice, and now England, and one of their worst recent batting line-ups, was falling apart. Neither team might have been good enough to actually force the other team to collapse, but the Ashes were helping out.

After lunch it didn't get better. Siddle, who had looked very dangerous in his opening spell, seemed to want to cash in on that, and luckily for him his mate Swann was at the crease. After a couple of bouncers, some steam coming out of his ears, he eventually drew an edge. It didn't placate Siddle, who hit Harmison on the head before getting him out in his next over. It was a shocking dismissal with Harmy backing away and then edging behind.

At 8/98 there was no guarantee that England would make it to 100. Hilfy was brought on to replace Clark. His first over leaked runs, all two of them, the last one getting Anderson off his duck again, dammit. Siddle seemed angered by England making it to 100 and tried to decapitate Anderson, who was caught behind off the gloves. And he went for Onions's throat first ball, hitting him on the arm guard but the England No. 11 was given out caught. It was a proper No. 11 decision: it hit something, he is shit, so let's give him out.

England had made 102. Exactly double what they had made when they collapsed in Jamaica. Siddle had ended up with an angry five-wicket haul, but Stuart Clark's figures of 10-4-18-3 seemed to be the major reason for Australia's turnaround. They never loosened the rope round England's neck, even if England had got up and put their head in the noose to start with. Matt Prior had finished with 37 not out, but a great deal of his runs had come off the outside edge.

When defending a total of 102, you need a pretty good start. Instead Anderson started with two wide ones that Watson used to gain eight. With two more runs from the over Australia had got almost 10% of England's score in six balls. Through much of the over Anderson was seen to be stretching his leg. It appeared that he had strained something batting.

Strauss took a huge gamble at the other end, giving Harmison the new ball. The crowd gave a great reception, but then quickly went quiet, perhaps remembering how he started his last Ashes. His first delivery was right on line and length and jumped up at Katich, making you wonder how batsmen ever play him. The crowd let go a sigh of relief and then got fired up for his second ball. He repays them with four byes down the leg side. Katich could only fend the third ball to leg, and Harmy must have been happy with the bounce he is getting off this wicket – Australia got four wickets with bouncers.

The next delivery was pure evil. It had a mind of its own, and that mind was in a vicious mood. It jumps back at Katich and all he can do is glove it to leg gully. Harmy was back, England were back.

Ricky came in, greeted by some of the loudest and most impressive booing I have heard. In Edgbaston the crowd really gave it to him, but now they aren't just booing Ricky, they are booing Giles Clarke. It is a boo to the evil fascist dictator and the pantomime villain. Had Giles and the media not made an issue of it I doubt the booing would have been more than a few drunks huddled together, but their indignation had galvanised everyone to boo. It was democratic booing.

Ricky didn't seem to notice the booing, but he did notice the first two balls from Harmy, one cutting him in half and the next one where he played a nervy pull shot and missed it. At the other end Anderson got massive swing, way more than any of the Australians. If Anderson could find a line and Harmy continued to bowl like this 102 might not be the nipple caught in a blender it appeared to be.

But England chose another path, the path of complete fucken idiocy. Anderson, perhaps because he was injured, was feeding four-balls every over. Harmy, way too excited at getting Katich with a short one had decided to bounce Ponting out. Onions, brought on to provide the control that Anderson couldn't, decided to bounce Ponting as well; Ricky tried hard not to snigger as he took 17 runs off his first over, including greeting him with a six.

After that over Australia were 1/57 after seven overs. Words failed...

England had only bowled 11 bad balls, but look at the total: Australia, even on a pitch with something in it, had put every one of them away. Ricky had scored 32 off 20 balls at this stage, Watson 20 off 18. That is why having a No. 3 like Ricky is a gift from the tribal elders. Other batsmen would have seen the Katich ball, looked at England's score and just let the bad balls go or defended them, maybe nudging the ones on the hip away. Ponting went straight back at England and tried to win the match there and then.

He wanted Australia to have beaten England, at least psychologically, by tea. And with some help from Harmy, Anderson and Onions, he had done that. England's hope of rolling Australia cheaply was gone. Their only chance of getting Ponting out came from a possible run-out, but they stuffed that up too.

To prove the wicket was still good, after Onions's horror over, England's next eight overs went for 12 runs. It was a slap in their own face, proof of what they could have done if not for a seven-over period of freaking out. At tea Australia were 1/69, 33 runs behind, nine wickets in hand, and no Freddie.

England went with Anderson and Broad after tea, and Ponting brought up his fifty off 63 balls. England seemed in awe of him. He hit one back-foot drive so well that several million people converted to it. About half an hour after tea Watson slashed at one and gave Australia the lead. Wow. Literally wow. How did this happen, is this happening, am I dreaming? Was Maggie Gyllenhaal about to come on and bowl so I'd know this was all just a fantasy?

Harmison came back on, and considering the whacking the English bowlers had taken earlier on, his figures of one for 17 from six overs looked pretty good. He celebrated this by giving Watson three of the easiest balls to smash he has had in a long time. If someone hadn't taken sharp objects away from Andy Flower, they should have considered it – the man is too much of a legend to die over wank like this. Harmy's next over went for only ten. He didn't get a third and Onions was brought on.

Watson brought up his third straight fifty – and the third of his Test career. But then Onions, like the Mitchell Johnson ball to Prior at Lord's, shocked the opener with a ball on a good length and Watson plays across his pad and is fairly out. But Australia were by now well in front, and the wicket meant little to anyone other than Onions and Watson.

But England were not finished. Ponting's flawless innings was brought to an end when he got a full straight one from Broad and tried to work it to the leg-side. An innings that good should have ended in a hundred, but his 78 was enough to get Australia the lead and walk over England's lifeless corpse. It was innings like this that made people swoon over Ricky.

Broad then got Hussey out. I know how surprised you are. It was lbw again, just to prove to England how their earlier length had been insane. Australia were now 4/151. They had lost 3/18 and England were thinking of getting out of their mess with a possible double-digit deficit rather than the 400 their shambolicness deserved.

After drinks, and two maidens, it seemed things were going more England's way, but then Onions got it wrong twice – not as badly as in his over to Ponting – but one on the pads and then one too full were enough for Clarke to take some wind out of their sails.

Asad Rauf then took an umpiring decision that I respected, telling Stuart Broad that he couldn't leave the field of play just because he felt like it. In this series, like every series, both teams have given their 12th or 13th men almost permanent fielding duty. The ICC said they had made it harder, but Rauf is the first umpire in ages I have seen actually stop a fielder going off. Broad wasn't happy, but neither is a kid when you slap their hand away from a donut.

Then Australia had a big slice of luck. Harmy dug a short one into Clarke's face, it hit something in his arm area and went through to Prior. England were all over it, but Rauf never moved. After about seven replays from five angles you could see his inner peaking out from his glove sort of do a little jump as the ball thudded into his arm. Hard to blame Rauf, it was not clear-cut, especially from straight on. But it was out. Clarke was one Australian batsman who could not whinge about the umpiring in this series.

Soon after it was stumps. Australia were 94 runs in front. England were deader than Bela Lugosi. What a day of Test cricket.

Even though the cricket hasn't always been top draw in this series there have been some great days of cricket. But surely a day in which 14 wickets fall and one team is already in front on first innings takes the cake. Could England come back? Why not? If you had told me that England could have been 94 runs behind on the first innings after the first day I would have spat on you.

Stuart Clark's nip

Every Australian in the know I talked to about Stuart Clark had told me he had lost his nip. Bumble and Beefy obviously had the same information as they mentioned quite often on Sky. It was a rumour based on VERY solid information, I was always told. The perception was he was not quite quick enough to make his good line and length count anymore.

It was in quite a few papers, and was hard to overlook. Even his wickets in the warm-up game hadn't seemed to convince anyone.

But he had bowled at pretty much the pace he always had done on the first day. And he took three-for. I'd say that he had his nip.

So who has been releasing the nip rumour? I honestly don't know, but my theory involves well-known names. But more importantly, why?

Was it something that was said so that the South African tamers – Mitch, Hilfy and Siddle – could be picked first, and then it got away from the person who first released it?

The rumour might have cost Australia the Ashes, and also probably didn't help Clark's bank balance or future career. Funny how quickly perception becomes reality.

Day 2

As you would expect, the English media were scathing after the team's first-day performance. Everyone was to blame, it was a national outrage, the players were soft, blah, blah, blah ....

There were also reports that the Australian Fanatics – their equivalent of the Barmy Army – had claimed responsibility for playing the fire-alarm prank. But it was actually caused by a woman's drying underwear. A poor effort from the Fanatics. If they were really fanatical they *would* have pulled the fire alarm. But then to claim it for their own notoriety. Opportunistic bullshit.

There was also talk about Anderson's fitness. The constant stretching and incredibly bloated figures were a sign something was wrong. England denied he wasn't fit, perhaps trying to make sure Australia didn't have more of a psychological advantage. His figures of 12 overs for 55 runs probably made that a bit redundant. It didn't take a person trained in the art of body language to tell you that Jimmy was struggling.

The talk from the England camp was about how fired up they were and how they were going to come out and take this Test match back. It was lovely, but no-one believed it.

England decided to open with Anderson. His first over was stiff. For a moment it looked like England had replaced him with Mecha-Jimmy, a robotic version that had roughly the same functions but without any flexibility or humanity. At the other end Harmy started – and started with a ball that showed that England were not really in the mood for the day's play.

Australia went about their job with ruthless professionalism. There was a time when they were just ruthless. Clarke and North were the new models; preparation and patience was how they operated. With England not really putting too much effort in, both batsmen just waited for the bad balls, kept out the very occasional good ball and put Australia into an unreachable position. Clarke brought up his fifty – and the England spinner, Swann, had still not had an over.

In modern cricket five-man attacks are the in thing. I understand why, especially with back-to- back Tests and flatter decks, but this was the second time Strauss had not used a bowler inside the first 50 overs of an innings. Yes this was a seamer's wicket, but that didn't mean Swann couldn't do some kind of damage, or even a containing job. Perhaps it was Strauss' way of punishing his bowlers. Swann had been ordinary in the series, and just like he had held Broad back, it could be that Strauss was trying to make clear that they were not playing as he wanted or expected them to.

When a team is being outplayed as much as England were they often turn on each other, so it was no surprise that when North dropped one on the leg-side and got two for it, Broad had a go at the fielder. It was just a shame that the fielder was Ravi Bopara. Poor little guy. How were people not running out on to the field to give him a nice warm hug. Ravi had let Australia get one extra run; but Anderson, Harmy and Onions had let in how many extra runs by bowling crap without Broad yelling at them.

The first 12 overs of the morning had cost 65 runs. No real chances of wickets. No spinner, and for England, the depressing feeling that all hope was not just lost, but found dead under an overpass, victims of the kind of brutality even the CSI team had never seen.

Swan finally got a good 59 overs in and started with a maiden. I thought it was funny; Strauss probably didn't. Swann and Broad then bowled well in partnership – well Broad bowled three feet wide of off stump as an obvious defensive tactic, and Swann kept the runs to a minimum. It was horrible to watch at times, like a football team who won't attack because they might lose possession, but it was what England needed. It didn't seem to worry North or Clarke, but at least England weren't being embarrassed.

Onions eventually replaced Broad, and he was rejuvenated. His new tactic of line and length bowling was improving his figures. Then, just after Clarke had moved into the 90s, Onions got a bit of reverse swing on a yorker and Clarke was gone. Australia, though, got to lunch without any further wickets falling and were over 200 runs in front. They had made 110 of them in the session.

After lunch England just wasted time until the new ball was taken. North helped himself to a fifty. Harmison was given the new ball, and eyebrows were arched everywhere, but second ball he got one into Haddin's ribs that was half pulled into the hands of leg gully. Harmison now had two wickets, both to leg gully, but I don't think Australia were quite as worried about this one.

For a time, every over had a predictable boundary in it. Mostly from North, but Johnson was chipping in as well. North just waited for balls he liked and then launched them to the fence. Then Johnson was out to Broad on the pull, again, and Siddle made a golden duck.

North had reached 95, and still looked calm, even with the tail. When facing Swann he gave the strike to Clark without too much worry, and Clark brought up Australia's 400 with a single. North was so excited he hit the next ball for six, bringing up his second Ashes ton and ensuring Australia were now more than 300 in front.

It then became party time for Australia, Stuart Clark is a great tailend batsman. I don't mean he can bat, I mean he can swing madly with no fear. Clark and Murali are by far the world's best tailenders. Neither of them really care about batting, and are as likely to hit their first ball for six as get bowled by it. The last thing England needed was Clark getting a few. Clark generally hits seven or eight big shots, or none at all. He can go about six innings without making double figures, but then he'll make a couple of entertaining 30s.

This was one of the days where he hit the seven or eight big ones. A four from Broad was followed up with a six off Swann and then back-to-back sixes off Broad. All slogged delightfully to different parts of the ground. And predictably, as he got into the 30s, he dragged one back on to his stumps, giving Broad a fifth wicket. In Broad's next over North tried to copy Clark's form of attack and was caught at deep mid-wicket.

Broad had got a fairly undeserved six-wicket haul. I suppose someone had to get the wickets, and he did bowl a good spell on the first day, and stuck in while North, Clark and Johnson were hitting him. Australia ended up on

445 from 104 overs, every single run seeming to looking at England's total of 102 and smirk. Tea is called.

The pitch, in case you were wondering, had now completely settled down and was an official shot-playing wonderland. But England would have to make 600 to make a game of it and that is a lot of shot playing. No-one really believed this would happen, but the Sky commentators kept mentioning Headingley 81 like there would be a repeat. I thought the best that could happen was for England to get bowled out easily so that Sky could show replays of Botham's greatest moment for two days while the team regrouped.

Hilfy started out with a great length, and Siddle was full of fire, producing the occasional brilliant delivery. Cook didn't inspire anyone with confidence, while Strauss was just solid. After 13 overs they were an unspectacular 0/25.

After the drinks break the runs started to flow a bit more freely, but Mitchell seemed to have found some sort of fire. With one ball he smashed a confused Strauss on the gloves. I can't remember a bowler since Curtly Ambrose who hits gloves as much as Mitchell, and he usually only hits them when he is at his best. England kept on plugging away steadily.

Hilfy came back on and started to get swing – I still don't understand why the Duke balls don't swing early – and he curved one back into Strauss and he was given out lbw.

Poor Ravi. I am sure there is a part of him that just wished that the opening partnership would never be broken, that he could be in a magical place where there is free candy-floss for everyone and people love him. Instead he was out in the middle with England still miles behind and the cricket world mocking him.

As he made his uncomfortable walk to the middle, I got a call from the ECB:

"If you want we have a spare seat in the press box for you for the last three days".

"Three days".

"Well, how ever long it lasts".

"SHIT, THAT IS OUT".

"Sorry?"

"Sorry, Ravi is out. Okay, yes, thanks, I'll see you tomorrow."

I'm not sure if as a young cricket writer trying to make your way in this world it is advisable to scream into the ear of an ECB media person when England lose a wicket, but Ravi had made a golden duck. He was probably, possibly, unlucky. He seemed to hit the ball at the exact same time it hit his pad, but it did look out. Ravi was gone. And not just for today. England could not take him to the Oval, or to South Africa now. Shane Warne was probably smiling.

It just struck me that Siddle had been on a hat-trick with his first ball of the innings. He didn't get it. Now Hilfy was on one, but despite giving it a red-hot go just misses the outside edge of Bell's bat. Oh it's Bell; with all the confusion I forgot. At Edgbaston Onions and Anderson had been on hat-tricks too. Must have been contagious.

At 2/58, I figured I might as well still go for the third day. Maybe I just wanted to go that bad that I didn't really think it through, but while I was on the net looking up the freakishly expensive train fares to Leeds, Bell got out. Prodding at one from Johnson with all the assurance of a crack head at a police picnic.

Next ball Collingwood was greeted with a throat ball; Johnson meant business. It wasn't long before he plucked out one of his ethereal inswingers and it curved in to strike Collingwood in front of middle stump. England were now four wickets down. I stopped looking up fares to Headingley. England send in Anderson as the nightwatchman.

Anderson got one off the first ball of Hilfy's next over – way to protect your top order – and then Johnson swings another away from Cook, who edges it behind. England had lost five for 20. What an amazing collapse, again.

I immediately decided that any trip to Headingley would be a waste of six hours of my life. England were probably worried about making it to stumps. Ponting went in for the kill and it was some of the best captaincy I had seen from him. Not worried about getting out Anderson he moved the field back so that he could get Anderson off strike and have a go at Prior. Brilliant, why hadn't captains tried this before?

Anderson looked confused, and left one from Hilfenhaus that was not out, but would have made a few in the English changing-room nervous. Most importantly Anderson could not get on strike for the last over, not that he tried very hard. Instead, it was Prior facing Johnson. Third ball, Prior guided one away and, perhaps not wanting to look like a pussy, took two. It was a nice, positive step, but one that made the decision to have a nightwatchman even more baffling.

The next one from Johnson was full and wide and Prior wafted at it. It was a stupid shot, perhaps because he was thinking he should have taken only a single, perhaps because people play stupid shots under pressure. The penultimate ball was simply left alone. Now Prior had to get through only one more ball. At any time during the series before this, he would have been comfortable facing this last ball, but this was the Johnson that the English thought existed only as a figment of South Africa's imagination.

For the last ball Johnson did that weird Cro-Magnon-like shoulder-hunched run-up, flailed his right arm up like an angry elephant and then slung his left arm as fast as he could. It was a top ball and Prior pushed at it and got an edge. It flew to third slip only for Marcus North to save England from further embarrassment by dropping it.

I closed all my Firefox tabs that have train information on them, took out my phone and called Patrick Kidd, the author of *The Times's* Line and Length, to tell him I can indeed play the next day in his charity game.

I know you feel let down, but this Test was over, and I'd really rather not watch the tail play futile innings when I could be playing in my own game. Even writing something about this day seemed wrong. England didn't put in any effort; why should I?

Torture

It was as if the entire English cricket-loving population were tied to a chair.

They had been punched, spat on, pissed on, kicked and force-fed their own sexual organs. Then they were made to watch their loved ones perform lewd acts with various animals.

This shit made water-boarding seem like cotton candy.

Horrible torture type torture. But the puffy-chested Australians did not do this.

Their heroes inflicted this. Then English team donned mischievous moustaches and became villains.

Harmy spat on them.

Anderson punched them.

Ravi and Belly pissed on them.

Collingwood fed them the organs.

And Strauss orchestrated the lewd Zoophilia acts.

You expect it from the opposition, but this was just wrong. Sick and wrong.

England took to the torture with such relish that you knew on some level they enjoyed it. Of all the fans in world cricket, English fans know what it is like to be tortured by your team, but this was a shock.

No one saw it coming. Michael Atherton had started the coverage by saying that England were five days away from possibly winning the Ashes.

Millions of English fans were excited; they willingly sat down to watch their team. They could sense victory. So this viciously obscene, unnecessary attack caught them right off guard.

It goes without saying that several English fans would never trust themselves around the English team again.

There was a reason this game was not on free-to-air TV. It had an R-rating.

Day 3 (Cricket with Ray Parlour)

I was very happy with my idea not to watch the last day of the Test; it was obviously going to be 1-1, and I didn't need to watch it to know that. The game I was due to play in was at a stately home called Audley End and was in the aid of some charity. I can't remember which one, because I wasn't there for charity, I was there for the cricket.

I was told this was an exciting match as we would be paying against the former England and Arsenal footballer – that is soccer, Aussies – Ray Parlour. I must confess that I had no idea who Ray Parlour was until the car ride on the way up. And this was his first game of cricket.

I was keeping when he came out to bat, and first ball one of Patrick Kidd's high, slow nude nuts bowled him. An embarrassing moment for an experienced cricketer, but someone in their first game probably wasn't too worried. The rule in this game, however, was that you couldn't be out first ball, so he was given another chance. The next ball, he sort of stumbled down the wicket and missed it. This time it missed the stumps and I took it clean with the gloves (perhaps the only one I did), but instead of whipping the bails off, I sort of mimed it, and then when he still wasn't in, I took them off, but didn't appeal.

I don't know why. I had been chatting with him as he came out, giving him some advice (which clearly hadn't sunk in), and he seemed like a good guy. But it wasn't very Australian of me. Instantly, I felt like I had committed some grave sin and the ghost of Ray 'Slug' Jordon, the former Victoria and Australia wicketkeeper, was cussing me out. Although Parlour said he would buy me a beer for it. It just seemed wrong that two balls into his first game he was out and hadn't hit a ball. So I let it go.

From there he went on to top score (with perhaps too much coaching from me) and was a large part of the reason that we couldn't win the game (we drew due to some fucked-up English rules). Once he started watching the ball, he really smashed it. I had to stop coaching him after a while as I was afraid we would never get him out.

I must say he was a top fella; but he does still owe me a beer for not stumping him. The game was such a big deal that *The Times* and the *Saffron Walden Reporter* both covered it. Football really does get into the news in the UK for almost no reason at all. Although for some reason the Saffron Walden paper forgot to mention the most important innings of the game – my 26 not out – and also the fact that only two people hit the ball into the moat surrounding the ground all day. Me and the Romford Pele.

My mate Suave, the author of republiquecricket.com, also played in the game, wearing a cravat. I just thought that deserved mention. Not enough people play cricket in a cravat.

Fourth Test at Headingley

Australia won by an innings and 80 runs

England first innings	Runs	Balls	Mins	4s	6s	
*AJ Strauss	c North b Siddle	3	17	16	-	-
AN Cook	c Clarke b Clark	30	65	104	3	-
RS Bopara	c Hussey b Hilfenhaus	1	6	10	-	-
IR Bell	c Haddin b Johnson	8	26	40	2	-
PD Collingwood	c Ponting b Clark	0	5	13	-	-
+MJ Prior	not out	37	43	76	5	-
SCJ Broad	c Katich b Clark	3	12	13	-	-
GP Swann	c Clarke b Siddle	0	15	21	-	-
SJ Harmison	c Haddin b Siddle	0	6	8	-	-
JM Anderson	c Haddin b Siddle	3	10	7	-	-
G Onions	c Katich b Siddle	0	1	1	-	-
Extras (5 b, 8 lb, 3 nb, 1 w)		17				
Total (all out, 163 minutes, 33.5 overs)		**102**				

Fall of wickets: 1-11 (Strauss, 3.6 ov), 2-16 (Bopara, 6.4 ov), 3-39 (Bell, 15.3 ov), 4-42 (Collingwood, 18.3 ov), 5-63 (Cook, 22.2 ov), 6-72 (Broad, 24.5 ov), 7-92 (Swann, 29.4 ov), 8-98 (Harmison, 31.4 ov), 9-102 (Anderson, 33.4 ov), 10-102 (Onions, 33.5 ov)

Australia bowling	Overs	Mdns	Runs	Wkts	Wides	No-Balls		
Hilfenhaus	7			0	20	1	-	2
Siddle	9.5			0	21	5	-	1
Johnson	7			0	30	1	1	-
Clark	10			4	18	3	-	-

Australia first innings	Runs	Balls	Mins	4s	6s	
SR Watson	lbw b Onions	51	67	121	9	-
SM Katich	c Bopara b Harmison	0	4	9	-	-
*RT Ponting	lbw b Broad	78	101	119	12	1
MEK Hussey	lbw b Broad	10	10	16	2	-
MJ Clarke	lbw b Onions	93	138	193	13	-
MJ North	c Anderson b Broad	110	206	321	13	1
+BJ Haddin	c Bell b Harmison	14	23	25	1	-
MG Johnson	c Bopara b Broad	27	53	70	5	-
PM Siddle	b Broad	0	1	1	-	-
SR Clark	b Broad	32	22	24	1	3
BW Hilfenhaus	not out	0	3	6	-	-
Extras (9 b, 14 lb, 3 nb, 4 w)		30				
Total (all out, 463 minutes, 104.1 overs)		**445**				

Fall of wickets: 1-14 (Katich, 1.4 ov), 2-133 (Watson, 27.3 ov), 3-140 (Ponting, 28.6 ov), 4-151 (Hussey, 30.3 ov), 5-303 (Clarke, 72.6 ov), 6-323 (Haddin, 80.2 ov), 7-393 (Johnson, 96.3 ov), 8-394 (Siddle, 96.6 ov), 9-440 (Clark, 102.5 ov), 10-445 (North, 104.1 ov)

England bowling	Overs	Mdns	Runs	Wkts	Wides	No-Balls	
Anderson	18	3	89	0	1	-	
Harmison	23	4	98	2	1	-	
Onions	22	5	80	2	1	2	
Broad	25.1	6	91	6	1	1	
Swann	16	4	64	0	-	-	

England second innings		Runs	Balls	Mins	4s	6s
*AJ Strauss	lbw b Hilfenhaus	32	78	97	4	-
AN Cook	c Haddin b Johnson	30	84	136	4	-
RS Bopara	lbw b Hilfenhaus	0	1	1	-	-
IR Bell	c Ponting b Johnson	3	12	12	-	-
PD Collingwood	lbw b Johnson	4	10	10	-	-
JM Anderson	c Ponting b Hilfenhaus	4	10	20	1	-
+MJ Prior	c Haddin b Hilfenhaus	22	29	40	3	-
SCJ Broad	c Watson b Siddle	61	49	95	10	-
GP Swann	c Haddin b Johnson	62	72	100	7	1
SJ Harmison	not out	19	28	43	4	-
G Onions	b Johnson	0	7	8	-	-
Extras (5 b, 5 lb, 11 nb, 5 w)		26				
Total (all out, 275 minutes, 61.3 overs)		**263**				

Fall of wickets: 1-58 (Strauss, 22.4 ov), 2-58 (Bopara, 22.5 ov), 3-67 (Bell, 25.5 ov), 4-74 (Collingwood, 27.6 ov), 5-78 (Cook, 29.6 ov), 6-86 (Anderson, 32.3 ov), 7-120 (Prior, 38.6 ov), 8-228 (Broad, 51.3 ov), 9-259 (Swann, 59.2 ov), 10-263 (Onions, 61.3 ov)

Australia bowling	Overs	Mdns	Runs	Wkts	Wides	No-Balls
Hilfenhaus	2	60	4	-	9	-
Siddle	12	2	50	1	1	1
Clark	11	1	74	0	-	1
Johnson	19.3	3	69	5	-	-

After Headingley

On the third – and last – day at Headingley, Anderson was out third ball, Prior a few overs later, and then Swann and Broad had a bit of fun. A 100-run partnership in 12 overs. I watched some of it on the highlights, but I never find the highlights that enlightening. There were some good shots, some luck, and some slogs, but it must have been fun to watch. At least the poor souls who turned up got some entertainment. Johnson picked up five wickets and this series of confusing fluctuations had ended up all square going into the final Test.

England's only positive was the six-wicket haul to Broad. He had gone into the match as player second most likely to be dropped. He would go to the Oval having taken wickets and made runs.

The paper thin batting line-up was England's major concern. Cook, Ravi and Bell had started to look like a tremendous waste of talent, dedication, coaching and resources. It was one of the worst line-ups from No. 2 to No. 4 that anyone could remember, although people never really think that far back when making those sorts of claims. Freddie would come back in, meaning that England's tail would once again be something that Australia would have to fear.

Australia must have been doubting their reality. England weren't great in the first three Tests, but they were okay. Then suddenly they rolled over and played dead. How do you prepare for your next Test against opponents like this?

And for God's sake, who had the momentum? Australia had won the Test, but by all accounts England had won the last day. Of course on the last day at Headingley, the Justin Langer dossier came out. Amazingly, it was a dossier prepared for the start of the series but it didn't come out until England lost a Test. Either the papers were holding it back so that when England won they could say, "stupid Aussies", or they were waiting for England to collapse so they could say Australians know more about cricket than we do.

It was the *Telegraph* who broke it, and I must admit I spent a lot of time taking the piss out of it on my site. I showed a youtube video of a young Indian kid playing like Sachin Tendlkar and then channelled the spirit of Justin Langer to write a review of him for future use. It seemed appropriate.

There was nothing that special in the dossier – England are good when they are in front; the Duke balls don't swing straight away; English players use Murray Mints for swing; English players don't believe in themselves; Andrew Strauss is a solid character and an excellent bloke, but conservative; Alistair (sic) Cook is average outside off stump; Ravi Bop is a street fighter who struts; James Anderson is a pussy; Graeme Swann doesn't like short bowling and is at least as good as N. Hauritz; Matt Prior has a massive ego; and Freddie has to be worn down.

It was obviously a bit longer than that – I am just paraphrasing. England are shit pussies who rub mints on the ball, but Freddie and Strauss are good. Why he decided to call little Nathan N. Hauritz I don't know, but I liked it. It was like his way of saying I don't know what his name is. You know, the little young bloke that looks like he is about to cry, that guy.

A lot of English people were pissed off with it. He takes our money, tells us he loves our country, and then sells us out. Boo hoo. It happens every tour. No team arrives in another country without a scouting report from someone who has worked there, played there, or knows the system pretty well. Greg Chappell was there for Australia's tour of India, which may have been the reason they lost. Langer's report wasn't even that in-depth. I'd be surprised if other players in the county system, like Ian Harvey, Michael Di Venuto and Stuart Law, didn't have some input as well.

For England I assumed that Graham Thorpe, former England and Surrey nugget of battingness, gave a dossier of his own. He was assistant coach of New South Wales, which provides about half the Australian line-up most of the time. So he would know way more than Justin Langer would being trapped at Taunton without any Test players in his line-up.

For some reason the Thorpe Dossier never made it into the media's hands, so I just made it up.

The Thorpe Dossier

Chaps.

Below is an intelligence briefing by an ex-English player by the name of Graham Thorpe; he once lived in Sydney. He contacted me with some observations on the Australian team. Take a read, take notes, and try not to leave it in your local pub or twitter about it.

The Australian team cannot handle swing bowling. Do whatever you can to make the ball swing. Borrow Atherton's trousers, buy shares in a mint company, use Jimmy's mousse, but get that ball swinging.

The way Australians are brought up means they believe they are better than you. Usually they are, but not that this time. Any squad with Andrew McDonald in it should be mocked, not feared. So when an Australian does macho posturing in your face, do it right back at him.

The team has signed some anti-sledging form. This will confuse them. You can use this to your advantage. For once we will be the team that can question their sexuality and talk about their family members in poor taste. Use every half-rumour against them, scour the blogs for material, make it personal, make it hurt.

Ricky Ponting is still a class batsman even if these days he struggles to score more than one hundred a series. Let him get the hundred out of the way early. His boys love him as a captain; they would follow them off a cliff. If you have access to a cliff, this is worth considering. Don't worry about getting Ricky angry, he will do so regardless.

Australia aren't very good, but Mitchell Johnson is. The best way to get him in trouble is to send a hard sudoku book to his hotel room; the more he thinks, the worse he plays. I met his mother once, a lovely lady; she said he was a very sensitive boy. He also has a tongue ring, not sure if that helps, but I thought it was weird.

Michael Clarke has a planet-sized ego. There are at least seven moons around it. There is nothing you can do to dent it, NOTHING. However, you may want to mention that it is footy season back home and slip in the name Brendan Fevola. I can't be bothered explaining it, just Google Lara Bingle + Brendan Fevola.

I have coached Phil Hughes over the years, and he has no weaknesses. The boy is pure batting perfection. Good luck getting him out.

Shane Watson will get injured. You can disregard him. okay, he may not. No, he will, disregard him.

There has never been a player in worse form than Michael Hussey. Apparently it isn't a technical thing, his pussycat died. He loved that cat, you wouldn't understand. But they had this bond, and now that Snapples is gone, he just can't get his mind right. Make sure you mention Snapples when he is coming out to bat.

Brad Haddin has fingers made of chalk; every player should make a special effort to go and shake his hand on the morning of a Test. Then send over the officials. Then the Sky team. Everyone. Squeeze hard boys.

Never underestimate Simon Katich. I know it is hard.

The Ashes reality TV singing competition

Cricket selectors are a weird bunch; on one level they are harsh men who ruin careers in haste, never pick others based on pettiness and seem to spend a lot of time talking up players from their home towns. But when they like you, wow, you are set for life. Sometimes regardless of talent.

They way cricket fans bag selectors is similar to how reality TV show fans bag the judges.

Even the players fill their roles quite well.

Nathan Hauritz: the young cute one who is oh so nice, and that everyone feels sorry for. Can sing okay, but seems to have no personality at all. Mums around the world vote him in, while everyone else can't work out why the fuck here is there.

Stuart Broad: has relatives in the business and is well known by the judges. He is a hard worker, and everyone thinks he is going to be a star. Seems to be promoted on work ethic and creativity alone.

Mitchell Johnson: comes in for his first audition and just blows everyone else away. He has an edge about him that the judges love, and makes the young girls swoon. Even though he never matches the level of his audition, he stays in the show.

Andrew Flintoff: the most talented singer, but one who doesn't like to look like he is trying too hard. Is too talented for the judges to get rid of him, and the fans love him because he is a bit of a lad.

Shane Watson: the sort of singer that the contest is dying for, a true all-round talent that can be a long-term star. Unfortunately, he is prone to emotional breakdowns, and no one feels pity for him.

Ravi Bopara: in every idol show there is one person who just does not make sense. They can't sing, they are kind of awkward, and people laugh at them.

Still they make it way further than others who can sing.

Phil Hughes: the judges like to take a punt on someone with a different kind of singing style sometimes and he is lucky because his style of Mongolian throat rapping is quite popular at the moment. The judges soon tire of him.

Ian Bell: looks like he came from the pop-star factory. Everything about him is right, and the judges expect big things. Problem is when he sings live he suffers from shocking stage fright.

Graham Manou: has an amazing soul voice, makes the old classics and the new pop songs sound amazing, but soul music isn't in right now, so is canned.

Middle-aged crisis

All my watching of England over the years had been from afar. This was the first time I had been inside the enemy's lair. For most of the Ashes they had been fine. Sure there was a great deal of unnatural pessimism, but nothing that you wouldn't expect from the English. But the Headingley loss sent them into a spiral of despair and panic I just couldn't understand.

Suddenly the whole team was useless, the batting line-up was the worst thing ever, and everything needed urgent changing. The batting line-up was terrible, but it was almost the same as that at Edgbaston. All they needed to do was take out Ravi and replace him with a batsman who could provide Australia with a contest. No panic was required.

Instead, the media and fans suggested that one man was going to come in and save England from this dire position of being 1-1 with one Test to play. The man was a 39-year-old who had played 52 Tests and averaged under 30; someone who hadn't played Test cricket since 2002; and someone who actually said that appearing on a reality TV dancing show would help him deal with Test cricket better.

Mark Ramprakash. The last man to make 100 100s in first-class cricket.

It was fucken bizarre. Even if it was not going to happen, it told you something about the mindset of the country. How could they pick him now? Why would they pick him now? How could a man with his Test record be the saviour? Sure he had been smashing people in both divisions of county cricket, but this was Test cricket. He wasn't going to be facing Mark Ealham.

Being that I am an almost Surrey fan who lives near the Oval, I have seen Ramps in full flight in county cricket. It is an erotic scene. He is like a naked sparkly God amongst men. County cricket doesn't look capable of having someone of his class. But he still hasn't played an attack of Test bowlers in years. And when he did, he didn't do well.

If, for some reason the selectors were to pick Ramps, they would be saying that they should have picked him all the time. They should be fired on the spot. They won't pick him, of course. It was only being suggested to make Andy Caddick mad. Jonathan Trott or Rob Key would be picked. Or they could stick with the young players they have been developing and backing. Getting the women and gay dudes on-side is important, but surely that will take more than a cameo Test from Ramps to make them all watch.

The pro-Ramps camp was saying he must play as this was a must-win Test. Fuck I hate that saying. Every Test is a must win Test. Anyone who doesn't think that is not thinking straight.

Geoff Miller decided to stop the Ramps madness by saying this: "I'm not ruling anybody out."

Why not? Can't a selector say: "We won't be picking Ramps for a one-off Test as that would be a panic decision and would also fly in the face of the sort of selection policies we have in place?" Not ruling anyone out is bullshit, Robert Croft, Ronnie Irani and Matthew Hoggard are all ruled out. Shaun Udal is ruled out, and my mate Suave is ruled out.

I knew women so excited at this non-statement by Geoff Miller that they went and bought special cricket-themed throwing panties just in case he played.

Ramprakash's dream

In his deepest sleep, he always dreamt of the same thing. The people wanted him; they screamed his name from every corner of the land. They had not seen him in a long time, but his legend had grown with every year he was gone. At first the wise old men were sceptical, but they feared their chance was slipping. He was the hope they needed.

They called upon him.

The telegram arrived on a Tuesday; what a glorious day for good news. The telegram had made him positively gay and giddy. So happy was he that he broke into a dance. His friends came over and asked how he felt about the news? He told them he was happy, confident, that he thought he had deserved this chance and would do his best for his country.

He had always hoped for this day.

There was not a moment during the long winter that he did not long to be back fighting the enemy, winning the people's hearts and taking the spoils. He knew this would not be easy; the first time he tried he went into many battles, and only twice did conquer his opponents.

While he was representing the same army as before, the faces had changed; there were new generals, lieutenants and corporals, but this was not of issue to him. His job was simple and yet dangerous: slay the enemy's mighty beasts. So many times when he was in the wilderness had he slain beasts, but these were puffed-up farm animals, and now he knew that these were, at the very least, angry dogs.

Would his powers, now dulled ever so slightly by his aging exterior, work against this toothy adversary? He knew not the answer. It tormented him.

Every day he grew more and more restless; he could see the battle coming up, would this be his last, would he even survive it? The gayness and giddiness was replaced by a grim foreboding.

Am I still the man to go into war for my country? Was I ever that man?

The torment of not knowing the answer would always wake him up from this dream. He would check his mobile, answering machine, and email looking for Geoff's message, but it was 3am, selectors don't get in touch at that time, they are still out clubbin'.

He tried to go back to sleep. His angst made him clutch his pillow just a little too tight, but his experience had taught him to just take deep breaths and sleep would come. As he fell asleep he said, "This will happen. I can do it. I know I can... Can't I?"

Soon he would be asleep, and the very same dream would happen again.

The Oval

Where Stuart Broad won the Ashes

The weeks leading up to the last Test were pretty hectic for me. Other than laughing at the Ramps story, doing a bit more research on Jonathan Trott and trying to work out who was actually going to win, I took a step back from the Ashes. Not from tiredness, or an Ashes overdose, but because my family had started to turn up for the wedding.

Hours and hours of trolling news services for Ashes titbits was replaced with hearing my dad whinge about Ponting's captaincy and warm beer – he wasn't drinking ale, he just didn't think the lager was cold enough. Then I had to get my clothes for the wedding. That wasn't as easy as it should have been as I had decided that I wanted to get married in old flannels.

You would think buying old cricket flannels in the UK would be easy. It really isn't. I even rang the Lord's Royal (real) Tennis Club, and the dude laughed at me. So then I went all around London with my best man looking for the fucken things, and the best I could side was some snazzy looking bowls trousers. They were white, not cream, but it took me so long to find them, I went with it. The cravat took a while to find as well.

Even while I was planning for the wedding, I was keeping one eye on the cricket. I knew, not because of research, just because I knew, that batting at the Oval was easier than waking up. A teenager – the very talented Leicestershire batsman James Taylor – had made a double hundred there only weeks earlier, and Ramps had opened a café at the Vauxhall end during Surrey matches. This isn't so much a bowling graveyard as a freeway paved over an ancient bowlers' burial ground.

England finally decided to leave Ramps out of the Test, instead choosing to honour their South African quota by picking Jonathan Trott, the terrifically in-form batsman who is over ten years younger than Ramps. The whisper was that Trott didn't like the short stuff, and with Australia probably playing the same unchanged attack of four seamers, he would get plenty of it.

The major change for the English was Andrew Flintoff. He was not merely the heart of the English team, he was almost every vital organ. Without him at Headingley the team looked soulless. And even though he might not have changed the result there, in his last Test he could be the difference. He was still a gimp, but I could only imagine the crowd reaction to him coming on to bowl would be so intense that he would forget about the fact he may never walk properly again and give his all. It looked like Graham Onions was the man who would make way for Freddie. He had taken ten wickets at 30 this series, but the Oval pitch does have bounce, so England wanted Steve Harmison instead.

It came out between Tests that Freddie had thought he was fit enough to play at Headingley. And by came out, I mean Freddie's agent – Chubby Chandler – announced it to the world. Agents are lovely creatures, as we learned in the Stephen Moore section, and here were England, two weeks before an Ashes decider, being caused headaches by one.

It didn't really matter if Freddie was fit in his own mind – it mattered what England wanted. Being that I have the same knee problem as Freddie, and I have continued to play cricket with it, I think I actually, for once, have a genuine insight here. Playing a game of cricket doesn't always hurt my knee, but playing back-to-back games is what really does it for me.

At the end of the Edgbaston Test, Freddie looked like a cripple. I've seen few players more genuinely struggling to move than he was. Even when standing still he looked in pain. All he needed was a Zimmer frame, some casual swearing and he was my Nan. I have already talked about how I think Strauss and Freddie might have had a falling out. And even though they have had their issues over the years, I think this falling out was mostly because Strauss was pissed off at Freddie's "fitness" and decided he wanted 11 men in top condition for the next Test. Although Freddie made a half-century at Edgbaston, he went wicketless.

Australia were more settled. The only change they were contemplating was whether they wanted a spinner or not. Australia wanted to go in with their four quicks, but the whispers were coming out of the Oval that this pitch was going to spin.

With Hilfenhaus safe, Siddle and Johnson coming off five-wicket balls, it seemed to be Stuart Clark that was the soft target. While he had taken three cheap wickets in a very Clarkesque performance on the first day at Headingley, he had also been smashed everywhere by Broad and Swann in the second innings.

There was one huge reason why Australia wanted to play Clark. In the three Tests that Hauritz had played, Australia were 1-0 down. In their one Test with Stuart Clark they had one win. To the Australian camp this meant one thing: with Clark they had a chance to take 20 wickets, with Hauritz there was no guarantee. On the one spinning pitch in the series Hauritz had taken six wickets, but failed to win the match.

It did seem that only the Australian camp thought that Hauritz shouldn't play. They didn't believe in him. It wasn't so much that they thought the wicket wouldn't spin, they just didn't think that playing Hauritz would help them win the game.

It was unintentionally hilarious that they played Hauritz when he didn't believe in himself, and once he did, they didn't want to play him. Ponting wanted strike bowlers. Australia weren't playing for a draw. They wanted to win. If Australia did play for the draw they would lose anyway. Some teams can play for draws, but you need a certain mindset, and this team didn't have it.

Also hilarious was the fact that England had Monty in their squad, and if this was such a spin-friendly track, why would they not bring him in? At Cardiff they went with two spinners, so there was no logical reason not to again. Monty had been in horrible form, not just at Cardiff, but in general. However, he was still in the squad.

I must be honest. My heart and head said Australia should retain the Ashes at the Oval. England's performance at Headingley had swayed me. I was hoping for a last day edge-of-the-seat, cliff-hanging, tight-roped contest, but I feared would be more of a turgid batting draw. England's biggest hope was for one more Australian batting collapse. It didn't seem likely but it could happen.

This series has been impossible to work out since Monty batted at Cardiff. Just when you think you have it worked out it turns into *The Crying Game*.

For this game I have no access to the press box and am in the outer for all five days. I suppose for the deciding game that is the best place to be. I don't want to be in the press box calling Mitchell Johnson an overhyped retard – that is much better said in the outer.

I still felt like the English team owe me one. For every Test match I had had to scrape and scrag to get myself into the press box. Heaps of emails, phone messages and unanswered calls just so that I could get in for the last three days. I could blame the ECB for not allowing me in for the first two days, but in truth the fault lies in the hands of the shithouse English cricket team.

I didn't get many days; I got none at Cardiff, and six for Edgbaston and Lord's. Three more at Headingley would have meant I would have seen a sizeable amount of Ashes cricket live. But you crapped on that, didn't you England? Your shithouse batting completely ruined my three days.

There is a way to make it up to me. Lose the Oval Test.

Dare to dream

With everything going on in my life, I hadn't noticed the one major event that was about to happen to me.

I was about to walk down Camberwell New Road, with my soon-to-be wife and my family, to watch an Ashes-deciding Test at the Oval. I have never been to an Ashes-deciding Test – in Australia they are usually decided at the Gabba toss.

Four Australians and an Englishwoman of Sri Lankan heritage and questionable loyalties – she claimed to be supporting England, but she doesn't really like Freddie – would go down to the ground and watch the match. Less than a week later we would all be back there for the wedding.

I'd never been one of those full-on Australian supporters who lives and dies by the team, but this felt different. I was on enemy soil. I had my family with me. It was the decider.

For me it was the most important Test match I had ever been too.

And that is when I got the Ashes. Or they got me. I might be an Ashes cynic, I might question the strength of these two teams, and I am not a mad Australian supporter. But even thinking of this match was making me nervous. At dinner the night before I hardly finished my burger.

I had butterflies and I wasn't playing. What must these guys have been going through?

You can be remembered for what happens in this sort of Test. You can fail twice against India, in India, in a deciding Test, and no-one back home will remember. Do it in this Test and the fans would eulogise you.

The Ashes should be just another series, but I just don't think I would have felt this way against India or South Africa. I want Australia to beat them too, but this is different. Like the difference between Britney and Madonna.

The Ashes, it's a motherfucker.

Day 1

The first battle for us was to get my cousin a ticket. He was one person above our allocation, and since my mum had started watching cricket and discovered the dreamy (her words not mine) Mitchell Johnson, she had decided to come to all five days. This was fine, except we still had to get him a ticket, so we did the tout thing for a few minutes, my cousin went out the back of some houses with an angry-looking man (with a scar) who tried to charge him over a hundred quid for a ticket.

Then on the giant Oval LED sign we saw tickets available at gate blah blah. How many poor bastards would have bought a ticket on the walk through off a tout at double or more the price and then looked up and seen this sign. Not many, to be honest, as you had to be looking at the sign at the exact nanosecond that it flashed up with the return tickets message Then we all entered the ground. This great old ground just near enough my house that I love it.

There was electricity in the air, a buzz, knife-edge tension. That is what you are supposed to say. The truth is that even sudden-death matches like this are like going on a blind date, but collectively. Everyone is nervous. Mostly you just really want the date to start so you can work out if you are going to get laid that night, find a soul mate, or be emotionally crushed by another human being. That is what I felt anyway – 27,000 people feeling a bit uncomfortable and just wanting the thing to start.

Strauss won the toss, four from five. Not bad at all. He decided to bat. At the Oval that is an obvious decision. Bat as long as you can, then hope the scoreboard pressure does the rest.

Jerusalem was played again. It is even more fucking excruciating when you are in the outer. I don't even get the song. People tried to explain it to me. Some said it was about Jesus coming to England to help the poor; others said it was about being British. I think someone might have even told me it was about a robo-Jesus who kills ninjas. Regardless, its shtick is to make the English crowd more English, in case they forget. I think a fat naked ginger fan wearing the Union Jack as a cape doing commando rolls could do the same thing – and entertain me.

Hilfy started to Strauss. In a lot of ways this had been one of the great battles of this Ashes. Every Test they have been at each other, both under-the-radar players, Hilfy as the working heart of the attack, Strauss as the class of the English line up. Four of the Tests have started this way.

This time Hilfy's first ball wasn't quite the incendiary device that it was at Headingley, and Strauss let it go.

Then there was that pushing and walking around each other that had happened every time Australia had started bowling to England since Mitchell was deposed. The Australian bowlers not quite making the play, the English batsmen not really doing much at all. Siddle was fast, though, noticeably faster than usual, and he beat the bat early on. Hilfenhaus looked medium pace in comparison.

Something had to give, and for the sixth time in this series it was Cook who faltered. Siddle was quick and on the money, but Cook just dangled out his bat, again, and Ponting took the edge comfortably. For all the talk about Ravi Bopara, Cook has had one lucky innings in this series, and even when he is set he looks likely to go.

To settle England down, Ian Bell came out. The man that less than six months ago was terminated at No. 3 for gross shitness, has now got the position back because one batsman got injured and another proved way more useless than him. All the talk of bringing Ramps in was madness, but it seemed almost as bad that for five Tests England came in without a No. 3 they could rely on.

When Johnson finally came on the Test felt like it had started. First ball at his new nemesis, Bell, he almost took out one of his ribs – and then appealed for the fun of it. Next ball Bell almost head-butted a ball I swear he never really saw. To top that he got one straight at the Adam's apple and fended it off in a way that would make Phil Hughes proud. The drinks break came, allowing Bell to start breathing again.

Strauss looked commanding at the crease – quickly in full wing commander mode. What I like about him is the way he puts away bad balls. There is an ease and calmness to it, but it is also dripping in authority. At the other end Bell looked more comfortable until Johnson got one to lift on him, and then he looked as if he didn't want to be out there. That said, he didn't give his wicket away, and he and Strauss put on a very good partnership. Ravi, who?

Just before lunch they both opened up a bit and Strauss smashed three
boundaries in an over off Siddle to bring up a very well played fifty.
Bell joins in the fun and England bolted to the interval with a very
respectable 108 runs off Australia's 26 overs. It was definitely a bowling
slaughterhouse, but Australia hadn't helped themselves, Siddle was well
on top, then just started donating boundaries, while Johnson was okay but
easy enough to score off when he wasn't trying to kill you.

Ponting obviously noticed the run rate, and decided to start with his two
most frugal men after the break. This should be a huge session and if
these two could bat for most of it, Australia could well be chasing tail for
the entire game. Instead Strauss undid all his work with a shocking shot
that got him caught behind. The Oval crowd still hadn't really settled after
lunch, and it shocked most of them.

Collingwood joined Bell in the middle. There is some sort of symmetry
there about both of them contributing nothing in 05, the MBEs and the
gingerness. This was the new Bell though, apparently, and he made it to
his fifty, not a convincing one, but in an Ashes decider an unconvincing
50 is still pretty good. In some ways it was the most low-down and dirty
innings Bell had ever played for his country.

Someone around me whisperered that Hilfy had overstepped in getting
Strauss out; my dad says: "Good." Served and returned. Mitch came on and
had one of his Ashes speciality overs: Wides, leg-side balls, and a boundary.
Only five runs come off it, but it does state that this is not the Mitch who
beat England up on the second afternoon at Headingley. Australia could
use that Mitch now. The game seemed to go into a bit of a lull. Bell and
Collingwood choked the life out of the innings, and the crowd talked
amongst themselves.

North finally came on for Australia when it was blatantly obvious that this
was not a wicket to keep ploughing through with quicks. From the few balls
the Oval big screen was allowed to show, it looked like he was getting some
turn. The Sky team would be frothing at the mouth over this. Especially
Warne. Before anyone could digest it Collingwood had a brain fade and

edged one to gully. The ball before he played and missed at a similar ball, and Siddle just went back to the top of the mark and replicated it, waiting for the error. And they say batsmen are the smart ones. The vampiric partnership was worth 52 runs off just a biscuit less than 20 overs.

In came England's latest South African. I'd seen Trott a few times on TV, and knew he was small, but for some reason he seemed to be wearing his bigger brother's pads. He looked like a ten-year-old kid promoted to the under-14s. Seeing a debutant, Siddle, now bowling seriously fast, decided to test out the middle of the pitch. Trott handled it all well except for a weird walk down the wicket that almost ran him out.

Somehow, even early on Trott looked more comfortable than Ian Bell, even though Bell was in his 49th (fucken hell) Test and well set. Australia really wanted to try Trott out with the short ball, so even North bounced him. Spinners don't bowl bouncers enough, and no, I'm not kidding. Trott took a lot of balls to get off the mark, but it didn't seem to bother him. Mature age South African batsman may be the future for England. At tea England are 3/180. The crowd were still strangely quiet; they were waiting for something to grab them one way or the other.

Almost straight after tea Ian Bell departed with a textbook bit of tentativeness. He barely poked at the ball, and Siddle crashed through his stumps. Siddle is the crashing type. Bell had had his luck again, and then toughed it out. He had made 72, which smacked of good, not great – and not enough.

Siddle's spell before and after tea was just great. This wasn't going to go down as a great Ashes debut series from him, but it was days like this that proved to the selectors that he is their man. Nine overs, five maidens, two wickets for 11 runs. Was that right? This was a flat pitch, no swing, no seam, and England were only two wickets down, and yet he had just pumped and pumped away at them.

Trott continued to look obscenely comfortable in Test cricket. He didn't play any big shots, or do anything risky, he just batted with a cool head. Prior did not look as good at the other end; you can usually tell after about five balls what sort of day he is going to have. When Mitchell hit him on the gloves he looked worried and next ball he fell to one of those Mitchell slower balls. Such an indignant way to go, I'd rather get an inswinging yorker or go down hooking.

Then the Oval crowd woke up. They knew who was coming out.

The man came out to the sort of applause that makes young men want to take up cricket and makes girls with dubious morals want to take up cricketers. It was as if Jesus had come in, dishing out beer and ice-cream.

They stood as one unit, they applauded, they cheered, they shouted, they awed.

He did what he always does, he left his helmet off for long enough for the warmth to wash over him. The crowd gave him the final inspiration he needed before taking on the filthy convicts.

The crowd loved every step he took. He was hope. Nineteen balls later he was gone. And the crowd ignored his exit. The hope was gone. All they were left with was a large northern lad with a fucked-up knee and seven useless runs.

The opposition's all-rounder, someone who knew something about hope, had humbled him pretty easily with a selection of short and full balls, and the cheer he got for coming onto the ground was going to have to be enough in his penultimate Test innings. The silence was not meant to be a slight, but it was. They wanted, expected, hoped for more, and he couldn't provide it, so they did the crowd version of turning their backs on him.

For thousands of people in the ground this may be the last time they ever see him play, and he exited the field to the sound of *The Times* being ruffled and chats about law firms.

Freddie's waft left England a bit stuffed. Trott was still doing the business, but at 6/247 on this pitch it was not the situation England would have hoped for. There looked like there were a lot of runs in this pitch. Not pretty runs, but grafting, head-down runs, and Trott looked set for them. He just needed a partner.

Marcus North had been bowling for a while now, and he did seem to be spinning the ball and making the batsmen check their strokes. In many ways he looked more dangerous to play than Hauritz, but he knew what his role actually was – to get through as many overs as cheaply as possible. He was an over-rate bowler, his job was to make sure Ricky didn't get suspended.

Shane Watson came on for the 74th-over mark. That is when Paul Collingwood usually comes on. I felt like I could hear the sighs of every Australian fan in the ground, and also some in the flats behind the stands. Second ball he got taken for four after gifting a leg glance to Trott, but last ball of the over he bowled one that hit Trott's pads and was given not out. It must have been close as there was no replay on the big screen. My lady, listening to the commentary, told me it was hitting HawkEye's leg stump.

But in the next over Trott got out in an even more bizarre way than being leg-before to Shane Watson, amazingly. He flicked a ball from North firmly off his pads and set off for the run, but his flick stuck in Katich's hand at short leg, and not only did it stick, but the Australian fielder got enough power to throw it back into the stumps and run Trott out. It seemed a rotten way for a debutant to get out when he had looked so good, but Watson probably thought it was an elaborate plot to stop him from getting wickets.

Anger seems to suit Watson, and he actually bowled at a decent pace, getting an inside edge from Stuart Broad that went for four and bringing another edge that fell just short of Ponting. I told my dad Phil Hughes could bowl this well. He grunted. With North having found a nice rhythm as well, Ponting held back from taking the new ball and let his two "all-rounders" have a real dip. It was a surprisingly gutsy move by Ponting, but the next three overs produced no real chances and it meant there were three fewer overs of the new ball for Swann and Broad to face.

Siddle took the new ball, Ponting rewarding his angry Victorian. But he resisted bouncing Swann too much in the first over and this allowed Swann to bring up England's 300 with a tasty cover drive. But he did not have to wait long to claim him as a victim, Swann edging behind a ball that was a few levels too good for him. It left England at 8/308 at stumps.

We went to the pub, The Black Sheep, to discuss the day's play. The general feeling was that England should have made way more on this wicket. Bell and Collingwood seemed to stifle the great start that Strauss made and, after that, only Trott seemed intent on batting positively.

There was a touch of déjà vu about the day; it reminded me of the first day of the Cardiff Test when you had all the build up but, at the end of it, few questions had been answered. Three hundred runs on the board was, wait for it, 300 runs on the board. England had underperformed, perhaps massively, but Australia still had to get there. Australia would have been happy that the match was still wide open, England would have been happy with over 300 runs in a day.

And there were other good things to come out of the day: my mum had her first Pimm's in 20 years, and neither my cousin or father got into an argument with anyone.

Tories and Canadians

I was very disappointed with the atmosphere at the Oval today. England's opening batsmen Andrew Strauss and Alastair Cook came out to polite applause, *Jerusalem* was played without any roar from the crowd, Ian Bell and Paul Collingwood were allowed to bat like cadavers without abuse and the crowd mostly talked about their (insert law/stockbroking) firms during play.

The last session was a cracker. But the crowd just couldn't get into it. Even the Barmy Army were amazingly quiet. There was no chanting, no singing, and no Aussie-bating.

With such an atmosphere it was very easy to hear the conversations in the crowd.

One of these was a cricket conversation so painful I wanted to pull the plastic chair out of the concrete, find out where the children of the people infecting my ears lived and smash them to death.

It was a guy explaining cricket to a Canadian with "baseball speak" and no fucken idea of cricket. I couldn't possibly explain every stupid thing he said, but this bit is so stupid it has to be retold.

She asked about runs, and after five minutes of trying to use baseball talk – a sport he clearly had no idea about either – he said this: "Both batsman run, so you can never have less than one run scored at a time."

Fucken hell. Who was this assclown to tell anyone about anything?

His tone of voice was the worst, he was so sure of himself. Dickhead. I didn't say anything, as I didn't want to get involved in a conversation that would hurt me this bad. I've done it before, and at the end I just feel dirty.

Luckily, another of his group came up with the correct information. But the dickhead couldn't accept that, so he then questioned the bloke who actually knew about cricket by saying: "Okay, if you know cricket so well, if the one batsman hits it, and they both run, who gets the runs?"

Just shut the fuck up you stupid little man. Shut up shut up shut up shut up shut up shut up shut up shut up shut up shut up shut up shut up shut up shut up shut up shut up shut up shut up.

I can still hear him talking in my head, and I am regretting not ending his life when I had my chance.

Day 2

I got gentle ribbing, mild mocking and some heavy abuse about my position on the game after day one for the pieces I wrote online. According to others, England's score was formidable and Australia would have to bat really well to get close to it. The pitch was falling apart, the Ashes were staying in

England and I couldn't read a game of cricket. Some did agree with me that the pitch was fine and England had underperformed.

I even went back and watched an illegal highlights package of the day to see what I had missed. The ball hadn't swung or seamed, it had spun, but England's spinner had taken only six wickets in four Tests. The pitch was good for batting: Strauss and Bell had shown that. And the conditions were placid enough that Trott, on his debut, could look extremely comfortable throughout his innings. To me Australia would have been happy to have England all but out for around 300 on a wicket like this.

To be honest, I think Ashes nerves had got to everyone. Players, fans, commentators, writers, even the strippers plugging their business out the front of the Oval looked nervous. It was just that sort of situation.

Everyone thought their way of reading the first day was correct, but when one side makes 300, but loses eight wickets, it is pretty damn even. If by the end of day two Australia were 3/300, 300 was a bad score; if Australia had stumbled to 150 all out, it wasn't.

Day two started well with my cousin now aware of where to get his tickets, but this time he had to sit behind the Barmy Army. This gave him a sense of trepidation. The rest of us were also seated close to the Barmy Army, and wondered if this would ruin our whole day. In general I have no problem with the Barmy Army, but I'd never sat near them, which could change things a bit.

The play began excellently, not just for Australia, but for cricket: James Anderson made a duck. I got up and screamed. I had been waiting for this day since the first time the "Jimmy no duck" stats started getting bandied around. At this stage I was probably the loudest person in the ground. Anyone not aware of the momentous occasion must have thought I was the most parochial man in the ground. They didn't know I was an anger-filled guy who really hated Jimmy's record for no particular reason.

Australia had a chance to wrap up the innings quickly as Siddle bounced Broad, but Johnson shelled it coming in from fine leg. Siddle fumed, but the crowd loved it. Harmy got away some nice shots and dirty slogs, and Broad picked up a couple of boundaries but eventually Hilfy got Broad slogging. Siddle ended with four wickets and England had made 332. Siddle had probably never deserved five wickets more.

If Hilfenhaus to Strauss was one great battle of the Ashes, then Anderson to Watson is its comic relief (apart from the occasional Johnson wayward spell). Anderson is a swing bowler of prodigious talent; he can win a game on his own when the conditions are in his favour. Yet in four Test matches he had only 12 wickets. He had postured with the best of them in this series, yet at the moment his greatest achievement was his batting with Monty at Cardiff.

Watson is comical at the best of times. He was injured before the Tests even started, stalked Phil Hughes's place, doubted Brett Lee's fitness, bowled the worst spell in the Ashes, then somehow turned himself into a punishing opening batsman. After a good shot, and sometimes a good leave, he seems to hold the position for just long enough for every cameraman to snap it. When Anderson takes on Watson they seem to be fighting out some sort of Realty TV male model show. And that is how the Australia reply started, Watson stuck at Anderson's end, and Katich at Freddie's end. Katich and Freddie must have shared a laugh as the Mimbos strutted around.

Watson struggled early on, Anderson and Freddie hitting him on the pads, and according to radio, and at least one of them was plumb. I didn't know. There were very few replays being shown on the giant screens and generally those that were not of the balls I actually wanted to see. What I wanted was boundaries, edges, lbw shouts, balls that swing, seam or spin, and close calls. But that didn't happen.

When you are at the ground, and not in a million-pound seat, you are dependent on replays for a feel of what the ball is doing. From square on you just can't really tell. So when the ball beats the bat or hits the pad, you really need a replay on the big screen. At the Oval they had two screens but both were useless fucken things because they hardly ever showed replays. I haven't been in the stands enough to know if this is a common thing, but it drove me and my family nuts. I've been in the press box or at home with unlimited replays. My family has come from the MCG, where sometimes you get to see three or four balls an over. What good is a screen if it is not used? Being that sponsors pay money to get their brand on them, it still doesn't make sense, because people would look at them more often if they knew there was going to be a replay. Instead the best you got was random replays that didn't tell you enough. My dad never failed to mention that a replay wasn't shown.

Australia got through the first 12 overs of Anderson and Freddie and then brought on Swann and Harmsion. Broad was still a third change bowler it assumes. Six wickets just wasn't enough to change that. Swann's first over was a tight, non-spinning maiden; Harmy's first ball was garbage. Australia looked to get to lunch easily enough, and then were helped by a little bit of rain.

The rain was just drizzle, but it stuck around for an hour. The chat suggested the game was now dead level. I do love cricket – everyone trying to work out who is in front before both sides have completed an innings. Other sports are too easy. Who is in front? The bloke leading the race, stupid. Who is in front? Well, India only made 236, but on this wicket, and considering New Zealand's batting of late, I'd say India. There were dozens of conversations like this going on. The break was enhancing the tension as fans had time to sit around and really consider how close the game, the series and the Ashes themselves were.

After an hour and a half of pontificating, we got some more action. Broad was brought on, third change, but it was still only the 23rd over of the innings, so not too bad. It got a lot better when he trapped Watson with a ball that faded back in. It was a good ball, but Watson was very late on it. Watson was out, for the third time in the series, straight after a break. Australia were 1/73.

Ponting's entry was greeted, surprisingly, with no real boos. Memo to Giles Clarke: see what happens when you don't tell people what to do. The wicket had also fired up the crowd. For the first day and a half, they have mostly been whisper quiet, but Broad has lifted them. The roar for him getting to fine leg was intense.

Even Freddie looked more with it now. Those weeks off have done him some good as well. He was now moving like a 40-year-old again. His first ball to

Ponting was greeted with an "ooohhh" from the crowd. It was a shit ball down the leg-side. I remarked on this, and got some looks from those around me.

Ponting looked nervous. Not that he always starts like a superstar, but sometimes he looks like he is not sure that it's his day. He got off the mark with a French cut that almost sent the bloke behind me into cardiac arrest. Freddie got at him too, putting in a huge shout for lbw, and everyone in the ground seemed to appeal with him. I can't see whether it was out or not.

And then Ponting was out. Chopping on a ball from Broad that cut back into him. It was not a great effort from Ponting, but he probably didn't expect the ball to rip back off the seam like that. Now Australia were in trouble – not so much because Ponting was out, but because the ball was moving. And their least reliable batsman was walking in.

Australia had been carrying Mike Hussey for over half of his career. On the day that the Ashes could effectively be decided he was coming in at two wickets down. Lots of people ask me why I am so harsh on Hussey, well this is why: this was the time we needed our No. 4 to be a fully functioning Test batsman, and instead we got someone coming to the crease who had not been in form for more than 18 months. Ponting could back Hussey all he wanted, but England knew he was a wicket.

Michael Hussey's numbers

41 Tests
3196 Test match runs.
First 20 Tests – 2120.
Second 21 Tests – 1076.
Average in first 20 – 84.
Average in second 21 – 30.
Hundreds in first 20 – 8.
Hundreds in second 21 – 1.
Number of back up middle order batsman Australia have in their squad – 0.
Times I have mentioned Hussey's shit form – 1076.
Number of times Australia has seriously thought about dropping him – 0.

Hussey had an over to watch Katich bat, before he had to face up to Broad. He left his first ball, showing a sly sense of humour, he defended the next on the back foot, but it was the third ball that did it. Hussey went to leave, but then seeing the ball straighten tried to jam his bat down. But it was too late, he was trapped right in front, and Billy Bowden practically appeals himself.

Fuck it. Such a pathetic effort.

The Oval was now screaming. The dull hum of work nonsense from day one had been replaced with a group animal intensity. They saw where this was going. And they wanted it.

Michael Clarke seemed to be letting the crowd scream itself out when he first got in. His first ball from Broad, was a shocker, down the leg-side, but the crowd "ooohhh" again. He mad it through his over, only to hear them scream more when Broad got down to fine leg. It was on the other side of the ground, but just for a second I thought I saw a young girl faint. Anderson was at the other end, but no-one cared.

For Broad was not finished. He tossed up an outswinger to Clarke, who reached for it and guided it straight into the hands of short cover. It looked like a plan. Clarke surely would have recognised it, but probably didn't think he would hit it straight down the throat of the fielder. But with the wickets coming thick and fast, it wasn't the smartest choice of stroke.

It should be mentioned that Simon Katich was still at the other end. The stoic, hirsute-chested man was looking very tight as his team fell apart around him. There was not much he could do, England were not giving him much to counterattack with, and Katich is not a momentum shifter, he is a rock, a krab, a tick. He was doing his job, but he was the only one.

Swann replaced Anderson, which was a good move from Strauss because North does not handle Swann well early in his innings, and Swann has two of his beloved left-handers to aim at. It didn't take long for North to go. Swann bowled his undercutting straight one and Asad Rauf shoots North straight out. Almost straight away you heard that tremendous phenomenon of everyone saying: "North hit it, Sky/TMS have just said". It hardly mattered, the ship was half fucken sunk anyway.

Soon afterward, Katich brought up his fifty, it is a terrific effort. He had somehow managed not to trip up on the corpses of the rest of the top order. However, he could only last so long, and next over he got a massive edge onto his pad that ended up in the hands of short-leg. When Haddin tried a clip to mid-wicket to a ball that swung away and took out his off stump, Australia have lost 7/35. That is a proper collapse and those experts in collapses, England, would have been proud of it.

With the Australia score on 111, I started screaming for Ponting to declare. It was insane, but my reasoning was that the only way Australia could grab some moral highground was to declare just under the follow-on mark and make Strauss look like a pansy for refusing to enforce it. Ponting, insulated in the dressing-room 150 metres away, didn't appear to hear me.

Siddle and Johnson did well to slow down the flow of wickets, but Mitch was undone by a lovely sharply spinning delivery that he didn't need to drive out of the footmarks and Australia were now 8/131.

Broad bowled the last over of the session. The expectation was amazing. He had bowled unchanged for the entire session, and he still almost slipped a yorker through Siddle. He was buggered though, bowling purely on emotion like England's other all-rounder does. But he couldn't make another breakthrough, and had to placate himself with the five wickets he had taken in this session – and the eight England have taken.

I suddenly realised that Australia were going to lose the Ashes. What a bastard of a realisation that was.

I turned to my dad and said: "Could be worse; we've gone past the follow-on." He tried to chuckle, but he didn't have it in him. My family is renowned for its black humour, but there was very little of it during the tea break. My cousin came over, swore and paced up and down. He only swears and paces when he is truly upset. My mum wanted to know how it happened. I tried to explain that Broad moved the ball, and we struggle with the moving ball, but she looked more confused so I stopped. My cousin enquired about the punishment for digging up the pitch.

After tea England went about cleaning up the tail, Clark came forward to one from Swann and it went to Cook at short-leg. Straightaway my dad screamed that he didn't hit it. Some English fans laughed at him, but a couple of seconds later it came through the headphones that Clark has missed that by a distance. How my 61-year-old-glasses-wearing dad saw it from 100 metres away square to the wicket, and Asad Rauf missed it from straight in front, I don't know.

Siddle proved, yet again, that he was a fighter, putting in some agricultural work to get Australia to 160 before Freddie swooped in to ruin Swann's hopes of a five-wicket haul by knocking Hilfy over.

When Australia came back out for England's second innings Ricky seemed to be giving them a right serve. And so he fucken should. What a shit performance. It didn't help though, because after ten overs of Siddle and Hilfenhaus both bowling decently enough, England were still none-for. Ponting opted for spin and North was brought on. I could only imagine that Nathan Hauritz was crying. Australia had no faith in him on this pitch? This one? North was spinning the ball a long way, and in his second over he got Cook – not that that is hard to do any more – caught at slip. It was a good ball, but Warne, on Sky, made it sound like his Gatting ball.

At the other end Australia went with Johnson, and he greeted Bell with a bouncer before, two balls later, the batsman clipped one on his pads into the freakishly good hands of Katich at short-leg. Katich was having some game: two pieces of freaky fielding to go with effectively batting on his own in the first innings.

Mitchell was looking brutal. I looked at the scoreboard, and thought about the pitch. Surely if the ball didn't swing again, any chase of under 400 was more than gettable. I started to believe again. Then just as I processed that Australia were still in this game, Paul Collingwood shat himself all over a short ball from Johnson and the score was 3/39.

I looked at my dad, but we said nothing because we didn't want to jinx this. But we knew that Trott was in next, and surely the pressure had to get to him eventually, and after that were the attacking batsmen.

I started taking deep breaths, trying to keep my head. There was no reason to get too excited. But there was hope.

England were now on the defensive. Trott and Strauss just had to get through to stumps. Johnson gave it a couple of big overs, but he couldn't break through and Nathan's sobbing must have grown louder when North and Katich were entrusted with the last few overs as Australia tried to rush through their overs and grab a wicket. They got the overs in, but they didn't get a wicket.

Being an Australian who had spent all day close to the Barmy Army I was impressed. They never pissed me off. Their songs, whilst being boring and monotonous, do give the ground some atmosphere. And since England had just realised they were going to win the Ashes, they were way more humble than I thought they should have been.

Just after stumps I heard that Collingwood was out off a no-ball as well. I quickly tried to calculate how many mistakes the umpires had made in two days, I think I got to seven or eight. The standard of umpiring in this series had been poor, even by poor's standards. More than a few people have commented that the top umpire in the world for the last five years, Simon Taufel, an Australian, is not eligible to stand.

As an Australian you left with some reasons not to kill yourself, as an English fan you left knowing that one decent day, not even a great day, and you would win the Ashes. I would have liked to know what that felt like. But I didn't.

We were all very quiet at the pub, even my Wife-Elect, as she didn't know what to say. I talked about how I thought Asad Rauf went off for a piss at one stage. But mostly we stuck to drinking. It seemed better than any conversation about the cricket.

None of us were really braced for being in this position

Mr Cricket retires

King Probot Michael Hussey has done something the selectors should have done a long time ago; he has sacked himself from cricket. Sure he is calling it a retirement. But we all know a good sacking when we see it.

He said: "I have struggled for a long time and I think this is the right time to go. I owe the guys better than what I am able to give them. I love playing cricket for Australia, but all good things must come to an end. My family has always been very important to me and it will be great to spend more time with them. Batting never came as easy to me as it did to others, but I am proud of what I achieved."

Hussey leaves the game with a batting average of over 50, the final statistical anomaly we will ever get from him. I have never been a huge fan, but he did make one of the best hundreds I have ever seen when Graeme Smith gave him boundary riders at the G and he and McGrath just batted as they pleased.

There are few people who love him or hate him, and this is what has always annoyed me about him. But when he was good he was better than you, and anyone you know.

When my grandkids say to me, "Grandpa Jrod, how good was Michael Hussey?" I will say something like this: "He was a frenetic overachieving earnest bastard who proved the existence of the Matrix for about 18 Tests, and for the rest he was a nervous wreck with a legacy position who should have been dropped long before he retired. Now go get me an iBeer.

I think it is good Test cricket has players like him, so that when the real class comes along we can see the difference. But how many people strangled out their talent as well as Mr Hussey?

I respect him, even if he wasn't my bag of skittles.

Disclaimer: Certain sections of this post, like the bit where Hussey retires, may have been fabricated. I apologise to the English journalist who thought this was real.

Bilal Shafayat isn't a terrorist... and has money to prove it

After the Cardiff Test a hard-hitting journalist brought your attention to a racist comment from David Penberthy over at The Punch, the Australian website. Now this from the ECB:

Nationwide News have agreed to pay significant damages and costs as well as offering an unreserved apology for offensive remarks made in a website article written by David Penberthy, an Australian journalist. Bilal Shafayat has generously decided to donate the damages to the Cricket Foundation's Chance to Shine initiative. The offending article has also been removed from the website on which it was published. The apology offered to Bilal reads as follows:

> *A few weeks ago I made a stupid and offensive joke in a piece written in the immediate aftermath of the drawn opening Ashes Test. It involved the alleged time-wasting tactics of the English side in the dying moments of the game, and referred to a private SMS exchange with a friend of mine that joked about the appearance of 12th man Bilal Shafayat.*

> *While I wrote the piece that the text message was clearly offensive – and had construed the piece as a self-deprecating look at the stupid behaviour of sports fans – the decision to publish this private SMS was of itself the truly stupid aspect of the article.*

> *This is because it was not only insulting and demeaning to a decent man and sporting professional in Bilal Shafayat, and anyone else who faces ridicule on the basis of their appearance. I was going to apologise at*

the time and shut the piece but I didn't, for two reasons. The first was that I didn't want to be accused of trying to whip the issue up to drive traffic to the website. And given that life doesn't come with a reverse button I thought that shutting the piece was a convenient out and that I should just wear it, as shown by our publication of many comments critical of the piece.

We have had a request from Bilal Shafayat through his lawyers for us to delete the piece from the website and we have now done that. I've also written to him personally and use this post to say publicly that I wish that life did come with a reverse button and that I'd never published this stupid joke.

We're not going to invite comment on this post because I don't want it to be a traffic-driving exercise, nor to open up a debate about whether the apology is warranted or not. I think it's totally unwarranted and it's offered sincerely and without reservation to Mr Shafayat and anyone else who found the piece distressing.

David Penberthy

Now I am glad that only a couple of sites ran with this story, because if I had got it in the news then the site would have got publicity, but this way I got to bag him, and Dean Jones, and Bilal got it taken down. Everybody won. Some who commented on my site pointed out that he said the apology was "unwarranted". This was a typo, a very fucken unfortunate typo that was fixed. I doubt it was Freudian.

I have not received my thank you from Bilal or the ECB, but I am sure it is forthcoming. As for Penberthy, nothing says I'm sorry like being forced to apologise by lawyers.

Broad's Barmitzvah

Bang. Pow. Kaboom. That is what the pitch was doing. Every single ball England bowled was a grenade, cluster bomb, or water balloon filled with rotten eggs. Wasn't it?

No, the pitch was fine. The puppy-dog boy-band member with a shocking bowling average and Test bloodline did the real damage. He may have won England the Ashes in one session.

There was always a chance Australia would lose the Ashes. That I could accept, even if I didn't like it. But Stuart Broad winning the Ashes? No, I couldn't handle that.

I thought Broad could chip in with bat and ball, maybe take a five-wicket haul, score a 60 or two. I didn't expect him to take five wickets in one session and completely rip out Australia's heart and leave it pulsating in the middle of the Oval.

At 0/73, on a pitch that still seemed to have lots of runs in it, Australia were cruising along. Katich had dug himself into the dusty surface, Watson had been lucky, but steady, and for a little while 332 seemed like a hurdle Australia could handle.

Then Broad was given the ball, and like some magical fairytale shit he turned into a real Test bowler. One who could lift his team above their average station and turn the enemy into a snivelling bunch of batting assclowns. Strauss was the fairy godmother character that took Swann off even though he was bowling well and let Broad loose.

It was quite a turn around from Edgbaston and bowling the 51st over.

What he did wasn't revolutionary: he bowled a good length, a great line, and he moved the ball in the air a little bit both ways. It wasn't the experimental Broad with the seam sideways, cutting down the side of the ball, or bowling revolutionary lines.

Simple swing bowling on a full length, he didn't even need to come around the wicket.

Stuart Broad can have a shit career from here on in, get caught with drugs and under-age Filipino dwarfs, start a crusade against pornography, or just stop playing cricket, but he will always be remembered for the second day at the Oval.

Day 3

Amongst some Australians there were some complaints about the pitch.

But it wasn't the spin or crumbling pitch that did Australia in, nor the two shit decisions. It was their 2005 nemesis, the swinging ball. Not massive swing straight out of the hand but late swing that moved just enough to hit the pad, or beat the edge. The only victim of Broad's that wasn't from some swing was Ponting, and his ball cut back in like a drunk driver.

Swann did take four wickets, but he only did the cleaning up once Broad had brought in the bulldozer. Two of his four wickets were blatantly not out in any case. And two of them came from no spin at all. Plus, and this is the kicker, Australia could have picked a spinner if they had wanted to, or believed in one. They didn't, and that is their problem. Abusing the pitch was wank.

And blaming the pitch was underselling the excellence of Stuart Broad. This Ashes has clearly changed me: beforehand I would have happily undersold anything to do with Broad.

My cousin got tickets again, three from three, all from the official gate for the ticketed price. Take that, touts.

The first ball of the day was one of beauty, mystery and ultimately unfulfilling for the Australians. Everyone at the ground seemed to assume that Siddle's first ball had taken the edge of Trott's bat. The Aussies got excited, the English dropped their heads. It took more than a moment or two for people to realise that Asad Rauf had given it not out. It was the correct decision, the radio said. Damn. Next ball, Trott sort of scooped the ball in the air, but safely.

I know it sounds weird, but after those two balls Australia looked like they were playing for the declaration. I am sure they weren't. But they seemed to lose any zip. They were inconsistent, and the English batsmen seemed to handle the lack of pressure very well.

Australia did try some interesting tactics. Clark bowled to Strauss round the wicket into the footholes with a silly point. Our tickets on that day were at fine leg, and we were looking straight into the eyeline of Simon Katich, who was the poor bastard in there. Because of the width that Clark was bowling, and the positive intent of Strauss, Katich spent most of his time trying to get into the foetal position each ball. It was hilarious.

This was a session that belonged to Strauss and Trott. Early on, they scored with the many opportunities Siddle and Johnson gave them, later they dealt with Clark's tactic and played North carefully. What Clark was doing was keeping the runs down, and it was bothering Strauss, even if he wasn't going to get out to it, so he started giving Clark the slow walk so he could get to the ball on the half-volley and smashed it though cover twice. It was great batting; Ponting took Clark off that over. Strauss was now past 50.

It also proved that for all the commotion over the pitch, it was a pretty easy surface to bat on. England were scoring quickly without taking many chances, and while you needed to think a little unconventionally at times, and ignore puffs of dirt, it was not a wicket that was likely to get you out. Australia tried Michael Clarke for a while, but it seemed the only thing he brought to the game was Trott's fifty.

Strauss could see this, he is a smart man. The walking down the pitch told you he was thinking about this more than most would. He knew that this was an important partnership, the one to knock back Australia's hopes of rolling England cheaply. There were plenty of runs in this wicket, and England would need to be a long way in front of Australia, especially with Australia's habit of making a great effort in the second innings.

The fact that Andrew Strauss was captain of a team that was probably going to win the Ashes is amazing. In late 2007 he found himself out of the English set-up altogether, partly due to selection and partly because he knew he needed a break. There was a chance he would be lost to the game altogether. Like many modern batsmen, he had technical flaws, and he had been worked out.

No-one had ever doubted his talent, or his determination, though. But a return of two fifties in 20 innings had meant his career could have gone either way. When he came back into the team he made a very scratchy, yet ultimately career saving hundred against New Zealand, and within 12 months he was the England captain.

It was down to his strength of character that few doubted this elevation. Strauss had now got himself into amazing form, and through luck, hard work, and talent he was about to write his name into the history books.

That is why it was such a shock to see him get out five minutes before lunch to Marcus North. Not that it was a bad ball – it spun out of the footmarks – but Straus looked so set for a captain's hundred, I couldn't believe he had nicked one to slip. It meant that England were now 4/157 with a lead of 329, and Australia still had some sort of sniff, however faint.
The last ball before lunch Matt Prior smacked a drive into the turf from North, and it kicked up and smacked Ricky Ponting, fielding at silly point, right in the mouth. The crowd was quick to "ohhh" and "ahhh", and then chuckle. Then there was the realisation that Ponting was actually bleeding. Some still laughed, even as he spat out a whole hunk of blood. I may, or may not, have been one of them.

I think Ricky just needs to accept the fact that the Oval does not like him. He was now on his way to a successive loss of the Ashes on this ground; Gayle killed Australia's Twenty20 campaign here. He got the only ball in the game that seriously seamed off the surface in the first innings, and now he has a gob full of claret from a cover drive that seemed to zero in on his mouth. Something about this ground hates him.

After lunch Matt Prior did an interesting thing. Sensing the crowd really wanted to see Freddie, he hit the ball straight to Katich, took off for the single and ran himself out by a long way.

Freddie came out to a huge roar. As much as I like Freddie, I have to wonder if anyone has ever received such adulation for producing so little. Jennifer Lopez, maybe. Ponting went over and shook Flintoff's hand . No-one boos that.

By now the crowd was well and truly humming. Their quietness in the morning was understandable as everyone knew how important that partnership was, but Freddie assured them it was party time as he heaved a ball from North over mid-wicket. The crowd applauded like Freddie had just given them each a new car.

At the other end Siddle was still fighting. I loved Siddle the first time I saw him bowl for Victoria. I loved him more when he took on the full strength NSWales team on a pudding pop wicket. My love went further when he started international cricket by sconing Gautum Gambhir, and I all but consummated the love when he took down South Africa. But today, I wanted to give him a hug. He hadn't always been on song in this series. He had struggled to control himself, struggled to control England, and too often hadn't bowled at his best. Today, he was 100% desperation. As always. Yet again he couldn't get the breakthrough he wants.

Luckily for Australia then that Freddie's desire for a stunning cameo led to him finding Siddle on the rope off North. He departed to a stunning ovation.

The amazing thing was that Stuart Broad got the same ovation for coming out. Obviously the baton was being passed. But what baton is that? Some still claim that Freddie was ruined by the adulation from 05, and even though Broad is a smarter guy, this sort of adulation leads to people standing naked on rooftops claiming they are descendants of alien warlords.

Broad's shots were also cheered with religious glee. He is probably the luckiest batsmen I have seen; almost every time I see him bat he gets dropped. I think he has a special way of mistiming the ball that makes it hard to read. Marcus North was the latest to let him off by shelling a simple caught and bowled.

The crowd didn't care. A drop got a cheer, a single got a cheer, a leg-bye got a cheer, and a four got a raucous roar. They were on their feet for almost every run. Those who noticed cheered the fact England now led by more than 400.

Broad, drunk on the acclaim, skied one from North and Ponting finishes him off. And then he got a standing ovation for his short innings. I may have just seen something special. Flintoff and Broad may have just played the two most celebrated innings of 20-odd in the history of Test cricket. One day I would tell my kids I was there when Broad and Freddie both made 20-odds, it was wonderful.

With the score on 6/243, Swann came in to what was his kind of environment. The atmosphere in the ground was more like a rock concert. He had always wanted to be a rock star. He got away a few big shots and the crowd jumped up and down.

Australia decided against taking the new ball, and even threw the ball to Katich before tea. England added 133 runs in the middle session for the loss of three wickets. These were the most celebrated 133 runs I've ever seen.

After tea the new ball *was* taken. It seemed to have been taken for the sole purpose of making Swann score quicker. And he did. He eased himself past a run a ball and was now batting like Broad or Freddie wanted to. Trott joined in with some boundaries, but mostly he got Swann on strike so he could slash, hoick and slap the ball around. He brought up his fifty from 44 balls.

Swann was so excited that he celebrated it like it was a hundred, taking his helmet off, saluting every last person in the stands. What the moment really called for was hundreds of panties to be thrown on the ground, while, with the lights dimming around him, Swann walked to the boundary edge to touch the hand of every last woman and took a few swigs from beers sitting on the fence.

That didn't happen, instead he just kept going for it, and that was cool too. But he got too close to the sun eventually and top-edged a hook shot of Hilfy. He left the ground to similar adulation afforded to the previous two all-rounders. If Freddie was a spiteful man, he would be a little pissed that he didn't get more of cheer than these new guys – I mean he was winning Ashes before Stuart Broad was shaving; I wonder if Broad shaves now.

Trott is still there. If Swanny was the rock star then Trott was the roadie. Almost all day he had been ignored as bigger names, bigger hitters, and bigger egos had come and gone. He had just played a proper dignified Test innings. Without him, England could not have got this lead in such quick time.

He still managed to get nervous in the 90s with an inside edge going close enough to the stumps to give his parents, who were in the crowd, heart attacks. Two balls later he flicked one away to the fence through mid-wicket and brought up his hundred. A top effort, but the crowd's reaction was different from what it was for the other guys. Their clapping matched his innings; it wasn't the fanatic hollering of before, but a solid line of applause. Trott had made a mockery of everyone who thought you shouldn't make your Test debut in an Ashes decider. He had assured England of victory.

After finally departing for 119, caught by North off Clark – obviously that was why Clark was playing, for that one wicket – England declared. The Australians didn't celebrate, they trudged off behind Trott, who soaked up the crowd love. England had set Australia a target of 546 runs. That was a biggy.

For the last time in this series Jimmy Anderson and Shane Watson wrestled with the new ball. I would miss this. Anderson dropped one short to Watson who put everything into a pull shot. I do enjoy the Watson pull shot; there is a masculine innocence about it.

Watson and Katich wanted to appear positive – and there is no better way of doing that than trying to run yourself out at every opportunity. Twice Watson took on Bell, and while on neither occasion could Bell hit the stumps, it was a shaky, unnecessary start. Strauss seemed to read the pitch well; he favoured catchers in front of the wicket rather than behind it. But it is still a defensive field considering the total to chase was floating in the clouds.

It took only eight overs of pace nonsense for Swann to come on. Harmison at the other end is leaking runs, but why would they bring Broad on, after all, he had struggled so far in this match. England were finding the edge, but none of them were carrying to slip. There was the odd play and miss and lbw appeal, but nothing to scare the aussies too much.

At 0/63 I heard this for the first time from an England fan: "Oh no, this doesn't look good." They are a special breed of fan. At stumps Australia were a spanking 0/80 with just 466 more to find.

I left the ground with hope, and quickly went to the pub to add beer to that hope. As Oprah would say: "What do you know for sure?" Well Oprah, I know that Watson will get out early in the morning; Katich is suited to the pitch; Ponting will bat like the world has molested his pets; Michael Hussey will try very hard, if nothing else; Clarke is the in-form batsman; North can chip in again; Haddin can score quickly on this pitch.

Also Oprah, I know that in a whole day of cricket, only five wickets fell to the bowlers; only one wicket fell in each of the first and last sessions; Swann is the only bowler who is a danger as this pitch is, although I know for sure that the height of Harmy, Freddie and Broad might be a problem if the pitch really starts falling apart.

Oprah, when I look it at, I know for sure that England will win, but this annoying coked-up koala keeps whispering into my ear that Australia can do it.

The pitch

While drinking Stuart Broad's spell out of my head at the end of day two I missed much of what others had to say. It seemed that a great deal of the Australian cricket media had bumped their head and lost their frame of reference.

"Fourteen years of world domination is in danger of crumbling with the

Oval pitch," wrote Malcolm Conn of *The Australian*. Really? Had that world domination not been raped and sold around the time Australia lost at home to South Africa after having lost to India only a few months before?

"Australia may be only a day or two away from handing over the Ashes after a shocking batting collapse of 10-87 on a dodgy and dusty pitch," Ben Dorries of *The Daily Telegraph* said. Perhaps I watched the wrong collapse; I saw a swing bowler take Australia apart by moving the ball in the air.

My mate Peter Roebuck, who I just realised I would never ever talk to, had this to say: "Although they are loathe to admit it, England ordered and prepared a dodgy deck," and "it turned out the talk about producing a typical Oval pitch was all smoke and mirrors."

Remember that Roebuck was one of the reasons I got into this gig, and that I loved that his opinions weren't of the standard Australian machine. Nothing hurts more than your hero turning evil.

It seemed only Shane Warne wasn't over-reacting, "He (the curator) overbaked it a little bit to make sure there is a result," said the Sky man.

Actually Warne was right; this was a result pitch, the bunch of pricks.

The Oval curator should be murdered. The ICC have been doing their very best to ensure all Test matches are played on the same wicket. The CEO brown five-day edition. Slowish. No grass. Great to bat on. Impossible to get wickets on. Stay true till the end. And guaranteed to get five days of gate receipts. Well this Oval pitch broke several of those rules. It had life in it; it was breaking apart; it encouraged the bowlers at times; it had uneven bounce; it may not last the full five days. And it will guarantee a result. This is bound to get the curator in trouble.

How many wickets had the Pitch claimed so far? Is none a fair answer? Not one wicket from vicious bounce, grubbers, unhuman-like movement, or shit pitch characteristics. Was it a shit pitch when Jonathan Trott made a hundred on it? Was it a shit pitch when England gave away their wickets and still made over 300 twice? Was it a shit pitch when Australia made 0/73 and 0/80*?

Give me a break.

Swann and Bell had made half-centuries on this supposed minefield. BELL. Minefield? England scored at four an over.

Dorries, Conn, Roebuck and anyone else could jump up and down as much as they wanted, but it was all bullshit.

If you could have found a wicket out of the 27 so far that had been due to the pitch's evil nature I'd have bought you a lollipop.

England should have made over 500 twice on this, Australia made 160. As for referred pressure, fuck off. Any batsman who got out on this pitch because he was worried a ball might do something unusual should learn to bat on uncovered wickets. Or cut off his hands.

As for England asking for a dodgy spinning deck, if that is the case why didn't they play two spinners? Huh? Exactly.

Day 4: The final day of the Ashes

I decided to watch the start of day four from my couch. Not just because I love my couch, and I do, but because I wanted to watch this killer pitch up close and personal. Every explosion, grubber, spitter, splitter, and splatter. Being close to the ground does have its advantages, and at lunch I'd stroll up to the ground.

My family all fucked off to the ground, and I was happy. I had got the house to myself and I started to count down the minutes until Shane Watson was due out. I figured Australia could afford to lose four wickets in the day, and I had his marked down for just after the start of play, and Hussey for just after tea. Yes, that'd do nicely.

Broad opened the bowling, and Watson survived the first over; Swann was at the other end and Watson survived that too. Maybe I had this wrong. Perhaps this was where Watson made a massive hundred, silences his critics, and goes on to propel Australia back to the top of world cricket. All this was dashed from my mind when Broad got one to hit a pebble off a length and smacked Watson on the gloves, but he survived.

Katich didn't.

Swann bowled his left-hander killer, the straight one, and Katich met it with his pad. That is one shocking fucken leave. How could he do this to Australia? He is the fighter, the street rat, the angry wombat. But he has gone.

Ponting came in to a standing ovation. Just then I realised I should have been there for this. If Ponting gets out I might not get a last time to say goodbye to him at a Test in England. I was being silly of course: Australia are playing Pakistan in the UK next year. The change from boos to cheers has been quick. England realise that even if they hate the hairy-armed goblin, you have to respect him, and when he is gone it will be a loss for the Ashes as much as the Australians. Either that, or they think the emotion will get to him, cunning mugs.

The emotion got to Shane Watson. Broad got one on line, and he gets smacked on the pads and is rightly given out, even if he doesn't agree. He almost lasted five overs. Four lbws in five innings, four times out after a break in five innings, and to think I spent years saying he wasn't consistent.

Mike Hussey and Ponting played tough for a while. It was a pitch you needed to go softly for a while on, but Trott and Strauss proved that once you were in it took something special or stupid to get you out. Runs were available, even if they were not piling up quickly.

Mike Hussey gave the Australian nation a scare when he left a ball from Freddie that seemed to go straight over the stumps. It was as if he had been reading my stuff on what a good pitch this was. I felt vindicated; most other Australians were having chest pains. At lunch Australia were 2/171, as good a base for a chase of 500 as you could hope for.

When I got to the ground my dad took me through the Shane Warne masterclass that he had been running for two county spinners during the interval. I doubt there has ever been a quick bowler in history that loves spin more than my old man.

Broad and Swann started again after lunch. Ponting knocked up his fifty, off only 76 balls, in the second over. A couple of overs later Swann got an edge from Ponting that went fast and low to Collingwood, but he missed it, it hit his foot and Prior scrambled for the crumbs. But nothing doing.

It took 0.00000000001 seconds for the first "has he just dropped the Ashes?" reference.

Swann switched ends, and Harmy returned, looking like he was bowling for his career. Hussey brought up his fifty thanks to some overthrows. He had been solid, but had never looked completely comfortable. Ponting had, and he had been dropped. Perception is a funny thing.

It should be said that at this stage there seemed to be thousands of English fans who were not only expecting the worst, but seemed to be almost perversely cheering it on. Australia had got to 200 with the loss of two wickets, but you would have thought it was 400 by the way some were acting. It seemed way too early to be freaking out.

Since I have been in the UK I have got to study this phenomenon close up. I don't think I'll ever truly understand it. The English tell me it is because of all the crushing losses and amazing defeats they have had over the years. But few sides have had more amazing losses than Australia. I have lived through them – although for one I was only one. Twice enforcing the follow-on and losing, coughing up over 400 a couple of times, plus they do like to fuck up chases of under 150.

South Africans know what it feels like to stuff up. Every international tournament they seem to choke and lose it. That is now a well established pattern that everyone is aware of, and yet before each tournament they back their side, and yes it is getting hollower. India also know how to collapse – they do it like drunken teens – yet the majority of their fans are the most positive I have ever come across. Until they collapse. Then it is put the boot in time.

The English pessimistic condition is absurd, and sort of sweet.

Michael Hussey shattered the pessimism. He ran out Ricky Ponting.

There was some weird symmetry global cosmic alliance shit going on. The man who should have been in the team in 05, hit the ball to the man that inspired England in 05, and ran out the guy who was trying like hell to atone for 05.

Australia's captain and best player being run out by England's National Drunkard Gimp, their Jesus.

Hussey had received a few good balls in a row from Harmy, but then got one on his pads and he hit it ever so slightly to the left of Freddie. He took off. Ponting was dozing, but it probably wasn't the sort of run you take when you are chasing down a total that will shatter all records.
Freddie moved quickly for a man his size with a knee made of cheese and hit the stumps. He didn't have much to do, the run out was there for him, three stumps to aim at, all he had to do was what Matty Hayden calls, "executing your skillsets" and the rest of us call throwing straight. He did it.

Freddie had hardly been a factor in the Test. He was moving better, but his bowling zest hadn't returned, and his batting seemed to be clouded by emotion. But this was huge. And he knew it. Freddie didn't need the replay to tell him Ricky was out. H was Freddie Fucken Flintoff, and he knew.

Ricky deserved better. Way better. The only ray of hope Australia had was this man, and he was on 66, in a huge partnership, and was in possibly/probably his last ever innings against England in England. He deserved a hundred, if not the win, he deserved it for the boos, for the fact his batsmen had failed him, for his bowlers falling apart, for the selectoral mistakes, Brett Lee's injury, or for the simple fact that for all the shit that was hurled at him he held himself with a dignity that in 05 he didn't even know he had.

Instead he left with a run-out and no hundred.

The crowd gave him an ovation that chilled me. It was like the ovation the MCG gave Sachin Tendulkar in 07/08. It was applause and respect on a different level. I could only hope that Ricky sucked some of it in even while he was hurting.

The crowd seemed shocked at what had happened, but to be fair, it just got weirder. The talk was still all about Ponting when Michael Clarke clipped one to leg and it rocketed to Strauss at leg slip, who flicked it back on to the stumps as Clark tried to get his bat back. We all waited for the decision and it felt like it was taking forever. People huddled around those with the 10-quid Sky radios, desperate for the news. The bat was on the line, but was it over? What was happening? My mum told me that the guy next to her was saying it was not out, too close to call.

All I could do was smile at her and the third-hand information I was getting. Others were saying the bat was not across the line. Everyone was standing, shifting nervously, and then the roar went up. Out. My mum was in a state of rage I had never seen from her at a sporting event, in fact at anything. She slammed her hat to the ground and that amused the English fans around us to no end. I looked at my dad, and he just looked let down, defeated.

We were.

For the first time since Cardiff I feel a bit relieved. This wasn't the result I wanted, but it was a result. No more analysis. No more uncertainty. No more Nathan Hauritz jokes. The Ashes were over. Australia had lost the key moments. England had won the Ashes.

I thought about something I wrote earlier about this just not being Australia's Ashes. How right I was. The Australians are as good at running between the wicket as anyone, so to have their best two batsmen run out in the space of a few balls while they are locked in on a big total just proved that this series was not destined to be theirs.

They might have dominated large chunks of it, but the important moments were won by the Poms, and the luck was on their side when it mattered. It seems unfair to them to say it was luck, but something had to decide this series – Mitchell Johnson wasn't going to.

England had to play themselves into the lead for the luck to mean anything, but they got the breaks, and they were going to win the Ashes. When you broke it down that way it all made sense.

This relaxed me, so I sat down and watched the rest of the Test, not as a writer or as an Australian fan, just as a spectator who was happy to be in such a joyous place because of the game I love. Plus, I was still getting paid.

Marcus North added to the English party with a stupid stumping. My cousin came down in his Essendon Aussie rules jumper to tell us he was going, he couldn't handle it any longer. Knowing him, it is for the best. My Wife-Elect offered to swap seats with my cousin so that he was not sitting surrounded by the English, but he decided to leave.

We had a chat with some English fans in front of us – they were still nervous, so we told them to sit back and enjoy it. Soon enough Brad Haddin played a stupid shot and the English fans finally started to.

Harmy, who had been a spectator for most of the match came on and demolished the tail. I have a soft spot for him. He probably doesn't have the emotional tools to survive as a modern cricketer, but he is a big, loveable guy. While he was on the rampage an Npower girl sat on a spare seat in front of me. She was obviously walking around outside, but the atmosphere had dragged her in.

Michael Hussey was the last man out, something I would never have guessed. There was no amount of runs that he could score that would make him feel better about his part in the Ponting run-out. But I was glad he got some runs, even if they were out of guilt. Huss is a great guy, but he shouldn't have been in this series. He will be remembered for the run-out now.

The crowd exploded as the last wicket was taken. People were hugging, screaming and jumping.

I gave England a clap.

I told my parents I was going to the pub, kissed my wife-to-be, leaving her to soak it all up, and left. I walked way too fast for my dad and his dodgy knee, hips and back. I knew I should slow down, but I just wanted to get away from there. Few words were spoken between us. I saw the camera crews trying to chat to Aussies as they left, so I took my parents onto the other side of the road.

Finally we got to the sanctuary of the pub, and they have the fucken cricket on the big screen. My pub never shows cricket, sometimes even when I ask. But I should have known better than to try and escape the Ashes.

My dad and I hit the beers hard, my mum hit the Pimm's hard (if you can) and were joined by my lady, and later my cousin who had gone shopping to escape. And we all got gloriously drunk and started toasting random things that amused us greatly at the time.

Fifth Test at the Oval

England won by 197 runs

England first innings	Runs	Balls	Mins	4s	6s	
*AJ Strauss	c Haddin b Hilfenhaus	55	101	128	11	-
AN Cook	c Ponting b Siddle	10	12	19	2	-
IR Bell	b Siddle	72	137	222	10	-
PD Collingwood	c Hussey b Siddle	24	65	89	3	-
IJL Trott	run out (Katich)	41	81	125	5	-
+MJ Prior	c Watson b Johnson	18	33	57	2	-
A Flintoff	c Haddin b Johnson	7	19	21	1	-
SCJ Broad	c Ponting b Hilfenhaus	37	69	89	5	-
GP Swann	c Haddin b Siddle	18	28	43	2	-
JM Anderson	lbw b Hilfenhaus	0	6	5	-	-SJ
Harmison	not out	12	12	17	3	-
Extras (12 b, 5 lb, 18 nb, 3 w)		38				
Total (all out, 414 minutes, 90.5 overs)		**332**				

Fall of wickets: 1-12 (Cook, 5.3 ov), 2-114 (Strauss, 28.1 ov), 3-176 (Collingwood, 47.5 ov), 4-181 (Bell, 53.5 ov), 5-229 (Prior, 65.3 ov), 6-247 (Flintoff, 69.4 ov), 7-268 (Trott, 74.2 ov), 8-307 (Swann, 85.3 ov), 9-308 (Anderson, 86.6 ov), 10-332 (Broad, 90.5 ov)

Australia bowling	Overs	Mdns	Runs	Wkts	Wides	No-Balls
Hilfenhaus	21.5	5	71	3	-	5
Siddle	21	6	75	4	-	4
Clark	14	5	41	0	-	-
Johnson	15	0	69	2	3	8
North	14	3	33	0	-	1
Watson	5	0	26	0	-	-

Australia first innings	Runs	Balls	Mins	4s	6s	
SR Watson	lbw b Broad	34	69	94	7	-
SM Katich	c Cook b Swann	50	107	169	7	-
*RT Ponting	b Broad	8	15	20	1	-
MEK Hussey	lbw b Broad	0	3	6	-	-
MJ Clarke	c Trott b Broad	3	7	9	-	-
MJ North	lbw b Swann	8	17	28	1	-
+BJ Haddin	b Broad	1	9	13	-	-
MG Johnson	c Prior b Swann	11	24	27	2	-
PM Siddle	not out	26	38	14	5	-
SR Clark	c Cook b Swann	6	8	48	1	-
BW Hilfenhaus	b Flintoff	6	21	10	1	-
Extras (1 b, 5 lb, 1 nb)		7				
Total (all out, 226 minutes, 52.5 overs)		**160**				

Fall of wickets: 1-73 (Watson, 22.6 ov), 2-85 (Ponting, 26.6 ov), 3-89 (Hussey, 28.3 ov), 4-93 (Clarke, 30.2 ov), 5-108 (North, 35.3 ov), 6-109 (Katich, 37.1 ov), 7-111 (Haddin, 38.4 ov), 8-131 (Johnson, 43.5 ov), 9-143 (Clark, 47.3 ov), 10-160 (Hilfenhaus, 52.5 ov)

England bowling	Overs	Mdns	Runs	Wkts	Wides	No-Balls
Anderson	9	3	29	0	-	-
Flintoff	13.5	4	35	1	-	-
Swann	14	3	38	4	-	-
Harmison	4	1	15	0	-	1
Broad	12	1	37	5	-	-

England second innings		Runs	Balls	Mins	4s	6s
*AJ Strauss	c Clarke b North	75	191	226	8	-
AN Cook	c Clarke b North	9	35	49	-	-
IR Bell	c Katich b Johnson	4	7	13	1	-
PD Collingwood	c Katich b Johnson	1	7	9	-	-
IJL Trott	c North b Clark	119	193	331	12	-
+MJ Prior	run out (Katich)	4	9	16	1	-
A Flintoff	c Siddle b North	22	18	24	4	-
SCJ Broad	c Ponting b North	29	35	43	5	-
GP Swann	c Haddin b Hilfenhaus	63	55	57	9	-
JM Anderson	not out	15	29	34	2	-

Did not bat: SJ Harmison

Extras (1 b, 15 lb, 9 nb, 7 w)   32

Total (9 wickets, declared, 408 minutes, 95 overs)   **373**

Fall of wickets: 1-27 (Cook, 12.3 ov), 2-34 (Bell, 15.4 ov), 3-39 (Collingwood, 17.3 ov), 4-157 (Strauss, 54.3 ov), 5-168 (Prior, 57.6 ov), 6-200 (Flintoff, 64.1 ov), 7-243 (Broad, 74.2 ov), 8-333 (Swann, 87.4 ov), 9-373 (Trott, 95 ov)

Australia bowling	Overs	Mdns	Runs	Wkts	Wides	No-Balls
Hilfenhaus	11	1	58	1	-	4
Siddle	17	3	69	0	2	-
North	30	4	98	4	1	-
Johnson	17	1	60	2	2	5
Katich	5	2	9	0	-	-
Clark	12	2	43	1	-	-
Clarke	3	0	20	0	-	-

Australia second innings		Runs	Balls	Mins	4s	6s
SR Watson	lbw b Broad	40	81	103	6	-
SM Katich	lbw b Swann	43	68	100	7	-
*RT Ponting	run out (Flintoff)	66	103	157	10	-
MEK Hussey	c Cook b Swann	121	263	325	14	-
MJ Clarke	run out (Strauss)	0	4	4	-	-
MJ North	st Prior b Swann	10	24	27	2	-
+BJ Haddin	c Strauss b Swann	34	49	97	6	-
MG Johnson	c Collingwood b Harmison	0	5	5	-	-
PM Siddle	c Flintoff b Harmison	10	14	14	1	-
SR Clark	c Cook b Harmison	0	1	1	-	-
BW Hilfenhaus	not out	4	8	8	1	-

Extras (7 b, 7 lb, 6 nb)   20

Total (all out, 102.2 overs)   **348**

Fall of wickets: 1-86 (Katich, 23.6 ov), 2-90 (Watson, 24.3 ov), 3-217 (Ponting, 63.6 ov), 4-220 (Clarke, 64.5 ov), 5-236 (North, 72.2 ov), 6-327 (Haddin, 94.4 ov), 7-327 (Johnson, 95.5 ov), 8-343 (Siddle, 99.4 ov), 9-343 (Clark, 99.5 ov), 10-348 (Hussey, 102.2 ov)

England bowling	Overs	Mdns	Runs	Wkts	Wides	No-Balls
Anderson	12	2	46	0	-	1
Flintoff	11	1	42	0	-	1
Harmison	16	5	54	3	-	4
Swann	40.2	8	120	4	-	-
Broad	22	4	71	1	-	-
Collingwood	1	0	1	0	-	-

The morning after

Waking up I still felt drunk. I had things to do; the cricket may be finished, but I had to go into Brixton to get the final seal of approval on the marriage from the registrar. I would really rather do anything else. While I wait for my lady to get ready I check my emails and find out I am quoted in *The Times* (the quote is "Well played England. You bastards.") I was pretty excited, but the it is dulled by all the waiting we do in the lobby of the Brixton Town Hall, or something like that, due to an administrative error.

Then I get this weird call from an Australian number, which turned out to be ABC radio in Sydney. They liked what I did on Crikey and wanted to interview me for a segment on the cricket. I was stoked (very pleased), and during the whole registrar process I didn't hear a word. Luckily he was a cricket fan, and didn't care.

Then as I left the town hall I got another call. This was from someone I couldn't really hear as the phone was cutting in and out. He told me he wanted to interview me, and that he would send a car for me. The two interviews were really close to each other, so I asked if we could do it on the phone. He said no, but that he would check to see if he could get me phone access to do the other one.

When I get on the bus I started putting all the parts of the phone call together and I realised what he had actually said. The reason he wanted me there was because this wasn't radio, this was TV, and the station was CNN. I think.

He called back and confirmed all this. I told him I hadn't showered, shaved, and was wearing a shitty T-shirt (it wasn't a shitty T-shirt, it was a Galaga T-shirt). He seemed excited by this as it would make me look like I got wasted the night before. So I rushed home and cleaned my teeth, because I didn't want to have bad breath on TV, and waited for the car.

I got there and first I had to do my radio spot with ABC in the CNN production truck. That went well, although I worried that I wasn't funny enough and from the moment Jim Maxwell was introduced, I couldn't get a word in. Then I was taken around to the front of the English team hotel and did a live five-minute piece with Nick Compton, Middlesex batsman and Grandson of Denis, and the CNN sports reporter.

People tuning in must have been a bit freaked out at the difference in our appearance. He the tall, skinny, blonde male model in his Savile Row clothes; me, the shorter, scrappy-looking, unshaven schlep bastard who didn't even take his hat off for the camera. Apparently I did well, although, to be fair, I did say, "to be fair" about four times.

Then my CNN driver pissed off without me. While we waited for a new one, the BBC heard my accent and also asked for an interview. I said yes, but only if they used my website name. They said they would (they lied). I did the interview, and I was shit. I need preparation time, and then I was asked me some stupid-assed questions including the classic: "Where to from here?" For who, you nut job? They then interviewed my cousin, who was only there as "my manager".

When I met up with my dad later on, he told me that superimposed on the screen while I spoke were the words "Australian Journalist Jarrod Kimber". Something I had never even called myself. My family all thought this was hilarious.

When he sat down later and watched the interviews, we pissed ourselves. Especially at the extreme close-up of my cousin. They had somehow made his head look even bigger than it is, and it is one big fucken head.

Somehow I had gone from a guy whose only media exposure had been as the Ashes guy for Kiwi FM's Saturday morning sports show, State of Play, and one midnight interview for Sport 927 plugging my book, to a star of radio, TV and newspapers in one day.

Not sure why no one had wanted to speak to me during the rest of the Ashes. If England could win the Ashes every six months or so I could make a living off this.

The media

I was just too busy during the Ashes to follow the media as much as I would have liked. But my mate over at theoldbatsman.blogspot.com was talking about the English media the whole time, so I asked for his take on them. This is what he wrote:

> *'He [Andrew Flintoff] is a country charging in to bowl, a culture brandishing a bat. To attack him is to poke the beehive of his nature, which survives the ravages of injury and calls to the night-porter to keep coming with the drinks'.*
>
> *The above paragraph is by Paul Hayward, the Observer's Chief Sports Writer. It appeared in the paper on 5 July, three days before the Ashes series began in Cardiff. It doesn't tell you much about Andrew Flintoff, but it contains everything you need to know about the British media and their agenda for the summer. The 2009 Ashes, more than any other, was one viewed through the prism of its predecessor.*
>
> *Odd-numbered summers in England are ones without major football tournaments in them, which means that the chief sports writer has dangerous time on his hands. Football is a monolithic thing that, in its written history, lacks the intrinsic romance of other territories: boxing, rugby, the Olympic Games and cricket are the places to stretch out and show the world your chops. In odd-numbered summers, watch out. The prose is usually purple.*
>
> *Before 2005, England had rarely been the type of cricket team to encourage it, but then that series became almost fictional; ridiculously filmic. Those five matches etched themselves deep into the collective memory, and there was a Pavlovian reaction to its return. It wasn't just Hayward*

who was at it. 'Sometimes Flintoff will turn himself into a Rodin statue,' wrote Simon Barnes in The Times, *'holding a vigorous pose to indicate extremes of emotion. There he stood, legs planted wide, head bowed, hands clasping head: Freddie Agonistes'. This after Flintoff had scored 30-odd and got Phil Hughes out in Cardiff.*

The English are in love with nostalgia, sometimes with nostalgia for a time and place that never really existed. The version of Flintoff in those paragraphs was not the reality but the image of him, the emotion he had once provoked. 2009 was a series that came with some heavy freight and the reporting of it was skewed by that freight. Cardiff was a good tight Test match finish with a fine last hour. Lord's was somewhat like Edgbaston 2005 in its first session and not unlike Manchester with a bolted-on happy ending in its last three – that is if you really screwed your eyes up and imagined it hard. But the truth, however unrewarding, was that these were two flaky teams deserving of their end-of-series rankings of fourth and fifth, rather than an ineffably great side being defeated by a very good one.

In a way, Flintoff was the Beckham-esque figure of the summer, a player whose occasional and valuable interventions were allocated a significance based on his legend. Flintoff himself understood that. He played the media like Slash plays the intro to Sweet Child O' Mine. *The drop on one knee at Lord's was, he admitted, calculated. The announcement of his retirement from Test cricket reset that agenda; the leaking of the news that he felt fit for Headingley added to the chaos. Now he is selling another autobiography on the back of it. If there is a cumulative effect of all of those throbbing passages from chief sports writers it is that this mediated vision of Andrew Flintoff is the one we are left with, and the one we'll come to believe existed.*

Connoisseurs of the noble art of space-filling were, of course, not disappointed. The Times *gave Gabby Logan a thousand words to discuss which side was better-looking ['The Aussies sent here to try to retain the Ashes just aren't as beautiful as our boys. Think about Bopara, James Anderson, Stuart Broad and Alistair Cook'];* The Guardian *asked Richard Williams to consider Lily Allen's attendance ['If the singer of* Smile *and* The Fear *is the shape of cricket supporters to come, then bring on the multitudes... She likes Flintoff and Onions and Broad']; Jonathan Freedland, the paper's political commentator, got stoned on the drama whilst on holiday ['I might be faced with a stunning Albegensian castle or the gorgeous sparkling Canal du Midi, but still my thumb itched to find out if Anderson had broken through']; Matthew Syed was awarded 900 words to run through the historical significance ['English and Australian cricket have what is known as a long-term relationship: it started not with a kiss but with the first Ashes Test in 1882']. It fell to the dependable, Strauss–like figures of the cricket correspondents to do the leg work, and as usual, that was great; the waspish Hopps, salt of the earth Vic Marks and as ever, Gideon Haigh.*

The best single piece of analysis though came on television: Shane Warne, replete with rails of mesmerising new teeth, called the unravelling of Ravi Bopara before it happened. On the radio, the other great and unexpected success was Matthew Hayden, who summed up perfectly the last sessions at the Oval. Welcoming fellow Australian Jim Maxwell to the mic, he said, 'mate, I just feel like giving you a hug'. Even big men crumble in the end.

The one edge radio retains over television is its refusal to blur the boundaries between commentary and analysis. On Sky, as brilliant as their coverage is, the 'comm box' is

just a hubbub of former players talking. Anyone who can
remember the great Arlott speaking gently but plosively into
the microphone, saying beautiful and perfect things like,
'here comes Botham, running in like a shire horse cresting
the breeze', feels a tug in the heart for what we have lost.
Those days, like Andrew Flintoff, are all gone now.

Test cricket's greatest blogger speaks

There has been plenty of what I think about the cricket, but I don't play
international cricket (I announced my retirement last year after years of being
overlooked). Iain O'Brien does play Test cricket. He even writes about it at
iainobrien.co.nz. Sure he is only a Kiwi, but like me he has an English missus,
and between defeats for Leicestershire he managed to watch the Ashes:

"James Anderson and Monty Panesar won the Ashes. Yeah,
they won the 2009 Ashes for England. Why, you know
exactly why? They did what everyone, and I mean everyone,
thought they couldn't do. They saved the first Test at Cardiff.
England did not lose that first Test. Australia did not win
that first Test. It was a draw. 0-0 after match one.

I predicted a 2-1 to England result before the series
started. I nailed it. I also said that of the two draws
one would be hugely weather affected; I nailed that one
too. I didn't really care who won to be fair, I just wanted
some good cricket to entertain me. I got entertained, but
it wasn't quite like the spectacle of the 2005 series. I also
predicted that England would win 2005 if they could keep
their bowlers on the park; they did and they did.

For me, the only match that got close to the feeling from
that 2005 series was the first Test in Wales; although
it didn't really heat up until that final day. It was
an interesting choice of venue for the first Test, but it
worked; good for them!

Panesar should be MBE'd for that innings alone. He did more than some in 2005, Fact! Of course I'm going to side with the tailenders, it might be obvious, but these boys did good. Bloody good! There were 18 overs to go when Anderson joined Collingwood, 11 to go when Panesar joined Anderson. Anderson and Panesar won the Ashes for England. Australia should have gone one-nil up in Wales. They didn't. It's hard to come back from a one down. That draw would have felt like a loss in the Australian camp and a win in the English.

England had to then play well to 'really' win the Ashes, but they owe it all to Anderson and Panesar, the bowlers that had their bats in hand."

A bowler standing up for tailenders? I am as shocked as you are. It should also be said that not long after this, Iain, who is a proper tailender, put in a herculean effort batting with Dan Vettori to almost steal a Test match from Sri Lanka after his New Zealand top order had thrown it away. Inspired by Monty?

The Australian selectors lose the Ashes

Before the Ashes I was critical of the Australian selectors, after the Ashes they were almost single-handedly blamed.

There are probably millions of Australians who believe Australia lost at the Oval because Nathan Hauritz didn't play. I am not in that camp. I have been racking my brain for ways that Hauritz could have won the Test for Australia; I just can't see it. Australia read the pitch badly, Jamie Cox apparently made the decision, and I think we can all say that he made the wrong call.

But was it the call that lost the game?

Graeme Swann took eight wickets at the Oval. Marcus North took four.

That is 12 of the 36 taken in all. A lot for two men, especially being that one is a part-timer. North's wickets led people to believe that Hauritz would have been the difference. At Cardiff Hauritz took six wickets, and North bowled seven overs. Mostly at the end. So if Hauritz had played would North have bowled much at all, would he have even have taken a wicket?

Would Hauritz really have taken more than four wickets in the second innings? He had never taken more than four wickets in an innings in 50 first-class games. Meaning that picking him, while quieting down critics of the selectors, would have made no difference.

Ponting just did not use North when Hauritz was playing. At the Oval North bowled 44 overs, and in England's first innings at Lord's, when Hauritz was in hospital, he bowled 16.3 overs. When Hauritz was fit in the second innings, he didn't use him at all. The only time North bowled when Hauritz was on the field was at Cardiff when Australia were trying to get in as many overs as they could. Why at the Oval would Ponting have changed this?

Because the ball was spinning? Was it spinning any more than Cardiff, a wicket that spun so much that England chose two spinners. At the Oval they decided against this. England used a lower percentage of spin at the Oval, because Swann is only one man, than they did at Cardiff, but the major difference was that Swann bowled well. Really well. At the Oval he looked like a Test spinner; at Cardiff he bowled like a homeless person given a pristine pair of whites.

England had two seamers that took one wicket between them – Anderson and Freddie – and Harmison took only three wickets, all in Australia's tail as they fell apart at the end. They also could have used an extra spinner, as bad as Monty had been bowling – either him, or Adil Rashid – because he might have taken a few more wickets than Harmison, Anderson and Freddie when the game was still tight.

In the first innings the seam bowlers were still the best options. Siddle should have taken five wickets; Broad did. Swann took four, but two weren't out. And you could argue that had anyone been bowling decently at the other end to Broad, seam or spin, they would have picked up wickets in that period.

The one time that Hauritz could have been useful was during the Strauss/ Trott partnership in England's second innings. That was a 110-run stand, and had Hauritz got an edge from Strauss early on that could have changed the complexion of the game. North did get Strauss though, and he worked on Strauss for a while to get it, something he might not have been able to do with Hauritz in the side.

We are all dealing in bullshit hypotheticals here, but I did say the Ashes brings out the wanker in people. I could probably write a novella on this particular argument alone – you should see how many notes I had. In the end the only way I could see Hauritz winning the game for Australia was if he'd put on 150 with Siddle in the first innings or if he'd gone out boozing with Broad at the end of the first day and rendered the England bowler useless.

To me, Australia's first-innings collapse was the difference. Andrew Hilditch and his merry selectors might have made a lot of mistakes – Hussey, Clark, the make-up of the squad and Andrew McDonald's free holiday – but the truth is the batting let them down.

It hurts me to say that, because I'd love to just blame Hilditch, who should be fired anyway. He certainly contributed to the defeat and for that English fans should thank him. But I get the feeling England would have won even without him, somehow.

If you still disagree, feel free to buy me several beers and argue it with me.

Numbers

There seemed to be a section of the cricket-watching public that believed Australia were very unlucky to lose, based on the statistics. Australia dominated the run table, they dominated the wicket table, they dominated the hundred table. It is amazing they lost at all. Of course cricket is very rarely played on tables (except in the case of the old Test match cricket table top game).

The one stat that isn't mentioned by people holding this theory is that

Australia collapsed more than England. And when they did it, it was worse.

Australia collapsed three times, England only twice. Being that one of Australia's collapses came during a rain-affected game, you could almost say it is even.

The difference was the timing, England collapsed twice in one match. On three occasions in their first-innings Australia failed to score 300: Lord's 215, Edgbaston 263, and the Oval 160. If you give the opposition three starts like that you are going to struggle in a five-Test series.

The batting and the bowling stat differentials are even explainable. Five of Australia's centuries came in the drawn games, and Hussey's came after Australia had lost all hope. English batsmen didn't make any in those two drawn Tests. So in the live Tests Australia made four to England's two.

When you include the tail batting, the whole thing swings massively back to England. Graeme Swann made 249 runs with a strike rate of 83 batting at No. 9. *NINE*. Stuart Broad made 234 runs batting at eight. Mitchell Johnson batted at eight for Australia and made 105.

There was also the bowling. Australia had the three leading wicket-takers for the series. Not by a long way, Hilfy took 22 wickets to finish on top, Broad had 18 and finished fourth. Australia's wickets were spread out over the whole series; England's were usually clumped around an Australian collapse.

The wickets were the reason that England won the Ashes. In five Tests only three times did a side bowl the other side out twice. England bowled Australia out at Lord's. Australia bowled England out at Headingley. And then England bowled out Australia at the Oval. That is pretty clear isn't it?

Two to one is that count.

Two-one is the final count.

The only numbers that really matter.

Sissy fight in the schoolyard

When I sat down and thought about that last day, I realised that two run-outs to seal the fate of the Ashes was probably the best way to finish the series. Neither team was really good enough to win it. It took a quirky sense of fate by the cricket gods to get this series over the line.

The series was close, the Tests were not. It was a series of artificial closeness inspired by the unrelenting fact that both sides are quite shit.

One of my headlines after the series was over was this:

The Ashes = Two equally shit sides fight out an ancient rivalry that no one understands, but everyone cares about.

Even Strauss said England were merely good enough, and he didn't say this naked on an open-top bus either.

Australians didn't even get the amazing entertainment of 05. This was a series of underachievement, missed opportunities and mental collapses.

I still enjoyed it, maybe in a perverse way more than I enjoyed 05. That had gladiators going at each other, two well-oiled machines clashing as the whole world watched. It was one for the ages, for the purists, for the casuals, for the highlight reels.

09 was more low down and dirty. Two teams of random blokes accidently bumping into each other that you could watch if you had a pay-TV subscription. It won't go down as one of the classics. But I have always been more of a fan of *Death Race 2000* than *Gone with the Wind*.

It had that great quality that you can only get from two opponents who aren't very good: farce. On Crikey I likened the series to two sissy boys fighting in the school yard. One is slapping with his eyes closed and rarely hitting, the other is pulling hair and barely staying upright.

An Ashes battle doesn't have to be two champions to make it good to watch. These teams were evenly matched. So even though it was slapping and hair pulling, it was a tight contest of slapping and hair pulling.

Freddie rises

It is now clear to me that I will never fully understand Freddie Flintoff.

I loved watching him play, but I also knew he was never as good as he could have been. I loved how his being in a game of cricket gave it something extra, but I can read statistics well and know England had a better record without him.

When I look back at this series I see that he was the reason it shaped the way it did. He might have not scrapped for the draw at Cardiff, or inspired any of Australia's three batting collapses, but under it all was Freddie.

His Test at Cardiff was poor, but his retirement announcement seemed to lift the English players at Lord's, and then just when Australia got victory in sight he stood up and took the game away.

At Edgbaston England's form seemed to slip away as his fitness did. By the end of the match he could not walk, and England were getting spanked in the field.

For Headingley he was rested due to concerns from the team management about his body, and England lost, looking unspirited and uninspired while they did it.

Then at the Oval, he rose again.

For most of the game he was nothing more than an interested spectator, then, just as Australia put in place a partnership that meant they can once again look for victory, he stepped up.

In fact he stepped to the side, then posed, and waited for his team and his nation to embrace him.

In the first three Tests Freddie's mortality was there for everyone to see. In the fifth, he became immortal. A spiritual cricket figure whose deeds will forever be outweighed by the love for him and his presence.

He did almost nothing at the Oval, and yet he did everything England needed of him.

In modern terms he is English cricket's Jesus. This man, a former cunt (according to Bob Simpson, at least), had transformed himself from likable English lad, to superhero, to saviour of a nation.

Freddie has now been invited on that pedestal with other such champions of the little people People, Princess Di and George Best. It is elite company, and odd company. But anyone who premeditates a Jesus at the Rio Grande-like pose wants to be in rarefied air.

Earlier in the book I used the term Jesus as a piss take. The crowd just built him up so much he had felt like the messiah. Now that I think about it, the Jesus tag might just be spot on. England's war cry in this Ashes was the song *Jerusalem*. I hate the song, and I hate it more when it is played three times a day. But think about the song. It is essentially an ode for Jesus to come and save the working people from the Satanic Mills of modern industry.

Perhaps my problem was I thought this was a match between two Test teams, and I didn't realise that William Blake and the New Jesus were on England's side.

It makes sense really; he died at Edgbaston and was reborn at the Oval. Bastard.

The Wedding

There isn't too much to tell. We were both on time. She wore white. I wore whites. Everyone loved being in the Oval long room. My mate read a poem I had written for the occasion bagging Alec Stewart. Iain O'Brien and Bryce

McGain sent telegrams. So did some of my unfamous mates. The tables were named after cricket grounds. We had a cricket bat for people to sign.

And we all had a great time and got proper drunk.

From the now-Wife

> Of course, there was more to the wedding than that. The groom's ring was much too small. The friend reading the poem hadn't realised that we genuinely wanted him to read the poem, and thought that it was all a joke, right up until the registrar called his name. And one of my friends composed a piece of music for us to the beautifully spare, austere words of Raymond Carver's poem Late Fragment.
>
> As I repeated the vows that we had agreed with the Registrar, I was facing the Oval pitch (although obviously gazing into the eyes of my new husband). There were still traces of confetti around the ground. Of course, lots of brides find traces of confetti at their wedding venue from the last celebration held there; mine, though, was leftover from the celebrations when Andrew Strauss lifted the Ashes urn. My first-ever comment on cricketwithballs, some 18 months previously, was about how I'd seen a crowd slow-hand-clap Rahul Dravid at the Oval. Our table name at the reception was "MCG", and featured a photo of Rahul Dravid in silhouette, playing in the match on which I had commented on cricketwithballs. Things had, in a way, come full-circle. Or oval.
>
> Later, at the reception, my speech included the telegrams from Iain O'Brien and Bryce McGain, both of whom had generously responded to messages from a virtual stranger imploring them to do a favour for her groom

(Iain O'Brien's being composed while he was in the middle of a Test match). It was the icing on the cake (in place of the actual icing that we didn't have because we had – of course – Victoria sponge).

Lots of people had asked how we, two cricket fans, one from Australia, one from England via Sri Lanka, would manage to get through the Ashes without falling out . I think (I hope) we're going to be just fine. Just don't get us onto Murali.

Loser

I know what you are thinking, sucked in Jrod, your team lost. You is a loser.

Huh, do you really think I'd lose. Of course not. After every day's play at the Oval there was a stand where they gave out free deodorant from one of the sponsors. By the end of the Test I had 16 of them.

Fuck, yeah.

That more than made up for losing the Ashes. Sure the deodorant doesn't smell that nice, and stings a little when applied, but it was free, and I took more than the one per day I was allowed.

Striking back at the industrial heart of England: you can take the Ashes, but I will defeat you, oh yes I will.

Oh, and I had gained a love for the Ashes and an English wife. That was good too. But that free deodorant....

Acknowledgments

The bands I listened to while putting the book together: Ola Podrida, Orenda Fink, The Sweet Serenades, Sweet Billy Pilgrim, Alias Diane, Pugwash, O'Death Bon Iver, The Distillers, Fanfarlo, The Duckworth Lewis Method, and Fugazi.

Thank yous: The newest Mrs Kimber. The parental units, Joel, Issy, Gazz, Mazz, and Sarge. All the Kimbers, Marshalls, Ahamats, Sarimans, Kilbys and Spehrs. For a piece of their mind, Rob, TOB and Iain. Thanks to Paul, Nigel and Pitch for bringing this together and keeping it as it was. Graeme and the boys at Kiwi FM. To Ed, John, Sampson and the TWC posse for getting me in. Leigh and Crikey for letting me be the chief. Patrick at the Times. Richard for putting in on the site. ©hinaman for keeping my site together. To Gideon, Dileep and Lawrence for their help. Campbellfield, Coburg and Barnes cricket clubs. And to everyone who came to my wedding, or wanted to.

Also to all my Twitter followers who answered my stupid questions like, "is Ian Bell a ginger?" And to goodcricketwicket.co.uk for answering a question about Freddie Flintoff's chest hair, and probably something more important. And finally to all the readers of cricket with balls, without you I'd just be ranting into a mirror.

No thanks at all go to my year 11 English teacher Ms Hooper. Two books now, you know where you can stick this one as well.